1 MONTH OF
FREE
READING

at

www.ForgottenBooks.com

By purchasing this book you are eligible for one month membership to ForgottenBooks.com, giving you unlimited access to our entire collection of over 1,000,000 titles via our web site and mobile apps.

To claim your free month visit:

www.forgottenbooks.com/free64490

ISBN 978-0-483-36021-1
PIBN 10064490

The Chameleon's Dish

A BOOK OF

LYRICS AND BALLADS

FOUNDED ON THE HOPES AND ILLUSIONS OF MANKIND

𝔗ogether with other 𝔓oems

By THEODORE TILTON

The King. How fares our cousin Hamlet?
Hamlet. Excellent, i' faith: of the chameleon's dish: I eat the air, promise-crammed: you cannot feed capons so.—*Act* iii, *Scene 2*

A NEW EDITION

With Preface, Foot-notes, and Appendix

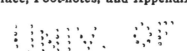

London   Oxford
T. FISHER UNWIN   B. H. BLACKWELL
11 PATERNOSTER BUILDINGS   51 BROAD STREET

Paris

MESNIL-DRAMARD ET Cⁱᴱ.

45 RUE JACOB, 45

1894

PREFACE

———•◆•———

It is the good fortune of this Book of Poems that its Shakespearean title is itself a poem.

In Shakespeare's time, the belief was common that the Chameleon fed on the Air.

Hence when the King of Denmark asks—

'How fares our cousin Hamlet?'

the Prince satirically replies—

'Excellent, i' faith: of the chameleon's dish: I eat the air, promise-crammed: you cannot feed capons so.'

Though Modern Science (which is steadily crumbling our pet illusions) has long since exploded the old and pretty notion of the chameleon's diet, yet down to this day, Hamlet's happy expression, 'the chameleon's dish,' remains one of those permanent and perfect phrases with which the greatest of authors has ornamented the noblest of languages.

By continuous currency for three hundred years, this expression has now become not only classic and venerable, but useful and indispensable; and to strike it from our present speech, or to relegate it to the limbo of the obsolete, would be to cast away a vital fragment of our mother-tongue.

A curious fact of Science, such as the strange digestion of the *Chameleo bifurcus,* may receive—in

265964

successive ages—new glosses or interpretations from fresh discoveries; but a quaint turn of Fancy—such as a pat line of our old poetry—suffers no change in its transition to modern times.

A Shakespearean word may drift from its mediaeval meaning; but a Shakespearean figure of speech remains for ever.

Hamlet's answer to the King has exactly the same purport now which it had at first.

Every credulous mortal who puts an over-eager faith in magnificent but illusory promises, too good to be true; in brilliant and flattering hopes, too grand to be fulfilled; in beautiful vagaries, tempting and plausible, but chimerical and vain; in theories Utopian—or in schemes Quixotic:—every dreamer of day-dreams—or dweller in cloudland—or hero of the impossible—is fitly said to feed on the Chameleon's Dish—the Air.

As this fascinating habit is common to the human race, Hamlet's metaphor is of universal application: and the last (and least) of its uses is to furnish a fine title for this book—a title better than the book—and justified as the aptest possible characterization of those unsubstantial and airy Hopes and Illusions which these pages are to chronicle and describe.

Perhaps under the good auspices of so suggestive a title—together with the help of the one strong moral of these many and diverse tales—this book may do something to remind our present hurrying, driving, and grasping generation

> '*What shadows we are,*
> *What shadows we pursue!*'

Paris, *January* 15, 1894.

TABLE OF CONTENTS

———•◦———

THE CHAMELEON'S DISH.

CARL OLAF'S CANTICLE.

'We are such stuff
As dreams are made of, and our little life
Is rounded with a sleep.'

Stave First.

I.

BEGIRT by Norsk and piny hills,
And interspersed with tumbling rills
Whose torrents are of melted snow,
There is a Valley that I know
Where herds of reindeer browse,
And troops of gay and barefoot maids
Go singing through the salty glades,
Jingling their pails at milking-time
To greet the far-off tinkling chime
Of home-returning cows.

II.

But let these merry maidens skip along
Nor loiter here in this my solemn song;
For though their eyes be blue,
And though their cheeks be fair,

B

And though their heads have each a triple tress
        Of golden hair,
And though these damsels be as sweet and true
As any mortal maids for men to woo,
     Yet I at once confess
   That this my Lay has nought to do
   With any lass of all the crew.

III.

I chant no madrigal of Love:
Full many a better bard indeed
Has piped upon that ancient reed.
But I shall do a different thing:
This theme of mine must mount above
The puny flight of Cupid's wing:
For what I now intend to sing
Forth-reaches to the furthest range
Of things most mystical and strange;—
Not things that *are*, but things that *seem*;—
    And which no bard before
    Has ventured to explore;
    Things whose remote domain
Lies beyond Lethé and its banks of ooze
      (Where spectres grope)
And merges in the utmost verge and scope
     To which mankind,
With its poor, meagre, unimmortal mind,
    Keeps evermore in vain
Pushing its earthly wish or worldly hope;
A realm beyond the dream of Druid[1] or of Druze[2].

---

[1] The Druids were Northern, and lived wherever oak-trees grew.

[2] The Druzes were Southern, and had their sunny seat in a mythical isle of the Sporades.

IV.

So lest my Fancy, wandering forth so far,
Should be misguided by an evil star,—
Till I, thus overbold,
My too presumptuous way should lose,—
Instruct me, O thou Arctic Muse!—
Who in the lore of runes art wise;
Who in the days of old
A runic rhyme didst not despise;
And who art gracious still to invocations
From all the bards in Odin's four-fold nations[1]:—
Nations of Northern mould,
Polar and bleak and lonely,
Which not Apollo and his Nine
Have seen or known,
But which, O Arctic Muse, are thine—
Thine ever and thine only;
Yea, thine to-day as thine of yore,
The whole quaternion, sea and shore!

V.

For thou dost still on mighty wing arise
Where Hecla[2] heaves her cinders to the skies
And Geysers leap
And Glaciers glide into the seas,
Chilling the Winds. And thou dost choose from these
A frosty breeze
Whose bite is stinging;

---

[1] Icelandic, Swedish, Danish, and Norwegian.

[2] Mount Hecla and the Geysers here represent Iceland; Lake Wener and the Cattegat, Sweden; the Skaw, Denmark; and the Naze, Norway.

And thence in Freyia's[1] feather-guise
　　Of plumage pure and cold
Dost rush to wreak thy wintry will
On Wener's waters till they freeze;—
And thence from snowy hill to hill,
　　From icy wold to wold,
Thou fliest softly to the Cattegat
　　Where never halcyon sat
Save thee, to lull a wave to sleep!
And thou dost still—in time of fog and thaw—
　　With drabbled feather sweep
To haunts of thine upon the Skaw,
　　Where murky vapours creep
　　With murrain to the sheep.
And thou dost still—on Balder's shining days[2]—
Love better yet, and ever best of all,
My darling country, with her ocean-wall,
　　Her billow-beaten Naze[3],

---

[1] Freyia was the Norsk Venus, or goddess of love; and Freyia's
'feather-guise' was a swan's plumage, which the goddess wore when
she wished to hide her identity—as Jupiter concealed his godhead
from Leda.

[2] Of the twelve great gods of the Norseland, Balder is called the
Beautiful. He represents the Summer. His annual reign lasts only
through the short bright season from June till August. He is then
suddenly slain by Höder (or Winter), who pierces him with a fatal
shaft of mistletoe. A cry goes up through all Nature, 'Balder the
Beautiful is dead!' He has a funeral-pyre of great splendour, in the
form of a burning ship. Nanna, his wife, during her brief union with
him, and before her widowhood, is the symbol of earthly bloom; and
when her husband dies, she weeps like Niobe. She will mourn for
Balder all the long winter—a fierce season of seven or eight months.
Her divine mate will then re-arise from the nether world, re-appear
in Norway, re-marry Nanna, and re-govern the North.

[3] The Naze is a sea-washed promontory at the extreme southern

Her precipices sheer and steep,
Her fiords a thousand fathoms deep [1]
And all her hills which many a Jotun's hand [2]
Hath flung together in a heap—
That Freedom there may make a stand—
For there indeed, as Guardian of the Land,
Full soon may Freedom have a watch to keep!

VI.

Meanwhile, since jealous Peace as yet abides
On all our goat-benibbled mountain-sides,
      Where Freedom loves to sit,
      I now will tune my kit [3]
And as a Norsker vaunt my boast
That nowhere else on Odin's coast—
With all its twenty-thousand bays
And grass-embroidered water-ways—
Can any other glen or vale be seen
That rivals mine in Nature's gift of green.

VII.

For there, throughout the whole year round,
The moss enamels all the ground,
And there the Arctic lichens grow [4]

---

point of the Norwegian coast. Opposite to the Naze, and across the Skaggerack, is the Skaw, or the extreme Northern point of Denmark.

[1] For instance, Sogne Fiord has already been sounded to a depth of 4,000 feet; and in many places, not yet sounded, the water may be deeper still.

[2] The Jotuns (pronounced Yotuns) were the primitive frost-giants—the earliest created beings on earth.

[3] A kit is a Norwegian fiddle.

[4] It is on these lichens that the reindeer feeds.

And there the mystic mistletoe
                    With magic charm
                    Protects from harm
The peasant and his hut and farm,
And yet presages Balder's woe.

VIII.

And so the bards of Balder's clime
Have named—in honour of his Queen—
This blooming valley Nanna's Heim:
For though it be a Boreal place,
            Yet thither Balder's spouse—-
The goddess of all earthly grace [1]—
            True to her nuptial vows
(The faithfulest of wives, I ween!)
Goes in the Spring of every year
To weave afresh her wedding-gear
And wed her Royal Lord anew
And dwell with him a Summer's space,
(For it is fated that the two
Be parted all the Winter through.)

IX.

O verdant Valley! joy of June!
(Where Nanna spends her honeymoon,
And where she drops a widow's tear
On Balder's all-too-early bier),
Thy Summer vanishes too soon;
Yet, while its fleeting glory lingers,
No Tropic turf in all the globe
Vies with the velvet of the robe

---

[1] Nanna was born of a bud.

Woven by Northern Nanna's fingers!

And I proclaim
In Nanna's name
That when the Earth shall re-assume
Its lost and primal Eden-bloom
(As once agen[1] on plain and hill
It must and will),
The universal verdure then
Will simply be the same as when—
Throughout the re-awakened North—
The word of joy goes wildly forth
That Balder weds his wife agen[1]
Whose bridal-robe is of a hue
So green that it is almost blue.

x.

——Here pause, O thou my lay!
Hush thee awhile, and let not Nanna know
On this her wedding-day
That the swift dart of mistletoe
Which Höder has let fly,—
Winged with the winter-wind,—is on its way,—
Coming from far yet speeding nigh
To pierce the bridegroom By-and-By.

---

[1] The old spelling (*agen* instead of *again*) is here resumed. Out of a hundred persons, ninety-nine nowadays pronounce this word as a rhyme to *wren* and not to *rain*. The old way, here revived, is seen in Dryden—who wrote:
'Borne far asunder by the tides of *men*,
Like adamant and steel they meet *agen*.'

Stave Second.

I.

Now listen to a tale
Of my Norwegian vale—
The sunny Vale of Nanna's Heim—
    Where I was born,
And where (a lazy youth) I dwelt
And loved to roam and learned to rhyme,
And where (to pass away the time)
I sang of all I saw and felt—
Until the very longest days
Were cut the shorter by my lays.

II.

There, in my native cot
(A humble one, God wot!
The humblest on the mountain-belt),
    One summer morn,
Before as yet a wakeful bird
In any nest had peeped or stirred,
I rose so early from my bed,
That when I knelt and bowed my head
The skies received my matin-prayer
Ere any sign of morn was there:
The East had not a ray of red;
    But fiery Mars
    And other stars
Were lingering still in flaming sight
As loth to ·pale and take their flight;
And all around me everywhere
That ghostly, furtive stillness lay

Which haunts the final hour of night,
    To hie away
    At dawn of day.

III.

It was the hour
When bud and flower,—
In recompense for lustres which they lose
By nightly obscuration of their hues,—
Receive a double fragrance from the night-long dews.

IV.

Their odours, now supremely sweet,
Were wafted to my window-seat—
    Where down I sat
    And slid the slat
And pushed away the vines, to greet
(When it should come) the first forewarning
    That faintly steals
On eyes that wait the chariot-wheels
And golden-footed hoofs of morning.

V.

Apollo's steeds, though thorough-paced,
    Made little haste:
They were so slow that as I waited
    They seemed belated:
Aurora, though she bears a brand,
Had not yet brought it in her hand.

VI.

All Nature, after all the light
Of all her longest summer-day [1]

---

[1] In the latitude of Nanna's Heim, a June day has about nineteen hours of daylight.

(And like a child worn out with play,
Whose sleepy head
Is heavier than a lump of lead),
Now in the deadest slumber lay!

In all the outdoor solitude
The stillness was complete :—
There was no breath of wind to stir
A pine or fir;
No owl to-whitted or to-whooed;
No lynx's whelp
Gave any yelp;
No dog barked in the village street :—

In all the house
No gadding mouse
Made any patter with his feet;
Even the very cricket slept,—
And I alone a vigil kept.

VII.

The hush grew more and more profound,
Till on my listening ear
There stole a faint and tiny sound—
Weird, muffled, strangely near;
And oh, most magical to hear!
It was my heart! I heard it beat!—
The throb was such a thrilling bound,
So full of health and vital heat,
That all my body, through and through,
Tingled at every breath I drew!

VIII.

At first I counted each pulsation—
Till every nerve within me woke

And quivered to the quivering stroke;
And ever as my keen delight
Kept mounting to a higher height
   I said, 'O smite me still
With greater throb and fiercer thrill,
And wreak upon me all thy will!'

And every stroke would re-commence
With vigour more and more intense,
More ravishing to soul and sense—
   Till I, half mad (or quite)
From such a wild exhilaration
(That made my poor and thatched retreat
A more than palace to my sight)
Now felt that just to breathe and *be*
     Was ecstasy!
—For Life appeared divinely sweet!

IX.

Still, hardly daring to rejoice
Lest I should find my joy too fleet
(A pleasure that had come to stay
    Not for a day,
    Not for an hour),
I sprang upon my jocund feet
And gathered up my dumb-struck voice,
And half in whisper, half aloud,
I said, 'O God, were I endowed
For just the length of one long breath
With Thy immeasurable might—
If just a moment were my own
To speak a mandate from Thy Throne—
   Thy voice to me thus lent
   Should instantly be spent

To countervail my dismal doom of death—
A doom which I would straightway undecree!

X.

'Ye fatal Sisters Three'
(Thus would I haste to say[1])
'Your killing edict I reverse!
Cut ye no thread for me!
Spin me no shroud!
Weave me no winding-sheet!
Plume me no hearse!
Dig me no mouldy bed!
Plant me no yew above my head
To whisper with a windy sigh
And say to every passer-by
"Here lies a loathsome thing of clay—
A mortal dead!"
Nay, O ye Trine, who arbitrate
On every mortal creature's fate,
I charge it on ye as your trust,
Keep me exempt from Death and Dust!'

XI.

Then with a throbbing brain
(That seemed to split with pain)
How can a living man, thought I,
But dread to die?
—Would that my mortal days, when done,
Might here on earth be re-begun
And lived agen for seven times seven,
Rather than bartered once for Heaven!

---

[1] The three Fates of the Norsk mythology are called Norns; and their names are Urd or the past, Verdande or the present, and Skuld or the future.

XII.

And if the choice of worlds were mine,—
If on some glorious morn
The Third and Wisest Norn
(The furthest-seeing of the Trine)
Should come in majesty and say to me,
'A boon is offered thee—
The right is thine
To choose the world wherein thou art to dwell—
Take either of the Three,
The Earth, or Heaven, or Hell—
Choose freely as thy spirit may incline—
Elect, if so thou wilt, to tarry *here*—
Here ever, endlessly, from year to year—
Here where these crags of spar and syenite
Frown from their awful height
Down sheerly on the sea-bombarded shore:'—

XIII.

Oh if some high angelic voice
Should with an accent strong and clear
Call out and offer me this choice,—
Then by the dozen Gods—or by a score,
Or by a hundred more,—
However rash, however strange
My paltry preference may appear,
My answer would be this:

XIV.

'Thou gracious sprite,
Be Asgard all for thee[1]!

---

[1] Asgard is the Garden of the Asas, or high divinities—the pleasure-ground of the twelve great Gods—and hence a general title for the Celestial Land, or Odin's Heaven.

Let all its heavenly joys be thine!
But as for me,
O let the world I have, continue to be mine
For if my choice be free
I never, never will resign
Nor quit, nor part with, nor exchange
This bright and bosky earthly sphere
For such a dim unearthly strand
As Pluto's shadowy port,
Where souls of men are loth to land;
Nor for the undiscovered hill
Where Jove, if he be reigning still,
Holds his Olympian Court;
Nor for the fabled heavenly plain
Where Odin's mortal heroes, slain,
Immortally resort;
Nor for the feigned Celestial City,
Whose gates of pearl and streets of gold
The dreamy Patmian thought he spied[1],
And babbled of (for he was old),
Yet which since then (oh, more's the pity!)
No other mortal man beside
Has been permitted to behold!'

XV.

After this burst of mine
I paused, and from a vine
(One of the honeysuckles at my eaves)
I plucked a branch and stripped it of its leaves

---

[1] According to Christian tradition, St. John saw his vision of the New Jerusalem in his hundredth year while he was waiting for his death, which occurred soon afterward on the Isle of Patmos—òr, as some say, in the desert.

(Having nought else to do),
And peered with steady view
Into the many-spangled arch on high,
And thus said I :

XVI.

' Now to a callous carl like me,
Whose faith is small,
Or none at all,—
Believing only what I see,—
Of course the unseen Heaven above
Is but a place for dreaming of:
The only world that I desire
Is not another and a higher;
Let me have leave to live upon this blooming ball,
I care not then
If gods or men
Inherit sun or stars or comets, one or all!
Indeed, however Earth-excelling
Be Heaven, with its divine perfection,
Yet I am mundane in my predilection,
And I would rather, as my place of dwelling,
Be tabernacled on the wettest side
Of watery Spangereid [1],
Or at the wildest foss and fell
Of windy Angervell [2],
Or by Mount Hecla's fiery roar,
Or where the Pole is cold and lonely,
Or anywhere upon the blessed Earth—if only
My earthly lease,

---

[1] The Spangereid is the low and slender isthmus connecting the
Naze with the mainland.
[2] Cave of the Winds.

My term of tenantry, might never cease,
But here go on for evermore!'

XVII.

—And now, O pause agen, my song!
—Of what avail
Is this my tale
That grows already dull and long
Ere yet a tithe of it be told?

The White Wolf[1] waiteth for me on the wold—
Whose breath is cold—
Colder than winter's wind upon the snow:
How can I know
If he will wait until I end my lay?

—So let me drop it now! But nay,
On with the rhyme
While there is time!—
Ere yet the White Wolf creepeth nigh
To hush the rhymer By-and-By.

Stave Third.

I.

In looking back through ages the beholder
Can see that as the world keeps growing older
The earthly span
Allowed to man
Keeps narrowing from its first-appointed range—
Narrowed by Nature in a way most strange;

---

[1] The White Wolf is a dreaded spectre among the peasantry, for
whosoever happens to see it, even in a dream, considers himself
thereby forewarned of the near approach of his death.

Whereof there is a mystery to be cleared
Ere Man can hope to think himself endeared
                    To Nature's heart;
        For cruel Nature coldly stands apart,
        And Man, poor wretch, is now denied
        His place of honour at her side,
For she has other favourites favoured more than he.

II.

    Thus, though by Nature's odd caprice
            Her sacred Cedar Tree—
    In her Sidonian forests by the Sea—
            Has greenly grown
            And borne a cone
    From days of Abram to our own[1];

III.

        Though in her ancient dell
        Where Jacob dug his well
            (That now is dry)
    She gives her Tortoise leave to dwell,
    Housed in a sempiternal shell—
    A tougher roof than triple brass!
    (As if the very Earth should pass
                Ere he should die);

IV.

        Though to her lazy Carp—
        Who never swims beyond
        The marble counterscarp
        That walls his palace-pond[2]—
She grants the leisure to outlive a line of Kings;

---

[1] Among the Cedars of Lebanon, some that are still flourishing are more than 3,000 years old.

[2] The Empress Eugénie used to feed at Versailles a few big-bellied

v.

Though to her ocean-roaming Whale
She portions out his mighty breath to blow
        While centuries come and go
    And navies rot and cities fail;

vi.

Though in her parks of pleasure in Cathay
Her agèd Elephant still swings
    (As in his young and frisky way)
His cunning trunk, and still unties his cords
After his many short-lived human lords
        Have had their little day;

vii.

Though she impels her Eagle to the sky
And gives his master-feather force to fly
Until his hundred years have all rolled by;

viii.

        And even though
        Her thievish Crow
Has her assistance to keep young and spry
Long after his most venerable foe
(The whitest-headed farmer) is laid low;—

ix.

Yet I declare that Nature, granting thus
        Such years of grace
To crowds of creatures of ignoble race,
Displays to *them* a doting prodigality
Which she with stinginess denies to *us*:

---

fish which, in their slenderer youth, had taken crumbs from the
hand of Louis XIV.

For, to her minion of the highest place—
Proud man—whom she is willing to abase,
She shows a niggardly illiberality
By dooming him to swift and merciless mortality.

X.

Or if not Nature's self be thus unjust,
Then Nature's God—a Power still greater—
   Is Man's inexorable Hater :
   For though I shrink, as well I may,
   From what seems blasphemy to say,
   Yet say I will, for say I must,
   That our Omnipotent Creator,
   In moulding us of mortal dust,
   Appears so fiercely to dislike
   His poor resemblance of Himself in clay,
   That always with an angry frown
   And vengeful hand He hastes to strike
   The much-offending image down,
   And with implacable disgust
   To hide it in the Earth away.

XI.

Or is it true, as some have rashly said,
   That the Creator's cruel will
In striking every living creature dead
Is for the stricken creature's own behalf?

      I know of priests who prate
      How God, for Love, not Hate,
   Awards to Man a mortal fate :
   An argument at which I laugh !

   I answer (contradicting still)
   That Death is man's supremest ill ;

That Life, if not a perfect good,
Is yet a blessedness so great
That reason cannot overrate,
           Nor fancy guess
           Nor tongue express
Its most exceeding preciousness!
—*Who* would not live if so he could?
Yet Providence or Chance or Fate
Is always tampering with our date,—
           Fixing our death-day nigh.

XII.

And might I screw my sagging Lay
Up to a shriller, keener key,
           My angry note would be—
           (Dispute it whoso may,
           Deny it whoso can!)
           The earthly life of Man
           Is of too short a span:
His term is scanted, and too soon goes by:
Ere he is born, he has begun to die:
And while he yet is putting forth his leaf,
           He fades away!
           His days, alas,
           Are as the grass!

XIII.

Now Man's too-early death is wrong—
           He should instead live long;
           For I am sure,
In spite of all that Man must needs endure
           Of pain or grief,
           Of toil or tears,

His end is premature—
He is defrauded of his years!

XIV.

A gaudy May-fly flits about
And we who watch him say,
He lives but for a day[1]!
A Moth has hardly time to flaunt his wing
Or show his head[2],
Ere he be dead!
But Man—proud man—beyond a doubt
Is after all, poor lout!
The World's most transitory thing—
Its most ephemeral worm—
Whose meagre temporal term
Should be benignantly increased
To twenty times its length at least!

XV.

Why should his vigour wane
Until his years attain
Once more—as once they did—the ample round
Of their first-measured and primaeval bound
When human life on earth—
In spite of sorrows hard to bear
(Whereof each heart hath ever found its share),
Had for its normal term, from birth to death,

---

[1] The May-fly, the typical insect of the Ephemeridae, is so *very* ephemeral that, as Wood says, 'A single day witnesses its entrance into the perfect state, and its final departure from the world.'

[2] The Moth, in fact, often perishes even more prematurely still—through his inability to break his chrysalis—the shell of which, in hot weather without rain, becomes so dry and hard that he cannot crack it open; and he dies *inside*, unborn.

No less a limit than the years of Seth—
That primal-born, that pious patriarch,
Third of the sons of many-childed Eve,
Heir to his brother Abel's empty place,
 And who (unless we disbelieve
 The sacred annals of our race)
Lived on this globe of ours so long a space,
That at the last in sooth he proudly found
His head most winterly and whitely crowned?
 For nigh a thousand years had *he*
 To hunt and fish and till the ground!

XVI.

 —Why not the same for *me*?
Why not the same for all my fellows here?—
 Herdsmen of cattle and of deer,
  Hunters upon the hills,
  And fishers by the sea?
 Are we not just as simple men?
 Each living in his native glen,
 Each toiling at his wholesome labours,
 And each at peace with all his neighbours?
 —Not scarred with self-inflicted ills,
  Nor wasting life's resources
  In brawls and evil courses?

XVII.

Now though the World was well-begun
(For they, the first who sowed its seed,
  Were men indeed),
Yet what did these, our first forefathers, more—
  On hill or plain—
  Than we ourselves have done
  Beneath as fierce a sun

And in a tenfold fiercer frore—
To make the ground less grudging than before
        To yield its grain?

XVIII.

    Have we not sown our barren rocks
        And coaxed them into green,
    And dotted them with herds and flocks
        The fattest ever seen?—
Taking the hues of day and night
To stripe our cattle black and white—
Like keys upon the ivory fingerboard
Of Saint Cecilia's harpsichord[1]?

XIX.

    —Why is our work cut short?
    Why is our time so scant?
The frailest ilex which we plant
On house-roof or on wagon-shed[2]
Outbraves the Arctic ice and snow,
Defying all the winds that blow,

---

[1] Cattle of these contrasting stripes are especially familiar to travellers in the Netherlands.

[2] Roof-gardens abound in Norway. They are seen not only on the out-buildings of the farm, but often on the cottage itself. The roof is covered with a rich loam, and this is thickly planted with evergreen shrubs. This house-top shrubbery includes a great variety of picturesque growths—such as dwarf birches, reaching to the ridge-pole—white lichens—red mosses—marsh-grass of vivid green—saxifrages with two or three hundred blossoms on a single stem—daisies by the million—violets of Alpine blue—sorrel of a claret-colour—and even yellow asphodel : and if ever a bold goat climbs by stealth to one of these roof-gardens for his regalement, he is in an earthly paradise for only a moment till he is pelted away and punished, and made to remember the danger of venturing upon such thefts in future.

And still has years and years to grow
Long after *we* are struck amort
   And shriveled and brought low
And shoveled under with the dead !

XX.

  I groan, I fume, I writhe
To see the fellness of Old Father Time
   Swinging his fatal Scythe
And mowing mortals down before their prime !—
   Slashing them off, indeed, .
   Each as a noxious weed,
Each as a cumberer of the ground
To be destroyed wherever found.

XXI.

  So Time—to his eternal shame—
Is known immortally to Fame
   By one dread patronym
   Belonging but to *him*:
He is the Fell Destroyer ! *Who* so fell as *he*?
Not Death—for like an over-gorging beast
   Death has a frequent glut,
And so allows a victim to go free—
   Or free awhile at least:
Not Fate—(counted as one or three)—
For Fate herself is doomed to lag and flag,
  To loiter and to hesitate,
To spin a thread which she is loth to cut:
Not Nature—for if man be in a strait
   She will suspend her laws
    . (For righteous cause)
   As when, to free a land,
   She said, 'Stop ye and stand,

Thou sun on Gibeon!
Thou moon on Ajalon!'

XXII.

But Time—the one supreme Destroyer Fell,
The ravening child of Chaos and of Sin
  And born in Hell—
Time—ever hungry, gaunt and thin—
  With ever-greedy maw
  And ever-crunching jaw,
Gloating at every chance to bite and gnaw—
 Time, with his same old appetite
  Fierce as before,
  Keeps munching still with all his might,
  Feeding galore:
For though the Earth be growing old
And now is failing (we are told),
Yet Time, despite his lack of youth,
  Preserves his pristine powers
Nor ever yet has lost a tooth,
  But still devours
  All that is ours.

XXIII.

  —Indeed, they say,
  He grinds away
The World in fragments day by day—
Impatient till his day be nigh
To pulverize it By-and-By.

Stave Fourth.

I.

O ye who seldom look
Into the Holy Book,
Go read agen and yet agen
Upon its earliest page
The annals of the earliest men,
The first of all mankind,
The mighty sires of all our race,
Who saw their Maker face to face
And knew His mind;
And in the record ye shall find
That in that primal age
In spite of all the sin and wrong
That lured poor Adam to his plight
And smote his Garden with a blight,
Still, even then,
The Earth was yet so fresh and new,
So full of splendour,
So goodly in its Maker's sight,
That He to guilty Man declared:

II.

'O thou offender,
Whom I have smitten yet have spared,
The loss that follows on thy Fall
Is loss of much but not of all:
The Fig-tree and the Vine
Shall still be thine—be thine;
The Earth is still for thee—for thee;
It is a gift from Me—from Me;
Take it, enjoy it long;

Make it thy blooming bower,
And I, with dew and shower,
Will wet it at the morning and the evening hour:

III.

'And lest thy hungry mouth
Should ever go unfed,
I, to provide thee bread,
Have laid on Nature my command
To lead thee with her guiding hand
Until, from East to West, from North to South,
Thou everywhere possess the land;
And thus, as lord of all the soil,
Thy daily toil,
Though seeming-slavish, shall be sweet:

IV.

'Thy summer, though it must be fleet,
Shall still be long enough
To head and beard for thee thy wheat;
Thy winter, though it must be rough,
Shall yield thee crops of ivy-leaves[1]
To round thy cattle into beeves:
And though thy years, like birds in flight,
Shall chase each other fast
And seem too quickly passed,
Yet vex thyself with no regret
Nor futile fret,
For what I give I freely give;
And so I have decreed,
To thee and to thy seed,

---

[1] Norwegian cattle sometimes live almost entirely on ivy.

That many a lustrum shall ye live
And many a child shall ye beget
     Ere reaching yet
     The limit set
For paying Nature's final debt':—

V.

If thus our Gracious God the Lord—
After the fierce Archangel's sword,
     Two-edged with fire,
     Had driven our Sire
     Forth from the Garden Gate
     And left him to his fate—
     Outcast and reprobate,
     A wanderer in the wild :—

VI.

If thus, in that forsaken hour,
Th' Almighty—pitying Man's estate—
Could say to Nature, ' Take him for thy ward,
     Make him thy foster-child,
Snatch not away from him too soon
     His one most precious boon ;
Give him ten thousand months to be his measure
Of mortal life (that he may not complain
Of lack of time wherein to work his will
     Or take his pleasure),
And let him all his largest plans fulfil,
That he may die, not having lived in vain ':—

VII.

If this be what the God of Nature deigned to say
To Nature's very self, in her primordial day,

Why then should Nature not be bound
To give the mandate heed?
Why should she now instead be found—
With miserable greed—
Assigning merely three-score years and ten
To be the limit of the lives of men?
And how, with monstrous malice in her act,
By dire extortion, can she dare exact
Man's final debt to her as falling due
So much the earlier now than when the World was
    new[1]?

VIII.

It makes me sick and sore
That now the Years of Man should be so few,
That were so many heretofore!
For, what can be the doleful need
Why Death should make so mad a speed?
Why, to our bitter cost,
Should the life-quenching frost
Be in such haste to freeze the vital marrow?

Why should the final agony and throe,
That came so late in ages long ago,
Be now as swift as Höder's fatal arrow[2]?

---

[1] The old men in the Book of Genesis were Adam, who lived 930 years; Seth, 912; Enos, 905; Cainan, 910; Mahalaleel, 895; Jared. 962; and Methusaleh (the oldest) 969.

[2] Höder's fatal arrow is a symbol of the *first frost*. The story in the Edda is, that while Balder (the god of Summer) was disporting himself with other divinities in Asgard—none of whom were suspicious of a coming calamity—Höder (the god of Winter) appeared unexpectedly in the distance, led by Loki (the spirit of Evil), and immediately let fly an arrow at Balder, piercing him to the heart. This Norsk fancy—illustrating the suddenness of Balder's death—is

Or why (oh shivering to relate !)
Should Nature's primal care for man abate
        Or seem to cloy,
As if she nursed her passion to create
        Just to destroy?

IX.

In spite of braggart bards whose rhymes
May boast of these our Modern Times,
And who with vain pretence avow
That Life is at a richer rate
And better worth the living now,
        I still aver
        That I prefer
No scanty term of earthly pleasure,
But all the patriarchal measure
Conferred by Gód with freer hand
At that primaeval happy date
        (Would it were come agen !)
        The time when mortal men
        Lived long upon the land—
        The goodly days of eld,
The best of days that ever were,
The days of Aaron and of Hur,
Who in the battle's roaring rage
        The drooping hands upheld
Of feeble Moses, faint with age,
        Until .the foe was quelled:

---

based on the natural fact that the Norwegian summer passes away
with lamentable quickness—apparently without the intervention of
an autumn: for while yet the roses are in bloom, the snow begins
to fall.

But where is now the Jew or Greek,
Or where the mighty faith antique,
That wrestles with gigantic wrong
To snatch the battle from the strong
And give it to the weak?

X.

— Man needeth knowledge: knowledge needeth
years!
—Each separate hair of Nestor's hoary head
Was worth a phalanx of a thousand spears!
But what if Nestor had been early dead?
—Except for Nestor's frosty pow,
Troy might have stood till now!

XI.

I hold the Brahmin's creed,
That Life, wherever it is seen,
Even in creatures small and mean
Yea in the very midge and mite—
Exists as by a sacred right,
A right which every man should heed:
For surely there is human guilt
In crushing with a wanton tread
The little house the ant hath built,
Or causing wilfully to bleed
The caterpillar's pretty head,
Or luring to the flame the midge's wing;
And so the God of Indostán
Hath blessings for the kindly man
Who pitifully every night
Takes pains to shade his candle-light.

XII.

Moreover, of all Nature's works
The most inanimate are not devoid
Of something like a Life—to be protected or
destroyed:
For not alone
Are flesh and bone
Of man or beast, by Nature's care,
Kept in replenishment and fresh repair,
But even in a very stone
The vital principle in secret lurks—
To keep the rocks from growing old,
To stay the hills from falling dead:
And even on the inner lids of Tombs
There is enscrolled
(Too faintly to be seen
Yet still in living green)
The legend of a life that buds and blooms
And has its time to love and wed.

XIII.

So even *I*
(Like any other moth or fly
Or crumb of conscious clay)
Desire to live, and not to die:
And though I borrow no distress
From thinking of the doleful day
(Not very distant, as I guess)
When underneath some willow-tree
There is to be a mound for *me*;
Yet now while I am still on fire
With multitudinous desire,
I burn to say

That could my frail and mortal flesh
  Keep young and fresh
(If not indeed for evermore,
Nor for the term of Seth of yore,
Nor like Tithonus¹, wasting with decay)—
Yet if upon this Earth of ours
I could be privileged to stay
Still on and on, through frosts and flowers,
Till I myself should name the day
When Charon and his muffled oar
Should scull me to the other shore :—

XIV.

Then by Saint Peter !—by the Pyx !—
Or by the Moon in perigee !—
By one or both or all the three !—
I here and now asseverate
That ere I finally would fix
My distant, dim and dismal date
For ferriage of the River Styx²,
  I first would wait
  Until by fate
The grim old Ferryman, not I,
Should be the victim doomed to die,—

---

¹ Tithonus, in praying for Immortality, forgot to ask for Youth and Vigour to accompany it; he was doomed to live for ever, yet all the while to grow feebler and feebler; and so he is portrayed by Tennyson as

  ' A white-haired shadow, roaming like a dream.'

² Of the five rivers in the lower world (according to the Greek mythology) Lethé was the river of Oblivion; Phlegethon, the river of Flame; Acheron, the river of Sorrow; Cocytus, the river of Lamentation; and Styx, the river of Abhorrence—that is, the river to be the most abhorred.

D

And till his barge and he be rotten
And both be utterly forgotten,—
And never after should a ghost
Be paddled to the Stygian coast
(That shady shore which mortals dread!)
And man no more should vex his head
   And sit and sigh
And feel a lump rise in his throat—
From awful knowledge that the boat,
However far as yet, or nigh,
Must come to take him By-and-By.

Stave Fifth.

--

Thus, in a silly strain,
I with my shallow brain
Allowed myself awhile to muse—
  A mortal weak and vain:
And thus I rashly judged between
This present visible Terrene
And the Celestial World unseen;
As if I had been called to choose
   Which of the twain
   I would retain
  And which I would refuse:—

And having flung my casement wide
I leaned my foolish head outside,
And looking to the mountain-tops, I said:

II.

'Though God Himself were dead,
And though His Heavens were rolled away
Yet still for me there would remain
The green-enameled Earth instead,—
Which is so fair
That I declare
(Hear it, ye spirits of the air
And of the forest wild!)
This glorious globe of hill and plain,
Of land and sea,
Is more to me
Than aught that all the whole domain
Of all the highest Heavens can be!

III.

'So, since I love Thee well, O Earth,'
Said I, 'Now therefore, as thy filial child
(With right to be maternally caressed
And by my Mighty Mother to be blest),
I make to Thee my heart's supreme request;
Yet not with supplicating tone
Nor plaintive cry
Nor sob nor sigh
Nor bending of my knee
Nor beating of my breast!
The Heavens are prayed to, every day,
With tear and groan
And head low-bowed:
But this my prayer shall be addressed,
O Earth, to thee alone;
And with my head uplift,
For I am proud!

I ask thee boldly for a gift—
    Deny not my behest!
—In every clime, in every zone,
Thou hidest underneath thy vest—
    Deep down within thy girth—
No end of treasures still unknown,
    Which all belong to thee!

IV.

'So, O thou generous Mother Earth,
Now listen to my daring plea—
    Enrich me with thy best!
Grant me thy very dearest boon,
Thy gift of most exceeding worth!
And if thou grant it, grant it soon;
That, as my days are but a span,
I may enjoy while yet I can
Thy crowning mercy unto man!

V.

'And yet, I know not what I beg of thee!
    For, O thou Mighty Mother mine,
    How can I fathom or divine
    Or reason out or guess or dream
    Which of thy gifts thyself dost deem,
    For mortal man, thy boon supreme?
    What can so great a bounty be?
    What hallowed title does it bear?
    How is it pled for in a prayer?
    Or how in Saga or by Skald
    Is such a precious treasure called?
    Can it be syllabled in speech?
    Or is it spoken not, nor sung

But interdicted to the Tongue,
Like that forbidden Holy Name
Which not a Hebrew dared proclaim[1]?

VI.

'And is the boon within the reach
Of common mortals, all and each?
Or is it hidden from the view
Of all except a favoured few?
Or is it vaguely veiled in doubt,
That none may wholly find it out?
Or by what token would I know it,
If haply on a bard like me—
Although of low degree,
Yet as a gift of grace
To one of Bragi's race—[2]
O bounteous Earth, thou shouldst bestow it?

VII.

Thus did I rant—thus did I rave—
And fancied, with my throbbing head,
That what I had so glibly said
Was wise and sober, just and grave.

VIII.

—A salty whiff from Strelsa Bay
Arose and smote me on the cheek,
And seemed to say,
'Poor fool, thy wit is weak!
Thy Mighty Mother will not lend

---

[1] In ancient Palestine, one of the names of God, though it was known to men, was too holy to be taken upon human lips; but in ancient Norseland, one of the gods—the god supreme above Odin— was too mysterious to have a name at all.

[2] Bragi was the god of poetry.

To such a dolt her listening ear,
   Nor will she condescend
To' make to such a dunce her mysteries clear.'·

IX.

Then for a space that one might name
The flashing of a meteor's flame
As it goes blazing through the sky,
I had a burning hope of a reply;
   But when no answer came,
     ' Alack !' cried I,
' O Earth, thou dost not reck my rede !
For though the Heavens, when mortals plead,
   Are pitiful and tender
   And listen and give heed,
   Yet never have I known
   A heart so like a stone,
O flinty Earth, as is thine own !
No recognition dost thou deign to render !
Thy softest breezes coming from the sea
   Have voices as they come ;
Thy weakest waves along the shingly beach
   Lack not a speech ;
Thy tiniest insect beats a busy drum
   Or makes a hum,—
  But thou thyself, O Earth, art dumb !
  Thou heedest not the prayer or hymn
   Of men or cherubim !
O thou ungracious Earth, I spurn thee !
Thou· harkenest not to my desire !
—I care not if the final fire
   Should come and burn thee !—
   Nor care I if, instead,—

(To thy far greater dread[1])—
Thy Fimbulwinter[2] now be nigh,
To freeze Thy vitals By-and-By.

Stave Sixth.

1.

Now all the while as thus I spake
(With none except myself to hear),
I ran my eyes along the rim
Of Queen Brunhilda's lofty lake[3],—
Impatient till its crystal dim
Should catch the dawn and glitter clear:
For when the tardy day should break
            (That now was near)
I had a task to undertake—
            A toil unique,

---

[1] In the far North, especially among the Lapps and Finns, the idea of a fire big enough to burn the world is rather pleasing than otherwise, but the fear of perishing by cold is awe-inspiring and dreadful.

[2] 'Fimbul' is great or mighty; and 'Fimbulwinter' is the short but terrible Age of Ice, which is to precede Ragnârok, or the final destruction of the world.

[3] Princess Brunhilda, or Brynhild, was the mythic maiden whom Sigurd loved, and for whose sake he rode through flaming fire. Despite their troth, the lovers were fated not to wed each other; for by witchcraft—that was powerfully practised upon Sigurd—he was induced to marry Princess Gudrun; while Brynhild was at the same time married to King Gunnar. The subsequent jealousy of Brynhild, who ceased not to love and to desire Sigurd, so overcame her spirit that in her anguish she planned and accomplished Sigurd's death. This tragedy is told in the Elder Edda.

Which, though it was a sudden whim,
    A hasty freak,
Yet bore so big a promise in it,
That I was feverish to begin it.

II.

For I had lately much lamented
How idly I had spent my youth—
A folly which I so repented
That now (though tardily forsooth) .
I said, 'The remnant of my days
Shall all be passed in Wisdom's ways—
    If I can find them out,
    Whereof I have a doubt;
For they are ways to me unknown,
    Untrod before,
And I have read that they are strown
    With flint and stone;
    And furthermore
They are so narrow and so strait,
That whoso finds them, finds them late,
And whoso treads them, walks alone.'

III.

    Thus for a livelong hour
    I in my window-bower
Impatient sat and mulled and mused
Until I found my mind confused:
'For what is Wisdom?' wondered I;
'Is it of Earth or from on High?
Is it for mortals to attain?
Or is their longing for it vain?'

IV.

—Whereat my Conscience, with a fierce reply,
Said to me chidingly, 'Thou fool, O fie!
  The World has from of old
  By Holy Writ been told
That Wisdom is a thing to be desired
  More than the finest gold,—
Yet in thy stolidness, O stupid kern,
It is a thing which thou hast yet to learn!'

V.

Thus by this self-inflicted fling
(Which pierced me like a hornet's sting)
  My goading Monitor within
Convicted me of folly and of misspent years:
  As much as if to say,
  'Thy youth hath fled away
And left to thee a fool's cap and an ass's ears.
So lest thou also fool away thy prime,
  Redeem the time;
  Arise and go—
  Go high and low—
Go ask the Wise to tell thee what they know
  And listen well
  To what they tell,
And all their wisdom heed and weigh,
Till thou become as wise as they.'

VI.

So spake my Conscience, with a tone
That chilled me to the marrow bone:
Whereat, as when a criminal in court
Is bidden to uplift his guilty hand

And take his sentence,
Not daring to retort,
I humbly took my reprimand —
Till my repentance
Began to burn within me to the quick;
When, in my shame at the deserved rebuke,
I found a tongue to say,
'Now by the holy heifer of Saint Luke!
O thou my angry Conscience, thy command
I will obey;
My rebel heart is faint and sick —
Obedience, I am sure,
Can be its only cure.
So I, without delay
And with all diligence, shall go my way
To do thy will;
And I shall take this livelong summer day
To traverse vale and hill,
And make a wide and searching quest
Whereby to ascertain,
On evidence most plain—
Confirmed by many a proof and test
What worldly good or gain
Is by the Wisest deemed the Best.'

VII.

So, for the profit of my soul
I planned a scheme
Which now may seem
(To sober view) grotesque and droll,
And yet it was not meant
As curious sport or cunning jest.

For though I always, from my birth,
Had had an overflow of mirth,
Yet now a cankered sorrow in my breast
　　　　(Not here to be confessed)
Had put me on a new and sober bent,
And deeply stirred me with a strange intent,
Which was, that I might now be clearly shown—
What in my wayward youth I had not known—
The thing most worthy of a mortal's thought,
That I might seek it, as a mortal ought.

VIII.

Now this is what I had devised :—:
I was to start at peep of day,
A Pilgrim on the king's highway,
Yet so ingeniously disguised
That I could pass unrecognised ;
Not guessed to be a dalesman of the Ampt [1],
But deemed a stranger who had thither tramped :
　　　　For I could talk at need
　　　　As Norsker or as Swede,
　　　　Or I could feign
　　　　To be a Dane ;
Moreover, in my cottage attic
　　　　I had for years possessed
　　　　A sacred Alb and Vest,
Together with an old Dalmatic
And other toggery brought from Elsinore,
Such as the Danish Monks once wore—
　　　　All made of Flanders cloth,
And now bemouthed of many a moth—
Save only where, against the breast,

---

[1] Ampt is district or shire.

A silken Holy Cross remained
    Which not a moth had spoiled,
    Nor any mould had soiled,
Nor Time itself had mildewed or had stained:
(As if the emblem of the Holy Cross
Had power to save whatever thereto clings,
Exempting evermore from wreck and loss
Not only souls of men, but souls of things.)

IX.

So I· resolved that I would go arrayed·
Not only as a man of humble grade
    (For such I was in very deed),
    Yet, since I carefully must heed
    How not to seem as of the rank
    Of mendicant or mountebank,
    Or costerman or strolling clown,
        Or thimble-rigging cad,
I would *religiously* be clad—
        A walking Carmelite [1],
With sandals and an amice-gown
        And scapular of white,
.And with a wallet, staff and shell:
        And thus bedight,
I meant to saunter up and down
Through every neighbouring thorp and town
From cock-crow until curfew-bell,
Accosting like a beggar bold
All whom I met, both young and old,
    · Both great and small:

---

[1] The Carmelites are among the very few Roman Catholic brother-hoods that flourish among Norwegians; for Norway is the· most Protestant country in the world.

Albeit not with hand out-thrust
To beg a pittance or a crust;
But simply asking to be told,
    By one and all,
What worldly honour, gain or prize
Each for himself, with longing eyes,
Was looking up to as the earthly blessing
Most worthy of his winning and possessing.

X.

The summer day, thought I, is long—
So if I give my feet no rest,
But chase the Sun from East to West,
And go where busy mortals throng,—
And if I gather as I go
The thrifty maxims which they know,
I surely shall not fail to find
In all the wit of all mankind—
    In speech or song
    Or homely tale—
Some precious proverb, hint or rune
    That shall avail
To point me to some blessed boon
To which I have as yet been blind;
Some greater gain, some grander good,
Than I thus far have understood;
Yet something not too great or grand
For just a carl to understand:
No visionary aim or end
    Such as a hind
    Of humble mind
Might find too vague to comprehend;

No glory too resplendent
Or rapture too transcendent
For mortals in their mortal state,
Or too preposterously high
For such a worm of Earth as I ;
No promised fortune in some other sphere
Whilst I as yet am unprovided here ;
No heritage too far away,
Or heritable far too late
For common earthly needs like mine ;
No goal celestial or divine ;
No Glasir Grove [1]
In which to rove
With Valkyr [2], Vala [3], Norn and Van [4]
(Companions hardly fit for Man) ;
No Asgard gate or peristyle
To which the towering stairs
In their ascent may stop
Before they reach the top,
And leave me in the lurch meanwhile ;
No super-earthly Paradise
Of man's invention and device,
Hung high above the noon of day,
For which the Saints on Earth may pray,
Yet which, despite their prayers,
May not at last be theirs ;

---

[1] Glasir Grove was a haunt of the gods, and lay adjacent to Valhal, the palace of Odin.

[2] A Valkyr (or Valkyrie) was a winged spirit who hovered over earthly battle-fields in order to bear the souls of the slain to Heaven.

[3] A Vala was an inspired prophetess—who, both before and after her death, might be consulted as an oracle.

[4] A Van was a sea-god.

No shining seat afar
In sun or moon or star
Where possibly the Angels are—
But whether they be there or not
I lack the grace
To want their place :
Nor do I pray to share their lot !
I seek instead some boon of bliss
Not in another world, but this !

—There *must* be such a prize, thought I,
And whether it be far or nigh,
I hope to win it By-and-By.

Stave Seventh.

I.

Forth at the screaming of the Swan
As she awoke and fled her nest,
I, with my ancient relics on
(A stranger to myself thus drest),
On my day's pilgrimage departed
Just as the Sun on *his* had started,
While yet Diana's silver horn
Was regnant both of night and morn.

II.

Already, busy as a hive,
The little Thorp was all alive,
For now came Market-day,
And carts and wains
And wagon-trains

Began by dozens to arrive,
    And more were on the way.

III.

Straight to the Market-place I went,
    And found a Gypsy-clan,
      With all their caravan,
Encamped thus early in their tent:
For as to Egypt's roving brood
        (As everybody knows)
No coast nor land nor latitude—
From Gilgit, where the Indus flows
        And Lotos blows,
To Finmark where the seven-hued night
    Flames with Auroral light,—
    No habitable place
    Upon the whole Earth's face,
No smallest town in any clime,
No hamlet on a hill or plain
Is ever suffered to remain
Unvisited in summer-time
By this forever-roaming race,
Who slily come and slily go,
And in their wandering to and fro
Leave many a subtle mark and trace
Hid like a rune—and unbeknown
Save to their tribal mates alone—
      To guide aright
      Even at night
      A Gypsy wagon-train:
And thus, before the break of day,
In carts bespattered thick with grime,

The ragged rogues had found their way
Into the thorp of Nanna's Heim[1].

IV.

Their dingy house of blanket walls
   Stood open wide,
Lit with a pitchy resin blaze,
And showing to the public gaze
   A gay inside
All hung with Roman scarfs and shawls
  Of yellow, red and blue,
And glittering glass-work, blown in balls
(A kind of work the Arabs do),
And osier-baskets fresh and new,
And clumps of willow-splints and reeds
  Ochred with every hue,
And ornaments in ormolu,
  And Spanish leathers,
  And peacocks' feathers,
And stalks of coriander-seeds,
And strings of peppers dangling down,—
  And here a rag,
  And there a tag,
  And there a velvet-gown ;—
For so these beggars came to town.

---

[1] During a ramble along the Loire, in the centre of France, in the autumn of 1891, the author met a great company of Norwegian gipsies, migrating Southward to get rid of their native Northern winter. The spectacle was a picturesque and ragged travesty of the original invasion of France by the Norsemen ! The wanderers had a well-thumbed passport, signed by a Norwegian burgomaster. Among six or seven wagon-loads of children—all native Norskers—not one had yellow hair ; but all were true to their remote and original type of Egyptian swarthiness.

V.

Their swarthy Queen (into whose cap
I dropped a coin) sat by the road
And held, half-covered by her wrap,
And yet half-naked in her lap,
A babe, who laughed and leapt and crowed,
Although the bantling all the while,
Despite his wriggle and his smile
(As I discovered by a peep)
Lay sunken in the soundest sleep.

VI.

Then to the mother, as she sat
And suckled her tumultuous brat,
Quoth I, 'Some vision, it is plain,
Is flitting through his baby brain—
Some glowing dream which, I confess,
I would I had the wit to guess,—
For he is mad with happiness.'

VII.

So, stooping low and bending near,
I kissed his rose-leaf of a cheek,
And in his sea-shell of an ear
I softly said, 'Bambino dear,
How can a bairn, although so weak,
Although so small,
Yet jump and jerk, and pull and haul,
As if beneath his pigmy size
He were a giant in disguise?
Thy hands are of a tender touch,
And yet are desperate in their clutch!
What can so fierce a fight be for?

What cause enlists
Thy little fists
In such a furious show of war?
Can it be possible, my pet,
That thou already dost descry
In slumber, and with fancy's eye,
Some glittering prize before thee set,
Which thou who art so young as yet
Dost at thy tender age begin
Thus manfully to try to win?'

VIII.

The Babe, awaking, looked about,
With first a smile and then a pout,
And answered, in a baby's way,
With croon and crow, as if to say,
'O yes, the merest midge like me
Can have a purpose, as you see:
Why need I wait till I be grown,
To feel ambition of my own?
I have a great and glorious aim—
And every baby has the same;
Our hopes are high, you may be sure,
For we are innocent and pure;
              Our hearts are right;
And so our weakness is our might:
For what though I be young and wee,
Yet mighty thoughts were born in me—
Thoughts that have ever since my birth
Been more in Heaven than on the Earth:

IX.

'So in my sleep
I often leap

E 2

To catch a thing that shines at night—
　　　Up yonder in the blue!
But I have never caught it quite!
The Fairies wash it with their dew,
And so they keep it clean and white:
　　　It is a silver toy—
And looks so spick and span and new,
That always when it comes in view
　　　I jump for joy,
And up to Heaven my arms I fling,
And wish my arms were each a wing!
You tell me that I roll and bounce
　　　And flop and flounce,
And in the middle of my nap
Seem leaping off my mother's lap:
This is because the shining thing
　　　Appears so near,
　　　So big and clear,
And all so beautiful and bright
That I am crazy at the sight!

X.

'Just now, although my lids were closed,
I saw it glitter as I dozed:
But always when I wake it seems
Not quite so big as in my dreams:
Yet it is silver, as you see,
And beautiful as it can be!
It is the Moon—Oh! what a prize,
If I could pull it from the skies!'

XI.

Then to the tiny tot I said:
'I marvel how thy little head

With huge ambition thus hath planned
To hold a world within thy hand!
Art thou so bold at Life's beginning?
In all thy later years thou never
Wilt plot so daring an endeavour!
Thy baby hopes are wondrous grand—
So grand, I fear, that they are flighty:
For not the Fates themselves, though mighty,
Have power sufficient to fulfil
The monstrous measure of thy will!
Or shall thy feebleness prevail
Where every other force must fail?
                    If so, be gay
                    And croon away
                    And laugh and leap!—

XII.

'For by Saint Birgit and her Bear¹,
Whilst yet thou art a babe, I swear
                    Thy slightest whimper,
                    Thy faintest simper,
Thy dreamy rollicking in sleep,
Thy waking crow, thy ogling stare,
Thy wondrous wise and ancient air,—
All these are powers of thine to coax
And win and wheedle elder folks!
A baby's ways are wondrous winning;
They captivate both friend and stranger.

---

¹ St. Birgit's day is October 7th—the day on which the 'prime-staves' (or notched almanacs) say that the Bear begins his winter-sleep.

XIII.

'Indeed there was a Babe that lay
A nightlong on a hutch of hay
And in no cradle but a manger;
And yet before the break of day
Came Wise Men to adore Him,
Who knelt so low before Him,
　　That evermore since then
　　Among the sons of men
A babe, however poor and lowly,
Is by his birthright high and holy:
　　And so art *thou*;
But He—thy manger-born compeer,
The Prince to whom the Angels bow—
Is Lord alike of sea and land,
　　Of earth and sky;
While as for thee, thou ragged thing,
Though thou art something of a king,
Yet thou art neither earthly grand
　　Nor heavenly high:
And so, Bambino, much I fear
That yonder haughty Lady Moon
Is quite too far away to hear
　　Thy cunning croon;
　　Or if she heard,
　　Upon my word
I think she is too proud and fine
To come at such a call as thine!'

XIV.

Thus to this infant at the breast
I jabbered in a mocking tone,

As if the child were grown
And could respond to me with jest for jest.
But though his mother gave a smirk
And smiled at all my merry chatter,
Yet he—as solemn as a Turk—
Received it as a serious matter;
And once agen, with jump and jerk,
He gave a baby's eager reach,
And with a quivering of the lip
 He said, if not with speech,
Yet in a language quite as plain,
'You are a full-grown man—but, sir,
You are not yet too old to err!
I do not toss my arms in vain!—
I wriggle and I never stop,
Because I must be always ready
To catch the Moon when it shall drop!
I cannot keep my elbows steady
Nor shut my fingers close and tight,
 For please to understand
That I am such a tiny fellow,
 And have so wee a hand,
That things that I would like to snatch
 Are hard to catch:
The hardest thing to catch, of all,
 Is yonder Silver Ball
(Which now is Gold, it is so yellow).
But I must catch it, if I can,
And I will tell you of my plan:

xv.

'The slippery Moon is apt to slide
Behind a passing cloud,—to hide;—

But out agen it has to glide—
And oft it has to glide so fast
That it must slip and fall at last:
                    Now hark!
            If it should slip—
            If it should fall—
It then would drop into my grip!
And that is why I strive and strain
To touch it with my finger-tip!
And I shall try, and try, and try!
You see, I have a shining mark!
        My little hands, I know,
Will not be always small,—
                And as they grow,
My Gipsy mother . . . *she* will teach
My cunning fingers how to reach
And how to clutch and how to hold
                Silver and gold!

Now look! the Moon is coming nigh!—
And I shall snatch it By-and-By!'

Stave Eighth.

I.

The fierce Norwegian Summer-Sun
(So bright we call it Odin's Eye—
And well that Odin has but one,
            For had he two,
Their double fierceness, I am sure,
We Norskers never could endure)
—The Sun, I say, had climbed so high,

That now from every flower that grew
He stole the dew;
But still in every leafy haunt
The birds were boisterous in their chaunt,
For still the day was young and new.

II.

I wandered on,
Until anon
By slow descent of crooks and turns
I traversed—shoulder-high in ferns—
The Bailiwick
Of Breidablik [1]
And wound my way, descending still,
Until I passed by Thorkel's Mill,
Where, fearless of its flapping sails,
A thousand hungry snipe or more [2]
Were picking seeds about the door;
And thither too the shyest quails
In covies came;
And even timid ptarmigans grew bold [3]
Whom human kindness rendered tame,
As if the birds had all been told

---

[1] This obscure bailiwick has proudly named itself after the god Balder's principal palace in the sky!

[2] These are the snipe that say—'chick-a-chick-a chic!'—in unmistakable English words.

[3] In Nanna's Heim, the fowl that is known elsewhere as the ptarmigan, is always called the *rype*: in Sweden, the *ripa*: it is the chief game-bird of Scandinavia: and Nature, to give it a chance for its life (for it is hunted by thousands of sportsmen) renders its plumage in autumn as brown as the bracken, and in winter as white as the snow.

That by the Miller's friendly will
They there might forage to their fill.

III.

The millbrook in its bed of gravel
Made music to me in my travel,
And here and there a frightened trout
Fled from my shadow and leapt out
(As if to show his flashing fin
A moment only), and leapt in.

IV.

An Urchin with a book and slate
(Yet not in haste to hie to school)
Stood angling in the Orkla Pool.

V.

Thought I, 'My lad, you will be late!
And what a shame to fool away
The fresh beginning of a day!
For if the precious morn be lost,
It is a blossom nipped with frost;
And never to the bough that bore it
Can even Odin's self restore it.'

VI.

Behind the bracken then I hid
To watch the drone and what he did:
I saw him idly stand and wait,
And whip the water with his bait,
And change the colour of his fly,
Whilst not a trout of all the brook
Came nibbling at his luckless hook.
And well I knew the reason why—
                For I, oh lackaday!
Had frightened every fin away.

VII.

So down the angler flung his rod,
And sprawling on the mossy sod
Looked up intently at the sky,
Watching a cloud go sailing by,
That soon appeared to lag and stop
Becalmed on Orkla mountain-top[1].
And there it lay—a stranded barque
That loomed aloft, as when the Ark
Hung high and dry on Ararat.

VIII.

Then from the bracken out I crept,
And up behind the rogue I stept,
And said, 'What ho, my bonny boy'
(As down in front of him I sat),
'Tell me the secret of thy joy;
For certes, at a glance I trace
A look of rapture on thy face.
What fancy sets thee thus aglow?
What cheery hope enchants thee so?
Thou surely hast some wiser wish
Than just to catch a silly fish;
So pardon me if I inquire
What is a boy's supreme desire?—
Or what is thine?—

IX.

'For I divine
That with a face so fair and fine,
And with a spirit so elate,
Thou art expecting something great!

---

[1] The hill that overlooks Strelsa Bay.

A youth like thee,
With eyes so bright, and thoughts so free,
Bewrays a lofty pedigree.
There cannot be in all the Earth
A nobler birth,
Or a more royal line,
O lad, than thine!
Thou art some goodly mother's son;
Some honest peasant is thy sire:
In God's own eye
Thy rank is high—
So high that none on Earth is higher.

X.

'But Nature is not Fate,—
So, though thy gifts be great,
Yet if thou wouldst pursue
(As other gifted mortals do)
Some worldly honour which thou hast in view,
Thy task will not be easy to be done,
For all thy honours are as yet unwon.
Now tell me from thy inmost breast,
What trophy seems to thee the best?
What is thy heart most set upon?'

XI.

The stripling, from my trist attire
(That now was torn
By many a thorn)
Mistook me for a begging friar—
An object of his merry scorn—
One of a tribe
At whom to jibe:

So first he whistled—then he sang—
And then to my astonished ears
He burst into a glib harangue
That showed a wit beyond his years;
I never heard a tongue more fluent.
Quoth he, 'O Father Capuchin,
I have not sinned a sinner's sin;
For though I angle as a truant,
              Yet much I doubt
              If catching trout
(Especially when none will bite)
Be wrong in the Almighty's sight!
Nor am I such an old transgressor
        As to be deft and glib
In honey-fugling a confessor;
        But by the Good Saint Tibb[1]!
        (Who never told a fib)
I never told to mortal yet
The thing whereon my heart is set:
           My secret is my own—
           Mine only—mine alone.
I keep it from the village-rabble,
For if I once in Nanna's Heim
Should make my great discovery known,
Egad, how all the geese would gabble!

XII.

'But I can ·see no risk or danger
In telling it to you, a stranger;
So I will reel it off in rhyme,

---

[1] It is to be suspected that this saint (like some others in the calendar) is a myth!

Which I can spin by foot or yard,—
For every boy is half a bard.
Moreover, though you may not know it,
Youth is the pith of every poet;
And you yourself, I dare premise,
Would give the wrinkles from your eyes,
And add the tatters from your hood,
To be a poet, if you could!
So listen, Padre, if you will.'

XIII.

Then with a boyish voice, as shrill
As when a widgeon in the spring
                    Attempts to sing,
'Sir Priest,' quoth he, 'confession true
                    I make to you:
My heart is set upon a thing
For ever old, for ever new,
And never twice the same in hue.
At daybreak it is orange-bright,
At noonday it is fleecy white,
At eventide it is vermilion.—

XIV.

'Thou shalt behold it if thou wilt:
It is a high and huge pavilion—
The biggest that was ever built;
A house of many a wall and wing,
And which no Palace of the King
                    Of Yan-Teping,
Nor Mansion of the Hospodar
                    Of Kandahar,
Nor white Pagoda of the Ming,
Nor gilded Kremlin of the Czar,

Nor Delhi's pied and mottled Fane,
Nor tinted Tent of Tamerlane,
Nor silken Barrack of the Cid
(That reached the length of near a mile
And shaded half of Sarak Isle),
Nor that now-perished Pyramid
Which once stood midway of the Nile,—
No, nor the Holy House of Gold
Built by King Solomon of old,
Hath ever equalled, I am told!

XV.

'O grand were these, but grander yet
Is yonder porphyry parapet
Upheld by pillars fairer thrice
Than any carved by man's device!
  And all the while
  The stately pile,
From topmost battlement to base,
Stands not on any ground or place,
  But sinks and lifts,
  And ever shifts!
For by an architecture strange
It is remodeled in a trice
And subject momently to change.

XVI.

'This very instant, while I speak,
It moves from yonder mountain-peak;
Look up and see the glorious sight!
Cloud upon cloud! height upon height!
What temple on this earth of ours
Hath such majestic walls and towers?

What human hand
Hath ever planned
A portico so rich and grand,
Or gate of entrance half so fair?
What boldest builder ever known
Could put the pattern into stone?
Its like is built in dreams alone!
It is a Castle-in-the-Air!
And I desire it for my own.'

XVII.

Quoth I, 'O urchin noble-browed,
I will not daunt, I will not dash
A hope so honestly avowed,
And yet so beautifully rash.
The thoughts of Youth should be sublime—
Its aspirations should be proud;
But there are heights too high to climb!
And if thy Castle be a Cloud,
However much thou mayst desire it,
Or dream of trying to acquire it,
It may turn black,
And go to wrack,
And fly asunder,
For Thor may strike it with his thunder!
O big-eyed boy!
Make haste! Employ—-
Before the storm—some brawny Nixie,
Or doughty Dwarf or mighty Pixie,
To bring to thee thy palace on his back!—

XVIII.

'Or wilt thou, for the lack
Of such a useful elf,

Attempt the pretty task thyself?
Hast thou a ladder of ascent
To yonder sky-built battlement?
Or wilt thou on the rolling mist
Walk to those walls of amethyst?
Or canst thou from the lowly ground
Leap thither with a skip and bound?
The strongest birds, as all the hunters know—
The mightiest wings that from the forest fly—
   Are ever loth to go
Where all the upper air is full of frost and snow:
   Even the Lammergeyer[1],
   The very loftiest flyer,
Mounts not above the middle sky;
And since thy Castle reaches higher,
Thou wilt not scale its walls, I think,
By sprawling on the river's brink.'

XIX.

The lazy lad, who did not cease
To gaze upon his Tower of Fleece,
   But lay and listened
   Until his eyeballs glistened,
   Filled with all Heaven's effulgence,
Replied, 'O reverend father Abbot,
In honour of thy holy habit
(Somewhat, it seems, the worse for wear),
I thank thee for thy good advice,
But have no pence to pay the price
   Of plenary indulgence;
Or even of a mass or prayer;

---

[1] This is not the Condor, but his kin—the Bearded Vulture.

So I must trust to luck instead:
Which, from the signs that I have read,
Portends for me a happy fate;
For my desire shall come to pass
Whilst I am lounging on the grass.

XX.

'So here I tarry to await
The opening of my Castle-gate:
A breath of wind, from near or far,
Will swing the mighty door ajar.
　　　　　The faintest puff
　　　　　Will be enough.
I know not when the breeze will blow,
Nor whence, nor whither; but I know
That I shall be the luckiest living mortal
When I behold the opening of the portal.'

XXI.

Then to the Boy I said in answer,
　　　　'O young romancer,
　　　　Thy fancy teems
　　　　With empty dreams!
It is the foolish faith of youth
To take these nothings for the truth:
Dost thou in very deed espy
A new Alhambra[1] in the Sky?
A Valhal like the one of old
That crowned the crest of Idavold[2]?
Thy Mansion of the Mist, no doubt,

---

[1] See appendix.
[2] Odin's throne was on Idavold—as Jupiter's was on Olympus.

Is very grand, both in and out,
And to its owner may appear
Not only beautiful but near;
Yet, though I have no measuring-rule,
I fancy that the vestibule
Is forty times too far away
For thee to enter it to-day.'

XXII.

'Why not this very day?' cried he,
'For you yourself can clearly see,
Just overhead, the tower, the wall,
The dome, the pinnacle, and all!
The vision is so plain in view
That I am sure it must be true!—
And for its confirmation, look!
It is reflected in the brook.
Sir Priest, I cannot be deceived,
For what is seen must be believed!
Good riddance to my slate and book!
   I were a fool
   To think of school!
Why should I have a wish or care
Save for my Castle-in-the-Air?
O Monk, in spite of all you say,
And even of the Cross you wear,
   I dare declare
That there be Gods more eld than thine,
  And therefore more divine;
And by the ancient faith, I swear
That be my Castle far or nigh,
I shall possess it By-and-By!'

Stave Ninth.

I.

The fleeting morning passed, and soon
The shortened shadows brought the noon:
The matins of the birds were over,
But all about me, in the clover,
I heard the hum of honey-bees;
And now, on all the resin-trees,
The strident, sun-adoring crowd
Of shrill cicádas[1] sang aloud;
Whilst far away, like echoing trumpet-calls,
A dozen tumbling waterfalls
Down from the Norska Fiellen[2] roared
And whitened into Flekker Fiord.

II.

I crossed the Ferry
To Hakon Skerry[3],
And from the sandy bar
I climbed the granite scar
Where now the twin lighthouses are,
Though then no wagon-road, as now,
Went winding up the mountain's brow.

---

[1] The peasants say that the female Cicáda deposits her eggs only in soil that has never been touched by a plough.

[2] A mountain-chain—the backbone of Norway.

[3] A skerry is a fragment of sea-coast, broken from the mainland, and wholly surrounded by salt water, yet too small to be called an island, and consisting, in many cases, of only a single isolated rock— the haunt of sea-gulls, snipe and gannet-geese. The skerries are 'a multitude that no man can number.' They are patriotically styled the coastguards or sentinels of Norway. Hakon Skerry was named from Hakon the Great, king of the Norwegians in the ninth century.

III.

The place was strange—I knew it not;
And yet I knew its history;
The haunt was quite a famous spot
    By reason of a mystery;
For in that lone sequestered place,
Sole occupant, now dwelt a Finn,
A hermit far from kith and kin,
Self-banished from the human race;
Not living in a house or cot
        But in a stony grot
        Hewn in the gabbro shelf[1]
        By Nature's cunning self;
A haunt which, as I ventured in
Half-blinded, seemed a narrow cave—
Less like a dwelling than a grave;
For in its dank unwholesome air
The solitary dweller there
Had grown so hollow-eyed and thin,
That now at last he looked almost
A walking skeleton or ghost:
I never in my life had seen
A living man so strangely lank,
So supernaturally lean.

IV.

This hermit, born to noble rank,
Had quit a vice-imperial court[2]

---

[1] This formation of rock consists essentially of diallage and white epidote.

[2] Called 'vice-imperial' for the reason that Finland is a political annex of Russia.

(Or so the gossips made report),
And to this barren bank—
This cavern dim and dank—
Half hidden from the light of day,
Had come a dozen years before
(From which they argued he would stay
A dozen more).

v.

I from my low and humble station
Looked at this lord with admiration :
He was a man whose mind
Was subtile and refined ;
And though the garb he wore
Was shaggy like the pelt
Of the Sæhrimner boar[1],
And bristled like the belt
That girt the great God Thor[2],
And though his sunken eyes were wild,
Yet noble was his every feature,—
And he was such a kindly creature,
So gracious and so mild,
So very scholarlike and meek,
That I was charmed to hear him speak.

---

[1] This is the mythic Boar on which earthly heroes, who have fallen in fight and been carried by Valkyries to Odin's banquet-hall, are said to feast in Heaven. According to the Eddas, the immortal animal is re-killed, re-roasted, and re-eaten every day for ever !

[2] Thor is the Thunderer. He fights the Frost-giants. He carries for a weapon a hammer called Miollnir. He wears for a talisman a girdle called Megingyarder. Whenever he flings his hammer, it comes straight back agen to his hand. Whenever he puts on his girdle, his strength is redoubled.

VI.

'Be welcome, weary Sir,' he said,
'And if you hunger, here is bread ;
For never shall a beggar say
I turned him from my door away.'
Whereat with quick and hospitable zeal,
And with those lively graces manifold
That marked the manners of a former day
(But which at present are in sad decay
          And almost dead),
   The noble thane began to spread
   A table-mat as for a meal,
And in the centre set a cup of gold.

VII.

    Quoth he, 'O Abbot,
    You wear a habit
Not often worn among Norwegians—
At least, in these unpapal regions :
Now pilgrims of your holy cloth
    Live not on faith alone,
But every priest must have his broth,
    As every dog his bone :
My larder is not fatly stored,
Yet you are welcome to my board.'

VIII.

'By wide repute, Sir,' answered I,
'Thou art to all the poor well-willed :
But see—my wallet is well-filled ;
So I, in turn, now ask of *thee*
To join in a repast with *me*.'

IX

He shook his head and answered 'Nay!'
And pushed my proffered fruits away:
'Whatever dainties you have brought,'
Quoth he, 'I must partake of nought;
      For I to-day
Must calculate a new assay;
So I must think, and think, and think:
Now fasting is the food of thought.'

X.

I weighed his abstinent reply,
And would have put my wallet by,
Save that he led me to a seat
    Upon a quern of stone,
    And with a pitying tone
That sounded charitably sweet,
He said, 'O famished beggar, eat!
Eat both the portions, thine and mine!
And that you may the better dine
(Although the feast will not be grand)
I offer you, instead of wine,
    A bolus of a brand
    Not common in the land—
    One of the priceless things
    Beyond the purse of kings:
For not King Oscar[1], I opine,
    Has ever yet been able
    To buy it for his table.—

---

[1] This is the present King of Sweden and Norway—a superio
man, who in addition to his executive ability, is a scholar of wid
learning and of varied literary accomplishments.

XI.

'I am the host
And should not boast,
And yet no fruitage of the vine
From any vineyard of the Rhine,
No sparkling Muscatel
From sunny Bingenfell,
No beaker which the burghers drain
In Aquitaine,
No cup the chamois-hunters sip
On Tontitip—
Can ever vie in power to cheer
With what is set before you here;
Which you shall taste before you go.—

XII.

'But wait awhile—not yet;
For ere your lips be wet,
I first, O Monk, would have you know
From what this precious drink was made,
And whence it hither was conveyed.
The tale is new
And strange and true:

XIII.

'Once in a dragon that was tempest-tossed
And nearly lost,
I too, I too,
Like ocean-loving Liff of yore[1]
Crossed over to that sunset-shore,
That continent most blest—

---

[1] Liff or Leif was the viking who is said to have reached the New England coast in the tenth or eleventh century, and to have named the country Vinland.

Discovered early, rediscovered late—
A land thus doubly the elect of Fate,
  The New World of the West.—

XIV.

'But there, far from its cities and their roar,
I chose to dwell in chilly Labrador,
  Where merry Esquimaux
 With snow-shoes lightly tread the snow
And chase the mighty moose, whose horny feet
  Break through the crust
Until he sinks (as he is sure to do)
Beyond escape if hunters but pursue;
  For fail he must:

XV.

'And when they bring their panting prey
  At last to bay,
He stands deep-buried to his thighs,
Whilst human tears gush from his eyes
  And seem, in rolling down,
 To be the weeping of a King
  At losing of his crown.

XVI.

'Now if before he dies
 His tears be caught and treasured up
(In conch-shells which his captors bring),
The liquid is a precious thing—
For, mixed with Bragi-mead and quaffed,
The potion is a magic draught—
  A drink for seers.

XVII.

'Here is the brew—here in this golden cup—
A Bragi-cup, mixed with a moose's tears[1]:
  So taste it, pray,
  And frankly say
What in your honest heart you *think* of it,
For I am certain that a *drink* of it
Will wash the cobwebs from your brain
And render Nature's mysteries plain.'

XVIII.

  So said the Eremite,
  And I, lest I should slight
  An offer so polite,
Ate both the portions, mine and his,
And also drank both his and mine
(A drink which for its foaming fizz
   Was quite divine).

XIX.

I thanked (with more than mere formality)
The Hermit for his hospitality,
And asked myself—as well I might
Concerning such a Troglodyte—
In such a cave, where every cranny
Appeared so spidery and uncanny,
What could this meagre mortal be?
For certainly—as I could see—
No scion of the Church was he,
With crucifix or rosarie

---

[1] A Bragi-cup is a health to Bragi, the god of Poetry: and the addition of the moose's tears—or the wine of the wise—renders the libation a joint homage to Poetry and Wisdom.

Or grinning skull or other sign
Of thoughts that ran on things divine:
But from the world he dwelt apart
In practice of a secret art—
A subtile craft of such finesse,
That what it was I could not guess

XX.

The anvil which he smote
Gave back a tinkling note,
Not of a sledge's iron clamour,
But of a slight and silver hammer;
The windy bellows of his forge
Made but a soft and mellow roar;
And round him in his rocky gorge
I noticed lumps of smelted ore
And crucibles and glass retorts,
And jars and vials of all sorts,
And books of magic by the score.

XXI.

Quoth I, 'O man of solitude,
To judge thee by thy musty books,
And by the lankness of thy looks,
Thou art a man of learnèd lore—
A ravening bookworm—lackaday!
No senex, yet surprising gray—
Thin as a rail, lean as a lath,—
Philosopher and philomath!—
Yet hardly of the sapient brood
Who sometimes hither stray
From old Upsála[1] or some other college,

---

[1] The University at Upsála, in Sweden, is now nearly five hundred years old.

And yet who seldom make a stay
Save only for a summer's day.
I mean no slur by the suggestion—
 (Take no offence, I pray!)—
But answer me a simple question:
 O lump of learning, say,
What good to thee is all thy knowledge
If thus it gnaws thy flesh away?
Forgive me if I seem too rude,
  But by the Ides and Nones!
 O Master Skull-and-Bones,
Tell me what cunning work, I prithee,
Thou now art forging in thy smithy?'

XXII.

The Hermit, balancing awhile
As if between a frown and smile,
Stood pensive in his chimney-nook,
  With puzzled look
And arms akimbo, as in doubt
Whether to let his secret out:
   Yet when at last
   His doubt had passed,
His spirit—with a sudden burst
(Like an imprisoned fount set free)—
Poured out its pent-up mystery—
A secret which the lone Adept
Had long within his cavern kept,
   Not only undetected,
   But never once suspected.

XXIII.

Cried he, 'I now no longer will conceal it,
But thou, O reverend Father, art the first

To whom I venture to reveal it.
Yet ere I lift the veil
I ought to say
Why I am moved to trust thee with the tale.
Thou art a stranger in these borders—
A pilgrim passing on thy way;
Besides, thou art in holy orders,
And therefore thou wilt not betray
To vulgar boors who dwell around me
The lone and weird vocation
And shady occupation
In midst whereof thou here hast found me:
So use thine eyes—watch and behold;
The thing is better seen than told.'

XXIV.

Whereat I gazed with awe,
And this is what I saw:
At first, as if to calm his thought
(Which my intrusion had distraught),
He stroked the fetlock on his chin
Till he was ready to begin:
He then—to make his cavern dimmer
(Though it was dusky dark before)
Hung up across his wicket-door
From side to side
A walrus-hide,
Thus shutting out some prying rays
That played the trick of peeping in:
Next, in the faint remaining glimmer
He fanned a thin ethereal blaze,
Not hot and red, but cold and green,
The ghastliest flicker ever seen:

And finally, and while it flared—
　　And while I stared—
He brewed in an enchanted kettle
A broth of many a molten metal,
And skimmed it off at different stages
As often as he saw it simmer;
And while he skimmed the broth, he glared
And gloated with an expectation
That showed a mad infatuation.

XXV.

I watched him, till at last I knew
The purpose which he had in view—
　　At least, I guessed it;
And when I boldly told my guess,
He answered proudly with a Yes,—
　　And thus confessed it.

XXVI.

It was the fad of fads indeed;
For if it only could succeed,
　　　　It was a thing
　　　　That was to bring
To the inventor an immense renown
And turn the world (he told me) upside down!

XXVII.

In fact, he hoped (like many a former fool)
That the Elixir, on its growing cool,
Would yield at last the calx that silly sages
Had sought for, down through all the darkest ages,
　　And which, if found, would be the Stone
　　Styled by Philosophers their Own—
　　That wondrous uncreated gem
　　Unknown to God yet known to them!—

A talisman to work the cure
Of all the ills that men endure,
Transmuting poverty to wealth,
Restoring the diseased to health
And even able (as he said)
To raise to life agen the dead !

XXVIII.

'So great a prize, thou wilt agree,
Is worth the striving for!' quoth he.

XXIX.

Then in his weazen face I laughed,
And said, 'O wizard, thou art daft!
The Wise Men of the Earth were seven,
But long ago they went to Heaven ;
Art thou the eighth, and wiser far
Than other pedants were, or are ?
Thy magic stone, O Alchemist,
Is one that never can exist :
How canst thou hope to find it then ?
O most deluded man of men !'

XXX.

Then in rejoinder to my jeer
The Hermit, with a haughty sneer,
And with a lip that proudly curled
Contemptuous of a sceptic world,
Replied, 'O doubter, thrones shall crumble
                And sceptres tumble ;
But whoso fixes his reliance
On the eternal truths of science
(Whose votary I am, though humble),
May bid, like me, a proud defiance
To all the riff-raff rabble-rout

Who use their little wit to scout
At what they know the least about.
Think not, O prelate, that I grope
In all this gloom without a hope,
For Truth is like a glowing spark—
The brightest in the densest dark:

XXXI.

'And though I work
In soot and mirk,
And though the fumes are thick and blinding
And make the secret hard of finding,
Yet what the wise of all the past
Made search for, must be found at last.
They waited long—and *I* as yet
Have not the perfect amulet:

XXXII.

'But day by day, whiter and whiter
Emerge the crystals of the nitre;
And hour by hour, little by little,
The calx grows harder and more brittle.
I am in darkness but not blind:
The seers of old
Have all foretold
That when by heat a hundredfold
The crispy crust
Is cracked and powdered and calcined,
And thrice refined and re-refined,
Until from every speck of dust
And every mote and flake of rust
The fire shall free it,—
That then the metal in its mould
Shall change its hue,

G

And pass from white to whitish blue,
From blue to yellowish red,—
When I will wager thee my head
That what went in as basest lead
Comes out as purest gold.'

XXXIII.

'O great philosopher,' quoth I,
'If so it be, so be it,—
And may you live to see it!'

XXXIV.

'And so I surely shall,' quoth he,
'For Heaven hath fixed a fast decree
Whereby no mortal man, not one,
Shall turn him from his toil, to die,
Till his predestined task be done.
I know by many a certain sign
That I shall live to finish mine.
The soul in solitary hours
Is gifted with prophetic powers:
In this my cell
I can foretell
As in a magic glass
What is to come to pass;
Truth, being mighty, must prevail;
Eureka shall be soon my cry;
Or if indeed not soon, but late,
I still am master of my fate,
And I can work, and I can wait:
My triumph may be far or nigh,
But I shall win it By-and-By.'

Stave Tenth.

I.

The afternoon, with dog-day heat,
Wilted the poppies in the wheat;
The lilies hung their languid heads;
The pansies sickened in their beds;
The very sun-flowers, one by one,
   Were all undone
   By too much sun;
Even the water-flags that fringed.
The meadow-brooks were scorched and singed—
   For all the shallow streams
   That caught the fiery beams
Were shrunken dry, or if they flowed,
   Their channels were not full:

II.

And now the oxen felt their load
Grown all at once too hard to pull;
The sheep lay sweltering in their wool;
The rabbit found his coat of fur
Too heavy, and was loth to stir;
   The shadow-loving grouse
   Stayed in his shady house
Nor had a partridge on the heather
The energy of wing to whirr!
I never knew such blazing weather—
A fiercer sunshine never glowed!
   I scarce could bear
   The burning glare,
Yet still I trudged along the road,   •

Till in the Stift
Of Algorift
I halted where a mower mowed,
Upon whose blade
A sunbeam played,
And from whose brow a sparkling crown
Of watery diamonds trickled down.

III.

'What mighty man is this?' thought I,
For he appeared
A Giant of a time gone by—
A Jotun of the years of yore;
Nor had I ever met before
A swinkherd of so thick a thigh,
Or back so brawny,
Or skin so tawny,
Or countenance so seamed and seared,
Or such a gristle of a beard.

IV.

At every stroke,
His naked arms
Grew knotted like the gnarly oak:
At every stride,
The swath he cut
Was more than thrice a cubit wide:
—And as his scythe rushed through the grain,
The noise was like the swash of rain.

V.

So fierce a labour (I was sure)
No mortal man could long endure:
But though in such a heat his strength

(I thought) would ooze away at length,
Yet on and on the reaper wrought;
    Nor did he flag
    Nor droop nor drag,
But seemed with ever-added ardour
To work the happier and the harder.

VI.

Quoth I, ' O tireless son of toil,
    Thy zeal is strange;
Thy meadow is of meagre soil
    And narrow range.
Moreover, though thy thews be strong,
The method of thy toil is wrong:
Thy energy—I plainly see—
Is mighty, but is misdirected.
    For list to me:
The winter in this land is long,
    And while it lasts,
This field of thine, through all the icy blasts,
    Lies bare and unprotected;
And so, through half of every year
Thy acres waste their life away,
    Turning from green to sere:

VII.

' For, like thy sires of long ago,
Thou too, as wrongly taught as they,
Dost to their ancient error cling—
An error that must cost thee dear:

Thou fanciest that the sap of spring
(Which mounts to make the blossoms blow
    And stays to swell the fruit)

Makes afterward, in time of frost and snow,
          A downward flow
       To warm and feed the root,—
As if in kindness Nature meant
          To have it so:
          But no, oh no!
There is in Nature no such kind intent;
She orders no such comfortable thing:

VIII.

'She bids the sap flow ever up ·
          To cusp and cup,
          To leaf and spray—
The sap flows never downward for a day.

What cares the Winter for thy Plant and Tree?
The care, if care they have, must come from thee!

          O farmer, be it known
That if thy farm be summer-fed alone,
     It never, never will afford thee
     Sufficient harvest to reward thee!

IX.

'So, seeing thee in such a stress
Of soul and sinew, I may guess ·
That when thy narrow threshing-floor
Is piled at last with every sheaf
          Which in so wild a way
          Thou mowest down to-day,
Thy heart is not to rest content
With merely what thy scythe hath mown:
Thy pay, for all thy labour spent,
Is not to be thy grain alone—

Thou art for thy reward expecting more:
  Thou hast in mind some intimation
  Of some far nobler compensation.
    Forgive me therefore if I ask
    What grand, what final hope in chief
    Can nerve thee to thy torrid task?
    For much I marvel how, in face
    Of yonder blazing orb of fire,
    Thou toilest at so mad a pace
    Yet seemest not at all to tire.'

X.

Then with a burst of laughter, loud and coarse
(That woke the lazy sheep-dog from his sleep
And set him barking at the blameless sheep),
    The brawny rustic said, 'O friar,
    I be a pinkel [1] born and bred,
    And you a wearer of the lawn:
    You lack some hardiness of bone,
    But have another kind of force,
    For you have brain, instead of brawn;
    Whilst as for me, a swinish drudge,
    Although the life that I have led
    Has made my frame as hard as stone,
    Yet I am very thick of head
    (An askefis [1] as some have said):
    But now my mind is growing clear,
        As will appear
        From what you hear,
    And you yourself shall be the judge.

---

[1] *Pinkel* and *askefis* are Scandinavian words signifying a dullard or stupid person.

XI.

'But first, O Gown-and-Band,
I do not care a rap
For flowing of the sap;
And as to this my patch of land
    And its fertility,
    Or its sterility,
        I answer, Fudge!
It is to me a thing of nought,
And does not occupy my thought.
My meadow, to its utmost marge,
Is neither very rich nor large;
But I can boast with all humility
That now it is about to yield
What neither any bigger field
Nor ranker garden ever bore—
A harvest of a kind unknown
To any harvester before:

XII.

'But not of grain, oh no, indeed!
Nor grass nor fruit nor flower nor weed,
Nor aught that springs from planted seed:
This harvest has been neither grown
        Nor even sown:
        Nor need I take
        A gleaner's rake
To gather it upon a cart!
        I laugh, you see!
There is a cockle in my heart
That makes my very midriff shake,
And tickles me with such a thrill

That I could jump, it seems to me,
Up to the top of Orkla hill !'

XIII.

'Thou art a merry carl,' quoth I ;
'So let me ask the reason why.'

XIV.

Then, in a stealthy whispered tone,
As if some sly eavesdropping ear
        Might chance to overhear
(Although his nearest neighbour was a mile away),
He said, 'O Sir, we are alone—
        Now hark to what I say.
        Down to this very day
            I still have tried
            To screen and hide
My great and glorious expectation ;
But now it nears its consummation,
So I will hush it up no more ;
For I am proud that now at last
The day for secrecy is past.
        It pleases me right well
        To think I now may tell
What I have never told before:

XV.

'I seek a hidden precious prize—
A hoarded, ancient, secret treasure,
A fortune fallen from the skies ;
And in this very field it lies,
And I am now about to find it !
And so my toil is but a pleasure—
Or if a pain, I do not mind it.'

XVI.

Thus answered he,
In words so strange and yet so candid,
That I was filled at once with wonder.
'What *is* this treasure?' I demanded,—
        When from a thickening cloud,
        Far distant and yet loud,
Outbroke a sudden thud of thunder,
        And with a cry of glee
        The reaper shouted 'See!
How fine a rainbow! How it bends!
And how its foot as it descends
Comes just to where my meadow ends!
Mark how the bright and sevenfold band
Leans on the limit of my land!

XVII.

'Now there—just twenty ells beneath the ground—
    Is where the secret precious hoard
    That I have told thee of is stored—
    Concealed for years from human view,
    But which I now possess the clue
        To lead me to:
A treasure easy to be found,—
For all that I have need to do
Is just to make a spurt, to mow
From here across the field to where
The shining foot of yonder bow
Is standing on the wheat—and lo!
        I then and there
(To pay me when my field is mown)
Shall find beneath a gammal stone

A hidden Bag of Money; yea—
    Why do you stare?
You have no faith in what I say!
The money—all of it—is gold,
Coined from a fallen star of old!
The tale is true—I know it well:

XVIII.

'There was a Pleiad, and it fell;
    And there were seven in all,
    And this, before its fall,
    Was brightest of the seven,
    And down it dropped from Heaven.
But though it dropped so very far,
And struck a mountain and was battered
And bent awry and split and shattered
And buried in the grimy ground,
Yet being such a golden star
    It was so bright
    That in the night
Some impish Elves (those thievish gnomes
That nightly from their bosky homes
Skip out unseen, to prowl around
And filch whatever may be found)
    Espied it and purloined it,
    And melted it and coined it,
And put the money in a bag,
And cleft a crevice in a crag
And in the crevice hid the swag.

XIX.

'And oh, the cunning rogues were wise!
It was a bag of otter-skin,
And having stuffed the shekels in,

And having put the precious prize
        Beneath the gammal stone,
        They left it there alone,
And set no mark upon the spot
To point it out to prying eyes;
        Yet, to forget it not,
They kept remembrance of the place
As being at the Rainbow's base—
Where still of course the treasure lies.
For never having been molested,
It must remain where first it rested.—

XX.

'It was an otter that was killed
        In Andivári Fall[1]:
And though he was a creature sleek and fat,
And bigger than the biggest tiger-cat,
Yet ere his skin was with the shekels filled
It needed to be stretched to hold them all:
But since the Elves were more than mortal-skilled
They well knew how, in stretching it and packing it,
To run no risk of spoiling it by cracking it,
        But cunningly to stuff and ram it,
        And press and jam it,
        And with uncounted coins to cram it.

It is a pelt that cannot rot—
        A pouch that cannot mould—
And is as full as it can hold:
The money that is in the sack

---

[1] Sometimes called Andvári, or Andvárifors—a waterfall in which the dwarf Andvári lived in the guise of a gurnand, or pickerel.

Will more than fill a pedlar's pack
Or pannier on a camel's back:

> And all this pelf
> Is for myself!—

This is the fee—this is the spoil—
This is the wage of all my toil.'

XXI.

Thought I, 'The man is surely crazed!'
And so, whilst at the Arch he gazed,
I answered with a sorry smile,
'From here to there is many a mile—
And many a meadow must thou mow
To reach the base of yonder bow.'

'Not so!' he cried—and swung his hand
Across his meagre patch of land:
'Do I not know the boundary line
Of this poor narrow farm of mine?
And since, at farthest, sooth to say,
The Landmark is not far away—
So too the Rainbow must be nigh,
And I shall reach it By-and-By.'

Stave Eleventh.

I.

The sinking sun was shining still,
Though now his disc had slid away
Behind the back of Orkla hill,

> Whose ridgy crest
> Across the west

Had caught the arrow of his ray
And slanted it to Strelsa Bay.

II.

I walked through worts and water-weeds
And pimpernels and ferny closes,
And saw the Burning Bush of Moses,
    Whose fiery buds were still aflame
      Since early June;
I heard the kittywakes[1] all cry in tune
    To bid me welcome as I came—
    For each announced to me his name;
I passed the orchards where the crossbill breeds
      (Who with his scissors clips
      The apples for their pips);
I met that rolypoly water-hawk,
    The gannet goose, who waxes fat
    By feeding on the oily sprat;
But much I missed the ancient mighty auk,
    Which in my childhood I had known—
      That dodo of the North[2]—
    But now (I fear) for ever flown;
    Nor did I trace in all my tramp
    That thievish, terror-spreading scamp
The hungry lemming[3]—for his marching nation
    Was not as yet on its migration,
    But tarrying with the water-vole[4]
    And hiding like the campanole[5].

---

[1] The kittywake is so called from his cry, but he is otherwise known as the tarrock.

[2] The great auk's last living haunt was the Orkney Islands, and he now resides only in the British Museum.

[3] For an account of this brave little animal, see appendix.

[4] The water-rat.   [5] The field-mouse.

III.

At falling of the evening shades
I crossed the Dyke of Koboloo [1],
Where now the flooding tide ran through,
And where a gang of Fishermaids
   Had come to set
   Their herring-net;

   For there and then
   In fiord and fen
The women had to toil like men,
And livelihoods were hard to get.

   And yet indeed,
   Despite the need
Of hauling till their fingers bleed,
These buxom Gammerkins are fair,
And at their salty toil they sing
   And gaily wear
   Their yellow hair
Bedecked with half the buds of spring:
And I am proud indeed to praise
Such healthy women nowadays;
And may their herrings bring them gold,
And may their hearts grow never old!

IV.

Around me, from a kelp-clad rock,
A thousand sea-mews in a flock
All in a screaming chorus flew;

[1] A small fishing-station on an arm of Strelsa Bay.

While all before me, broad and blue,
The glittering ocean lay in view:
      The mighty deep
      Was fast asleep,
Save where the breakers round its rim
Chanted their never-ending hymn.

v.

Along the shingle, through the spray,
      I picked my way
To where, upon a dry-foot ledge
That overhung the water's edge,
An agèd man (whose head was bare
And face was scarred with time and care)
Stood beckoning with a frantic motion
To something out upon the ocean—
Although I saw no vessel there.

VI.

On nearer view I grieved to find
That his regardless eyes were blind:
I felt a pity—then a pain:
      'Ah me!' thought I,
'His other senses may remain,
But he has lost the very best—
The one indeed worth all the rest.'

VII.

I made him an obeisance low
(A courtesy of poor avail!)
And said, 'O honoured head of snow
      (For when a head is hoary
      It is a Crown of Glory),

Accept the homage that I owe,
And tell me what I wish to know.
　　　I see no sail
　　　For thee to hail—
Why therefore dost thou beckon so?
What can thy blank and sightless glance
Discover in the void expanse?
Art thou a conjurer, conjuring up
Some lost transcendent precious thing
　　　Long cast away,
And many a fathom sunk and hidden
　　　In gulf or bay,
Yet which shall rise to thee when bidden?

VIII.

'Is it the King of Thulé's Cup?
Is it the Wizard Merlin's Ring?
Is it the nine-years' prize which Guinevere
Flung down in rage into the middle-mere?—
　　　Or is it Fafnir's gold [1]
　　　That slipped the holder's hold
And over which the Rhine-wave rolled?

But be it what it may—
Even Saint Peter's Key
　　　(Which some are wont to say
Lies shining at the bottom of the sea)—
Hast thou come hither with a hope to-day
　　　That these obedient waves will bring it,
　　　And at thy waiting feet will fling it?

---

[1] Fafnir was the guardian of a fabulous treasure on Gnita Heath. He was slain by Sigurd. What became of the gold? This question was the theme of many different and contradictory fables.

IX.

'For though, O agèd sire, the sea indeed—
With all its mighty maw, with all its endless greed,
   With all its vessel-whelming wrack—
   Is never like to have a lack
   Of precious treasures such as these—
         Which it is swift to seize
         And slow to render back;
Yet, oh, thou dreamer, dost thou dream
That yon relentless Ocean Stream,
Yon miserly and gloating Deep—
With such a wealth to hoard and keep—
Will listen to thy crazy plea,
And yield its booty up to *thee*?—

X.

   '—Thou frownest, sire!—
   Thou art in ire—
Thou art offended with me now;
But tell me, Why dost thou thus knit
An extra knot into thy brow?
What Club of Hercules hath hit
      Thine ancient skull
And knocked away thy native wit
      And left thee dull?
Forgive me—I am over-bold:
But thou art venerably old—
A man so agèd should be wise—
For with thy threescore years and ten
Experience ought to make thee sage.
O time-worn mortal! tell me, then,
         What worldly prize
         Thy stony eyes,

That stare with such a vacant ken,
Can look for in a blind old age?'

XI.

Then he (still standing as before,
Above the rollers and their roar)
Said with a voice as hoarse as theirs,
'O stranger, in the happy time
Betwixt my youth and early prime,
 Ere yet my later cares
 Stole on me unawares,
I launched on yonder mighty main
An Argosy in quest of gain:
There never was a gayer craft,
For she was furnished fore and aft
With silken sails and silver ropes,
And freighted full of golden hopes!—

XII.

'Not Sæmund in his Iceland cell [1]
(Wherein he wove his fancies bold)

---

[1] Sæmund was the collector (and in part the re-writer) of those early Icelandic poems which are grouped together under the title of the Elder Edda, and which are the classic fountain-head of the Scandinavian mythology. Though a priest of the Christian faith, Sæmund had a passionate love for the pagan myths of the North. These he rescued and restored just at the critical time when they were wellnigh forgotten, and when they seemed about to pass into oblivion.

'He was born,' says Thorpe, ' at Oddi, his paternal dwelling in the South of Iceland, between the years 1054 and 1057, or about fifty years after the establishment by law of the Christian religion in that island: hence it is easy to imagine that many heathens, or baptized favourers of the old mythic songs of heathenism, may have lived in his days and imparted to him the lays of old, which his unfettered mind induced him to hand down to posterity.'

Dared in his boldest lay to tell
(Nor any Saga since has told)
Of mortal barque or caravel,
Or dragon-ship or yarded brig
That ever boasted such a rig
Or ever bore a bill of lading
    Of things so fair,
Or of a fairness so unfading!

Indeed my vessel's "manifest"
Was all of articles so rare—
And so unlike what ships are wont to bear—
    That save myself alone
No mortal could have dreamed or guessed
The curious items which the list, if shown,
    Would have surprisingly made known.—

XIII.

'What did this bill of lading show to *me*?
    To me it showed
That all I had—all I could call my own—
    Was outward bound at sea:
For never had I paused or rested
Till in my ship I had invested
    My total stock and store.
And when I had embarked the whole,
    I wished it had been more!

XIV.

'In sending thus away
    All I possessed,
I shipped it, strange to say,
    Unpacked in any chest—
    Unwrapped in any roll,

Unbattened by a hatch, unstowed
Like any other vessel's load;
Nor did my ship and cargo need
    (As other vessels do)
The service of a captain or a crew;
Nor had she any pilot—for she went
    Self-guided, self-intelligent: :
I wished my wishes—these were her commands—
    She sailed as she was sent:
And what she bore was mystic merchandise—
A sort unseen of human eyes,
    Ungrasped of human hands,
And therefore which no rude or careless touch
    Could soil or smutch,
And which no accident could break or bruise
    (Being infrangible
    Because intangible),
    And which no storm could shake
    Nor ruin overtake,
Nor even Loss itself could lose!

XV.

    'My vessel's filmy freight
    Had not a feather's weight!
For it consisted all of things of air—
    A load of dreams and expectations!—
    A cargo of imaginations!
    My ship in fact
    Was crammed and packed
With all my worldly aspirations—
An invoice far from being small!
Indeed my hopes were each so great,
And in their multitude so grand,

That just to furnish ship-room for them all
My vessel had to be of huge dimensions.

XVI.

'She was the largest ever planned,
A bigger barque
Than Noah's Ark!
And thus was able to contain
All the pet projects of my brain—
All my chief hobbies and inventions;
All my magnificent intentions;
All my sure prophecies and guesses;
All my deep secrets known
Unto myself alone,
And taken from my heart's inmost recesses;
All the sublime anticipations
Which, though they seemed unfounded,
I yet had safely grounded
On never-failing signs aerial—
(As when the Bird of Calm [1]
Takes for his nest
A wave at rest,
And utters from the sea
The things that are to be);

All my far-sighted figurations
Drawn from the Human Palm—
(That tell-tale palimpsest);

All my sagacious observations
From things half-mystical and half-material
(Like salt that sparkles sprinkled on the fire,

---

[1] The halcyon, or kingfisher.

Or like the throws and counter-throws of dice,
   Or omens from the squeaks of mice,
Or lowings of the phantom-ox [1] heard in the byre);

All my new notions, fanciful yet feasible;
      All the fond ravings
      And feverish cravings,
      Which were the fierce delight
      Of my soul's appetite,
And fed it to a hunger unappeasable;

All my clear visions manifold
      Of every name,
      Whether of fame
Or happiness or wealth untold;
Together also with each airy
And beautiful vagáry
      Of every kind
      Known to the mind
In all the triple necromancy
Of mingled Hope and Faith and Fancy.—

XVII.

'All these and more I put on board:
And when my ship, thus stocked and stored,
Seemed shrewdly freighted for a trade
Whereby I thought my fortune would be made,
   I sent her forth to seek a mart
   Not dotted down on any chart—
A port unnamed, a coast unkenned,
A region hid from mortal view,
And whose discovery would be new;
A shore beyond the utmost trend,

---

[1] The 'Phantom-Ox' is another form of the fatal spectre of the White Wolf, mentioned on page 16.

Where sky and ocean meet and blend,
And which had loomed upon my sight
In visions of the middle-night!—

XVIII.

'I saw it oft—I saw it well;
Yet where it lay I could not tell;
　　Nor did I care,—
For whether to the West or to the East,
Or whether to the windward or the lee,
　　Or otherwhere,
　　It mattered not to me;
My simple purpose was to send
My vessel to the Earth's far end,—
　　That mystic place
Where then the World's chief wonders *were*,
And where (unless I greatly err)
They *are*, and evermore will *be*:
And the course thither is by sea
　　And hard to trace—
　　A devious way
　　Which I may say
Full many a ship is like to lose;
Yet mine went forth upon her cruise
　　Without the faintest fear,
And she has now been gone so many a day,
So many a month, so many a year,
So near a lifetime, if not quite,
That when she started forth from here
　　Bound to that distant haven,
My hair was of the glossy hue
　　Of Odin's younger raven!

(You know that Odin's birds are two,
And each as black as Grani's[1] shoe.)

XIX.

'But afterward my head grew grey,
And now (you tell me) it is white—
As white as Fimbulwinter's frost;
And others say to me (with censure)
That I was foolish in my venture,
And that my ship is surely lost:

XX.

'—Which cannot be,
For I will not believe it, No!
And yet it keeps me on the rack:
For why should I have let her go
If she was never to come back?
But I rebuke my tongue for such a strain;
For why should I complain?
The winds at sea are oft ahead
And every ship must beat and tack
And jibe and wear,
And hunt her channel with her lead,
And make her progress like a snail;
But I will swear
That neither winter's gale
Nor summer's hurricane
Can blow my vessel from her track,
Nor long prevent her coming back.'

---

[1] Grani was Sigurd's horse, which could bear the rider through flames of fire.

XXI.

Quoth I, 'Tell me what name, O sire,
So strange an Argosy may bear?'

XXII.

'The name,' said he, 'which first I gave her
Was Fortune's Favour;
But hardly had she sailed
When all my fortunes failed;
And now, since kindly you inquire,
I call her simply Heart's Desire.'

XXIII.

Quoth I, 'Perhaps I do not err,
Old man, in venturing to infer
That thou hast seldom heard from her:
But tell me, good or bad,
What tidings hast thou had?'

XXIV.

'Alas!' cried he,
'Since first my vessel put to sea
I have not heard
A single word;
But hope is hope, although deferred.
Moreover, though the world be wide,
And though the distance be immense
From here to its remotest side,
It now is time my vessel thence
Should bring me back my recompense.'

XXV.

Whereat, although I now had learned
That certainly his brain was turned,

Yet still I tried
To save his pride,
Pretending I was much concerned
In what was likely to befall
An Argosy that held his all ;
And so, with an affected zest,
—'What is she laden with ?' asked I.

XXVI.

'With jewels!' was his strange reply ;
Which seemed a pleasantry—a jest ;
For surely neither in the East nor in the West—
No, nor in Niphon[1] nor in Aiden[2],
Nor in the Great Mogul's abode[3],
Nor anywhere on any strand
Or isle or coast where ships may land,
Was ever any vessel laden
With only jewels for her load !

XXVII.

I shrugged my shoulders and demurred :
Said I, 'It is beyond credulity!'

XXVIII.

Whereat the Greybeard loftily averred
(With Age's proud garrulity)
'I am not making a pretence—
I tell no lie—
I hold a falsehood a disgrace—
It is a thing I spurn ;
And so, however blind I be,

---

[1] Japan.   [2] On the Persian Gulf.
[3] Near the Yellow Sea.

I look you squarely in the face
(As if I had the power to see)
   And of my ship I say,
She now is on her homeward way
And crowded full, from stem to stern,
With gems and jewels—these alone:

XXIX.

  'And each and every stone
    Is of a size unknown
In any travelled land or zone:
      Pearls of a whiter sheen
      Than those of Egypt's Queen[1];
      Rubies of richer red
Than those for which the dove hath bled[2];
      Sapphires of brighter blue
      Than woman's eye
(As I remember it in days gone by);
      And diamonds too,
    Like drops of water in the light
    (For I have not forgot the sight);
    And countless gems of every hue—
    A shipload!—and the ship is due!

XXX.

'I care not therefore that my head is hoar,
For I am glad that I am young no more.
    A man is but a fool, forsooth,
    To whine at waning of his youth:
      Youth has been oversung.
    What did my boasted youth for *me*?
    What but to push me into plans

---

[1] Cleopatra.   [2] Pigeon-blooded.

That were as grand as any man's,
Yet always failed and kept me poor!
I was no idler in my early days
(As most of all our younkers be);
I sought my fortune in a hundred ways;
  But though I wrought
  With care and thought,
Yet my reward was nought—or less than nought:

XXXI.

  'I burned the midnight oil,
  Yet all my toil and moil
In making plans and schemes and wonderful devices
Was but a hatching of the eggs of cockatrices—
  Till I was bit and stung
  For simply being young!
  Beware thy youth—it is a lure!
For it will bring thee losses to endure—
  And worse than losses—debts—
  Which by their manifold increase
Will wear thee out and rob thee of thy peace!—

XXXII.

'I better love my white and wintry age,
When now my work is sure to have its wage,
  For I am shortly to receive
  (Perhaps upon this very day)
  My long-deferred and honest pay!

Of course you cannot quite believe,
  Or even understand,
  A boast that seems so grand:

Besides, permit me, sir, to say,
Your voice is yet no scrannel-pipe;

You still are young—jejune, not ripe,
　　Perhaps not even grey.
What know you yet of life, who are not old?

　　The heart of youth is bold;
But though you feel it beat and pant
　　In search of gold,
Yet how can any Stripling hope to win
Those precious treasures hid beyond the main,
Which Far and Orient Climes are richest in?—
　　Climes further East than the Levant,
　　　And quite beyond the reach
　　Of mortal ships or human speech;
　　Lands far away—requiring years
　　　Of toil and tears
Ere any certain knowledge can be gained
Of how their treasures are to be obtained?
Hope is not hope till patience tests it long;
Faith is not faith till trial makes it strong!—

XXXIII.

'There comes at last a moment in our lives
Worth all the weary years that went before—
It is the moment when our ship arrives
That brings our long-expected wealth ashore.
　　So here beside the ocean's foam
　　I wait until my Ship comes Home!'

XXXIV.

Quoth I, 'Thy waiting may be long!—
The sea hath sirens, and their song
May lure a venturous craft like thine
And whelm her in the boiling brine;
Or she may burst her silken sails

And scud in rags before the gales;
Or prove (like many a hope, alas!)
To be a brittle ship of glass,
Which suddenly the slightest shock
May shiver on some hidden rock.

The heavens are often unrelenting,
And lend themselves to the preventing
Of man's desire:
A thousand keels, O wrinkled sire,
Shall come from Tarshish and from Tÿre,
From Cancer and from Capricorn,
Ere thine shall bring thee Plenty's Horn!

Remember how the thick-ribbed Argo,
Though built of oak and fifty-oared,
And with the Golden Fleece[1] on board,
Was smitten of the tempest's ire:
So tremble for thy ship and cargo!
Thou hast a vain possession;
For by thine own confession
This Argosy of thine is far more frail
Than any other craft that ever spread a sail;
The very least disaster
Must cripple and dismast her.
Indeed I more than half suspect
That either she has long been wrecked
Or else that (bound, as thou dost boast,
To an enchanted sea and coast)
A cruise like hers, so far away,
Will last for ever and a day!

---

[1] The Golden Fleece was found hanging on an oak-tree in a grove near Colchis; and Jason snatched the prize and carried it off in the Argo.

O blind old man, thy hopes are great ;
But is it wise for thee to wait
For such a ship and such a freight ? '

XXXV.

Then with some childish, happy tears
(Such as the old are proud to shed
At hearing mention of their years),
He stiffly raised his haughty head,
And speaking arrogantly, said,
' O stranger, I am not cajoled !   .
One grows the wiser, being old ;
One sees the further, being blind :
There is a forecast in one's mind
Whereby one's fortune is foretold.
I have for many a year foreknown
What wealth would one day be my own ;
And now the hour has come to which
I long have looked to make me rich.
Oh how the world will envy me !—
I shall be rich as rich can be !—
Richer than any prince has been—
For now my ship is coming in ! '

XXXVI.

' O visionary man,' I cried,
' And will this present wind and tide
Bring to an anchor—in this road—
This vessel, with this wondrous load ? '

XXXVII.

Whereat the tottering patriarch
(Still making signals to the main,
Although it bore in sight no barque)

Replied, 'O Sir, the case is plain :
A ship that sails the world around
Must soon or late be homeward bound ; .
    And so must mine ;
    And as I reckon,
She now perhaps is near at hand,
And waiting to receive some sign,
    Some signal, some command
To warrant her to anchor and to land,—
And that is why I stand and beckon.

Or if she be not here as yet
(For tidings, Sir, are hard to get),
    Yet this I know,
    That breezes blow
    And waters flow,
And whether she be far or nigh,
My ship is coming By-and-By.'

Stave Twelfth.

1.

The Sun, reversing now his beam,
Shot up a final fiery gleam
From where he just had fallen down
Into the depths of Strelsa Bay ;
And I beheld him sink and drown.

His dying glory was supreme.
I love the death of such a day,
That dies, yet all the while is bright,

And seems (like Holy Writ) to say
'At evening time there shall be light.'

II.

I gazed, and to my dazzled sight
The half of Heaven took fire and burned;
    The crystal Skaggerack [1]
    Flashed the refulgence back,
      And all the Naze
      Was in a blaze.

III.

The tinkling cattle homeward turned;
The weary sea-mew sought her nest;
      I too was tired,
      And half desired
To make a finish of my quest.
And yet how little I had learned!—
    Just what I knew before!
    Not an iota more!
In every thorp and ampt and region
    Which I had travelled through,
The fools that I had met were legion,
    The wise were none, or few:
And sage or simple, young or old,
They each had innocently told
(And all their several tales agreed)
What ninnies they had been indeed!—
Beguiled and duped and led astray,
    Not once nor twice,
    Not twice nor thrice,

---

[1] This strait, between the Naze and the Skaw, is very deep—about 400 fathoms: on the contrary, the Cattegat, between Sweden and Denmark, is very shoal—varying from fifty to thirty fathoms.

Not for a day, nor now and then—
But all the race of mortal men
Without exception, as I found,
Were April-fooled the whole year round!

IV.

So while the glow was in the West
(And made the eve a softer noon)
    I further wandered,
      And mused and pondered,
And sighed, and said, 'I marvel much
That every mortal's dearest boon
(Or what appears to him as such)
Should prove as false as it is fair,
And always at his grasp or touch
Should melt away and not be there!

V.

The Babe shall see (and oh how soon!)
How hard it is to catch the Moon;
The Youth shall marvel when and where
His Castle vanished in the air;
The Sage shall waste his flesh and bone,
Yet miss at last the Magic Stone;
The Reaper shall repent his whim
Of mowing to the Rainbow's rim;
The Greybeard shall not be alive
To see his Treasure-Ship arrive.

VI.

Thus viewing life through all its range
Of mortal years, I said, 'How strange
That Infancy and Youth and Prime
And Hoary Age, each in its time,

Each in its turn, with eyes uplift
And hands outreached as for a gift,
All seem to struggle, strive and strain
For just a phantom of the brain—
A mere vagáry of the mind—
A thing to seek but not to find!
The more they follow it, the more
The fleeting image flits before!

VII.

So every man, a giddy lout,
Goes ever gadding roundabout,
        Chasing with vain persistence
            Some gilded butterfly,
        That seems at no great distance,
        Yet which has no existence
            Save in the gazer's eye.

VIII.

Back through my Native Vale profound,
While evening shadowed it around,
And while I listened to the sound
        Of twenty water-falls [1]
That sprang, white-footed, with a bound
        Over their jagged walls,
            I trudged along
(Returning by the Orkla Weir
        Across the Skong),
Still reasoning with myself, but reasoning wrong.

---

[1] The water of these falls, after it has fallen, is carried off by the Skong—a deep, narrow stream that empties into Flekker Fiord.

IX.

'What though,' thought I,
'A man must die,
Yet is it therefore clear
That Life is but a thing of nought?—
A vanity and nothing more,
As Solomon proclaimed?

Now Solomon was wise, they say—
The wisest mortal of his day;
And yet his wisdom I am half inclined,
In sober thought, to estimate
At not a tithe so great
As it is famed.

X.

'Who was this vaunted King so wise?
This cock was many-damed!
A man so wived and concubined
Could not have known a quiet mind!
He had his Vanities indeed!—
Whereat he eloquently vented
A spirit vexed and discontented.
A note so cynic I despise:
For I maintain
That in the main
This Life and World are not in vain.

XI.

'And yet—and yet,
The World seems empty, after all!
It has a lack
Of something gone that never will come back!

The very sunshine lies upon it as a pall!—
.As if the Sin of Man had cast a shade
On every goodly thing that God hath made!

XII.

'Deep down within my bosom's core
    I feel the pang of a regret
That now the Gift of Insight, which of yore
    The Prophets had, exists on earth no more.

Things outward we are quick to see,
But to things inward we are blind:
    Our spirit, for its sight,
    Hath need of heavenly light;
Our spirit's eyes are bandaged, and through life we go
According as we grope and guess, not as we see and
    know.

XIII.

'Why should such ignorance be?
    Is it that Eden's Tree
Has come to fruitage for a second time,
And bears agen on Earth a fruit forbidden?
Is every kind of knowledge to be known
Except the noblest and the best alone?
Must all the highest mysteries still be hidden?
Is man's desire for truth once more a sin and crime?'

XIV.

Thus, in a humour for complaining,
    And with a heart unhumbled,
    I railed and scoffed and grumbled,
    And (what was worse)

I fancied with a proud disdain
That God—the King of Kings—whose reign
Extended once through the domain
    Of all His Universe—
Was now unheeded and unknown,
And ceased to occupy His Throne.

XV.

And self-complacently I also thought
(In looking through this universal frame)
That every evil of whatever name—
    Each social ill, each civil wrong,
      However deep-inwrought,
Or dating back however long—
      Could suddenly be righted
If only certain noble schemes
Which I had fashioned in my dreams
Could once be put in operation—
      Schemes which, of course,
      By magic force
Would soon and certainly work out the World's
salvation.

XVI.

But all these schemes of mine were wisely slighted
      And justly put aside ;
—For I had made the same mistake
Which every other human being,
      Through vanity or pride,
Is pitifully prone to make :
    —I thought myself far-seeing,
And called the world short-sighted !

XVII.

And now I gnawed my nether lip, and said,
'I cannot scorn
The humbly born
·Lest I should scorn myself—yet I admit
That through the whole of Nanna's glen,
From Lister Ridge[1]
To Mandal Bridge[2],
From Hyndla to the Water-Shed,
Thence westward to the Water-Spout,
And on from Klapperpad to Klaybers,
My rude and rustic mountain-mates—
My hunting, fishing, farming neighbours—

---

[1] The village of Lister gives its name to a wide maritime district called Listerland.

[2] Mandal is the Southernmost town of Norway—as Hammerfest is the Northernmost.

And if the reader has a taste for minute topography, he may now —once for all—be appropriately referred to the Ordnance map : or if he would prefer an easier reference to Baedeker, here it is :

Speaking of Carl Olaf's country, Carl Baedeker says—' The Mandal river, which falls into the fiord at Mandal, descends through a valley . . . the *upper* part of which is inhabited by *a very primitive and pastoral people.* In summer they migrate to the neighbouring mountain-pastures . . . where they are not unfrequently attacked by bears.'

Baedeker, who seldom misses a fact of historical interest, has failed to mention that at Mandal (in a dungeon still to be seen) the Earl of Bothwell—the hunted lover of Mary Queen of Scots—was imprisoned while unsuccessfully trying to flee from the Orkneys to Denmark.

Nanna's Heim is about half a degree to the north of Mandal—and is the favourite latitude of holly, hazel nuts, wild strawberries, and the campanula flower. The streams are mostly of fresh water leaping down from the hills, though others are estuaries that reach far inland from the sea, and make salt meadows for the cattle and goats.

Are folk not favoured of the fates:
    Their mother-wit—
Their native sense—may not be small,
    But, one and all,
These honest carls are poorly taught--
    So ignorant indeed
    That they can hardly read;
    Their lot is low;
They are but dalesmen of the Ampt,
Who never pass their mountain-wall,
And never see the World at all,
    From which they dwell aloof;
    What can they know?
    Their minds are cramped;
Their evidence must go for nought;
    I must have ampler proof,
    I must make wider search.'

XVIII.

    Then from a lofty perch
Upon a thousand-year-old oak
A Raven hailed me with a croak.

This bird is wise (the Sagas say),
And being cousin to the Pie,
Has foresight and can prophesy,
And often bids a traveller halt
To set him right if he be wrong,
Or else to give him good advice
When he most imminently needs it;
And if the hearer seldom heeds it,
The babbling bird is not at fault;
The fault is his whose churlish mind
Rejects a service meant as kind.

XIX.

My Raven did not chatter vainly;
I understood his lingo plainly.
  'Sir Pelerine,
  Or Peregrine,
Or whatsoever name,' quoth he,
'Your travelling cognomen may be,
  The reason why
  I hither hie
From kingdoms of the East and South
(Where I have visited the Cham),
Is just to bring thee, in my mouth,
A word of magic—which is Fram![1]

XX.

'I brought it to thee years ago
When thou wert lazy, dull and slow;
  For thou wert then
The idlest of all idle men,
And all thy days were spent in pastime;
But though I come to thee agen,
Yet *this* time is the *last* time;
  And now I say,
  Keep on your way—
You cannot be benighted;
You will not need to grope or halt;
The little lamps of Odin's vault
  Will one by one be lighted.

---

[1] *Fram* (in the Norsk) means 'forward.'

XXI.

'Go on, for after all your pains
I know that all your gathered gains,
　　Through all this livelong day,
　　　　Have been but *Nil*:
You have not found the pearl of price—
　　　　Go seek it still!
For you shall find it if you will!

—My manners are not over-nice,
　　Yet I who warn you so
　　Am not a common crow:
My name—as probably you know—
Is Munin[1], and I live on high:
My brother Hugin[2]—he and I—
For ever come, for ever go
On Odin's errands through the sky;
And every word I say is true:
So Fram! Go forward! And good-bye!'
—Whereat he flapped his wings and flew
　　Straight up into the blue.

XXII.

The Raven's speech
　　Was such a screech,
That after he had stopped his croak
I still imagined I could hear him;
And though I had no cause to fear him,
I felt so creepy and affrighted,
That I had knockings of the knees;

[1-2] Of Odin's two ravens, Munin is memory; Hugin, reflection.

Until, to my relief, I sighted
Not far away a whiff of smoke
That curled above a clump of trees—
A sign to which I onward pressed,
For what it signified I guessed:

—And oh that I could now infuse
　　Into my lagging, flagging Lay,
　　By help of some superior muse
Like high Urania (last and most divine
　　　　Of the Parnassian Nine),
　　　　Some of that happy thrill
　　　　(Which I remember still)
That came to me to cheer my heavy breast,
Just at the ending of that dusty day.

XXIII.

Up from the bank of Orkla Brook,
And at the very bend and nook
Which in the morning I had passed
And now had reached agen at last,
Arose a clang of noises made
　　　　By cudgelled asses braying
　　　　And fretted horses neighing
　　　　And fly-stung oxen stamping;
For there, amid a mirkwood shade,
Some Tourists, after a day's tramping,
Had halted for their nightly rest,
　　　　And had commenced encamping.

XXIV.

It was a motley cavalcade
Made up from many a different land,

Especially from South and West :
The troop had formed at Christiansand [1],
And thence, with cream-white ponies and a guide,
Had started for a fortnight's sylvan ride
Up through the narrow North to Hammerfest—
That Arctic town
Of high renown—
A meagre thorp more celebrated
Than many a city walled and gated :
For of all villages, however small,
That dot the cincture of this earthly ball,
This tiny one—
Almost the tiniest one of all
(Yet strong enough to smell for leagues away
Of rancid fish-oil on a summer's day)—
Sits on its crag,
And for a brag
Puts forth the mighty boast
That it is Northernmost !
And once a year its promontory
Borrows a transient gleam of glory
From the uncertain Midnight Sun !

XXV.

So ships from everywhere
Go creeping to the misty little port
To anchor off the feeble little fort
And tarry for a week or fortnight there,
With patient passengers, who learn to wait,
However long, however late,

---

[1] This thrifty city, which was lately devastated by a conflagration, is briskly recovering, and will soon look all the brighter for the fire.

To see—or try to see—that baffling sight,
The orb of day shining at dead of night!—
A glorious miracle!—yet seldom done!

XXVI.

The Midnight Sun, I fancy, would be fine
If only it would condescend to shine:
But every ship that goes there (see her log)
Always reports a never-failing fog!
   —Yet where, oh tell me, tell me where,
In any region of this Earth below,
Is there a Human Hope, if bright and fair,
That does not disappoint exactly so?
—Fulfilment never hurries nigh,
But always waits till By-and-By.

Stave Thirteenth.

I.

The Tourists to whose camp I went,
And who amid their forest-haunt
Were setting up their canvas-tent,
   Had finished now their first day's jaunt,
And being hungrier than a troop of bears,
Their supper now was their supreme of cares!
   I joined their bivouac for a bite,
   For I too had an appetite!

II.

I sat with the carousing band
And asked of each and every one,
   According to his mood,
   What aim he had pursued?—

What fancy had allured him most,
And led him on from coast to coast?
And how his travels, far and wide,
Had satisfied,
In whole or part,
The hungry hankerings of his heart?

III.

The answers I received
Were hard to be believed;
They staggered me and struck me dumb!
Each man narrated with a serious face
What all the others heard with a grimace!
The first who spake—and all thereafter—
As soon as they had said their say,
Were paid in plaudits of sardonic laughter;
For each narrator but repeated
Whence he had come,
And how, while on his way,
He had in open day
Been most egregiously beguiled and cheated
And lured astray!
So each, at what he sheepishly confessed,
Became the boisterous butt of all the rest.

IV.

One, with a smile-bepuckered mouth
(A Swabian from the silly South)[1]
Said, with a self-convicting candour,

---

[1] Swabia is the butt of jests on account of a supposed thickheaded-
ness inherent in the typical Schwab—who is likened to the dull
Bœotian of the ancient Greeks.

'I sallied forth with a desire
To catch a living salamander[1];
   But to my rue,
   All I could do
Was just to burn my fingers in the fire!'

This speech was odd, and made a hit,
And seemed to be a stroke of wit:
For speeches often pass for good
Through lack of being understood.

v.

The next recital was more grand,
And harder still to understand.

A Magyar, with an owlish face,
Had been to what was ancient Thrace:
'I crossed the Caucasus,' said he,
'On purpose just to hear and see
   The Singing Tree[2],
   Yet never found it,—
And so it never sang for *me*;
   Or if it did,
The hum of all the world around it
   Completely drowned it.'

vi.

We gave our Magyar a guffaw,
Which changed into a loud hurrah:

  For now a keg came rolling in;
  Inspired by which, amid the din

---

[1] Like the chameleon, the salamander is a small lizard that has given rise to a strange fable—being long supposed to live unharmed in a flaming fire—even in a sevenfold furnace-heat.

[2] The Singing Tree is in the Arabian Nights.

Of many a jingling dekkel-lid,
That oped and shut and banged and snapped
Against the beer-mug which it capped,
A Spanish student from Madrid
Said gravely, with a mock salaam
  (Doffing his scarlet fez
  Which he had bought at Suez),
'I made on foot a whole year's tramp
Through all the realm of the Nizaam
To Bilso, for Aladdin's Lamp,—
Yet never could I find a trace
Of such a lamp or such a place.'

Whereat, to chaff the speaker, we derided him,
And said it must have been a fool who guided him.

VII.

And now the ale, with flaky foam,
Made every stranger feel at home;
And ever as the jug was passed
Each tongue grew louder than the last.

Amid the noise, a Muscovite,
  Of dwarfish height
(In fact the man was but a mite),
Said, with a self-important air,
  'I left Yrkoutz¹,
And went to Cairo, to a fair,
To try to buy myself a pair
  Of Seven-Leagued Boots:
But shut was cobbler Hassan's shop,
And all his trade was at a stop—

---

¹ In Russia.

K

A trade whereby, although a master,
He earned no longer a piastre;
    For as the times now go,
    Such travel is too slow;
There being in its stead, you know,
    The newer notion,
    That locomotion
Should be like lightning, or a little faster.'

VIII.

Outburst a squall of Ahs and Ohs
From all the board, and then uprose
    A pious Croat
    (A priest of note,
And high at Agram in the Church,
For he was Padre to the poor).

'I undertook,' quoth he, 'a search
Through all the ancient shrines at Tours,
In hope to find within the town
(Or in the caverned rocks outside)
Some remnant which those caverns hide
    Of old Saint Martin's gown [1]—
    That garb of eider-down,
Which once the Saint, upon a winter's day,
    Cut with his sword in twain,
And to a nak'ed Beggar (so they say)
    Gave half the robe away:
'Yet,' quoth the priest, 'through all Touraine
    I sought in vain
To find the half that must remain.'

---

[1] A sumptuous and costly tomb has just been built for St. Martin in a new church at Tours.

IX.

After some mock applause
A Runen Magistrate,
Grim-visaged and sedate,
Full of judicial saws,
And ripe in all the lore of all the laws,
Gave to the table such a knock,
That all the tankards felt the shock.
And thus he spake : 'You all will laugh—
You all will jibe and jeer and chaff—
For once, in dread of Ragnârok[1]
I swam the Ormt[2],
I leapt the Kormt[3],
I plunged into Ginunga-gap[4];
I risked all hazard and mishap,
To reach the brink of Mimir's Well[5];
But when I stooped to dip my shell
And drink my draught, and so be wise,—
The fount dried up before my eyes!'

X.

Then came a Swomian[6] discourse
By one who hailed from Helsingfors
(Whose mellow native tongue
Is called the sweetest ever spoke or sung)
—A scholar bred,
With many a ballad in his head,
Which he had learned from Kalevála's Lay[7],

[1-5] Ragnârok is doomsday; Ginunga-gap is chaos; the Ormt and the Kormt are mythical rivers which the god Thor crosses daily; and Mimir's Well is the typical Fount of Wisdom.

[6] Swomian is another name for Finnish. *Suomi* means a marshy country—a fen land. Hence, Finland.

[7] Kalevála's Lay includes the greater portion of the folk-lore of Finland; and it furnished to Longfellow the metre of Hiawatha.

And which in cunning style
He on his kantali could play [1]
Bringing a tear and then a smile.
And this is what he strangely said:

'I tried,' quoth he, 'to solve the riddle
Of Bragi's spirit-haunted fiddle,
That played itself without a bow,
    Or touch of hand,
Till folk who chanced to hear it played
Said that the music which it made
Dropped down from Odin's Upper-land, ·
And that the instrument had wings,
    And came and went
    Divinely sent
Alike to palaces of kings
And huts of shepherds on the moor;
    But I am sure
That some unlucky, sad mishap
Has finally occurred to snap
Those now for-ever-silent strings.'

XI.

This rhapsody fell flat and dead;
And then a Munich pedant—pale
Through much addiction to a pipe,
And to an orgie called a Kneip—
    Arose and said:
'I chanced to read a crazy tale,
How that the wand of Prospero [2]

---

[1] A harp of five strings—the national instrument of Finland.

[2] If Prospero carried out his intention, he buried his staff in the earth and drowned his book of magic in the sea.—Tempest, Act v. Scene 1.

Still lay in the Trinacrian Sea—
As if it waited there for *me*.
In a felucca off I flew
To where the water was a sapphire blue,
And there I shortened sail
To slacken speed,
And dragged most cautiously and slow
A hair-knit, triple-knotted net,
With double dredges interset;
Nor zeal nor labour did I spare,
But swept the sea-floor everywhere,
As when a hussy plies her broom
In every corner of a room.
—And yet, from all my care
What profit did I reap?
I brought up nothing from the deep,
Save only here and there
A snapping crab, or wriggling worm, or slimy weed!
So fiddle-faddle! is my cry—
The thing called Human Hope, say I,
Is what no Human Soul should heed!
I lost my net, for it was torn to bits,—
And folk there be who dare declare
I also lost my wits.'

XII.

A young Rumelian, who was lame
(Which mortified
His manly pride
And grieved his spirit overmuch),
Said softly (in a tone to touch
The sympathy of all the table):
' I had in life a single aim,

Which was, to rid me of my crutch :
I grew to hate it—scorn it—scout it !—
So I resolved to do without it.
And this is how I set about it.
I could not walk, and so must ride ;
      And hence, of course,
I first must learn to mount a horse.
    And learn I did,—till I was able
      To mount at need
      The wildest steed,
And spur him to his highest speed.
     "Aha !" quoth I,
     "My crutch, good-bye !
I will go gallop to the sky !"

XIII.

'Whereat I climbed upon the back
      Of Al Borák—
      Mahomet's horse—
A roan with wings, a hippogriff,
Whose hoofs had such a facile force,
That he could bound from cliff to cliff,
      Touching the rock
      Without a shock,
And who, at every leap he took,
Sprang farther than a man could look !

XIV.

'At first, low down along the shingly shore,
      With pinions strong,

---

[1] The Korán makes Mahomet ride a mare, but the Northern
imagination assigns him a stallion.

My shivering soul full tenderly he bore,
    Skimming along
Where I might view my Native Vale once more:

    Then up into the ether far
    He madly shot from star to star—
Passing the stars till he had passed eleven:

And then, when all these blazing orbs were passed,
    Except the twelfth and last,
    I came so near to God's abode,
    That, at the rate at which I rode
        (Oh, it was breathless fast!)
        I would in just a moment more
    Have galloped straightway into Heaven!
    But suddenly there came a flash
        And then a crash,
    And while the white and fiery levin
        Streamed in its wrath
        Across my path,
    My startled stallion broke his girth
    And flung me to the flinty earth—
    When I awakened lame and sore,
    Needing my crutch as heretofore.'

This tale was staggering; listeners hardly knew
With what amount of credence to receive it;
Till some one said, 'Of course the yarn is true,
For not a mortal creature can believe it.'

XV.

A Cracow gownsman, growing jolly,
    Kept up the fun:
'A wisdom-loving man,' quoth he,

'Delights to do an act of folly,
    Yet stops at *one*.
But one was not enough for *me* —
    I did a score,
    Or even more:

At first I sought with rash pretension,
By diagrams of my invention,
To formulate a Fourth Dimension—
    Though all the things that be
    Are measured by the Three.

Then next I tried (yet soon despaired)
To coax the Circle till it Squared;
And ever vexingly I found
It would persist in being round.

At last I had the natty notion
    Of making a machine
For running by Perpetual Motion:
    But though I planned
    A scheme so grand
That not the like was ever seen,
Yet ere I solved my final doubt,
The Sheriff came, and sold me out!'

XVI.

    The ale flowed on,
    Until anon
A Paris painter, who had reckoned
To win a medal, first or second,
Yet who (as gaily he averred)
Would feel more honoured by a third [1],

---

[1] The third medal is the least and lowest.

Went to the jug
And filled his mug;
But though he drained it to his Native Land
(For Frenchmen are for France, you understand),
Yet with hilarious glee
He satirized the present tone of taste
In Paris Art as woefully debased.
'It is a taste,' he said, 'no longer pure,
Rejecting Troyon and Couture:
And so I had a hope,' continued he,
'That it would welcome *me*!
My passion was the gloomy grand:
I cared not that the grass was green,
Nor that the sky was blue;
I sought for luridness of scene,
For lividness of hue:
And so, to prove my thesis true
(And what ambition could be greater?)
I clambered down a burning Crater;
And if I had not choked and fainted,
I would immortally have painted
A scene original and new—
Vesuvius: an Interior View.'

—Whereat, in duty bound,
We all haw-hawed,
And caustic laughs went round
(For critics thus applaud).

XVII.

And then a Yankee, with a nasal tone,
Said, 'Be it known
That other countries than my own
Are tending to material things:

As witness Venice—where no more,
    As once of yore,
Her Doges with their marriage-rings
    Espouse the sea ;
    For now,' cried he,
'By Jupiter ! you hear a scream
    And then a clatter,
And see a smoke upon the stream,
    —And what's the matter?
—The Gondola of which you dream
Is now a Tug, and goes by steam !'

XVIII.

Then, amid quips and smiles and shrugs,
And much refilling of the mugs,
A youth who had not spoken yet
(Though he had kept his whistle wet)—
A son of Erin, who, I ween,
Was from the City of Dasheen [1]
Had roamed (he said) his island over
To find a sprig of Four-leaved Clover,—
Yet when he came to where it grew,
The leaves, instead of four, were two !
—This Irish bull was so Corkonian,
That the applause was Pandemonian.

XIX.

Whereat, ere ending of the shout,
Uprose—magnificently stout—
A glum Professor from the Cam,
Who said : 'I freely must admit
That Britons lack the Irish wit ;

---

[1] Cork.

Our heads are more opaquely made,
More stolid, yet perhaps less weak :
Now I—a dunderhead by trade
(Like *all* professors, so to speak !)—
Will show you what a fool I am !
I had an itching (let me say)
For things most Attically Greek,
      And so one day
      I took my pay
And went and hired a ten-oared ship,
Wherein I made a moonlight trip [1]
Along the banks of the Illissus
To see the Image of Narcissus—
But found the beauteous figure flown,
And in its stead my ugly own !'

XX.

This put the roysterers in a roar :
      But I replied,
'O no, it cannot be denied
That Englishmen have handsome faces,—
      The reason being plain :
You spring from blue-eyed Northern races;
Your blood has Scandinavian traces;
Your Shakespeare's Hamlet was a Dane;
And Shakespeare's self we proudly call
The noblest Goth among us all !
Your Latest Bard of great repute,
Whose harp as yet is hardly mute,
Was one whom Norskers love to claim
As Northern both in heart and name.
So while his grave was being made

[1] From Athens.

Where England's greatest dead are laid,
The pickaxe hewing in the gloom
Struck sparkles from the flinty tomb[1];
For all our trolls, with pious care,
With all their lanterns lit, were there.'

XXI.

The learnèd Briton then inquired,
'What know you of this bard of ours?
For though he was by Heaven inspired,
Yet as a singer, he was England's own,—
And, being English to the marrow-bone,
How, out of England, could his song be known?'
Then answered I,
'We knew his gifts—we felt his powers:
He drank indeed
From Bragi's cup of heavenly mead;
And to a bard so high
All honours we accord
Save one alone—
He was a Laureate and a Lord,
And sang a Throne:
He bowed too humbly down
To Sceptre and to Crown.

XXII.

'We simple Norskers think a skald
Divinely called
To sing his country's Liberty,
And not—oh not as he,

---

[1] In digging Lord Tennyson's grave in Westminster Abbey, October, 1892, the grave-diggers encountered a rock, which they cut through with great difficulty.

To wear in courts a gilded chain
And bid the whole world hear it clank;
Nor stoop, like him, to bear the train
Of feudal royalty and rank.
       A poet should be free!
We say that sceptre, throne and crown—
The tyrant's symbols—are to be abhorred
Like tyranny itself, and are to be cast down!
We Norskers have (for yet awhile) a King—
To whom we wish no ill or harm;
Yet Royalty has lost its charm,
And Kingship is an ended thing!
Yea, hither now on flying wing
Its day of doom is coming fast;
       For now at last
From fell to fiord, from mount to main,
No more in Norseland shall be known
       A King or Throne,
But Freedom shall arise and reign!'

XXIII.

As thus I spake, my rasping strain—
Unwelcome to unwilling ears—
       Awoke some sneers,
       And even jeers,
With no approving voice save one.
Yet one there was amid the groans,
And I remember still its tones:
For first, ere my harangue was done,
A big shillaleh thumped and pounded
And made confusion worse confounded;
And high above the racket then—
With voice exploding like a gun—

The Son of Erin cried 'Amen!'
—Whereat I flung my cap on high!
—'Hurrah,' quoth I, 'the day is nigh
For Erin's freedom By-and-By!'

Stave Fourteenth.

1.

'Has no one,' I inquired,
'A tale of Love to tell?'
Whereat a Pomeranian, fired
With memory of his Mirabelle,
Responded tenderly, and said,
'I fell in love and wished to wed:
The maid was beautiful and pure,
        And loved me, I was sure;
But *she* was of a noble line,
        And *I* was poor;
So, for that noble damsel's sake,
Ere I could ask her to be mine,
            I journeyed to Cathay,
            And wore my youth away
To find the Jewel of Jamschidd,[1]
But never learned where it was hid;
And she—my unpredestined bride—
Pined in my absence till she died.'

II.

This tale was of a sorry sort,
And had no jest and made no sport;

---

[1] Mentioned by Lord Byron.

Whereat a Frisian said, 'I too,
When I was younger, went to woo;
But she, the damsel I adored,
Had woman's wit, and she implored
That ere I bought and brought the ring,
I first of all would buy and bring
(In token that my love was true)
The Wishing Carpet of Tangoo
(Which, if you sat upon it, as you know,
Would waft you anywhere you wished to go).
And so, to please my prudent lass,
I started off upon a mule
(Myself, I think, the greater ass!)
And rode away to Istamboul;
Where not a tongue in town could tell
What merchant had the rug to sell:
And while among the Turks I tarried
　　　　To search bazárs,
The maiden jilted me and married!
　　　　—I thank my stars!'

III.

Thus through the supper ran a rill of fun,
As if the driblet never would be done.
For table-talk is never like to flag
Where every talker is a witty wag
　　　　(Or thinks himself to be);
But while so many voices all were chattering
Each in the language of a different land,
The wit (if wit it were) grew so diffuse,
　　　So helter-skelter, and so scattering,
　　　That I, whose native tongues were three
　　　(With some few added as a smattering),

Found that to listen was of little use;
For I could hardly comprehend a tithe:
•So I began to wriggle and to writhe,
And felt abashed and awkward and unnerved;
Which when the guide
(That shrewd and wily dragoman!) observed,
He squatted at my knee
And, bargaining for a fee,
Made in a whisper a translation
Most cleverly of each narration:
For *he* was not
A Norsker clot,
But Russian, and a Polyglot,
And had a mouth that opened wide,
With twenty languages inside!

IV.

Thus with the merry travellers at their meal
(To which in kindness I had been invited)
I sat an hour or more,
And while the evening wore
I lent my ear as each in turn recited
His crazy tale;
And now at last,
And while the talk was still increasing fast,
And ere the laughter, with its peal on peal,
Had time to fail,
I sprang to my impatient feet,
And as my task was incomplete,
'Adieu!' I said,
And off I sped,
And left them to their pipes and ale.

V.

—'O thorp of Nanna's Heim,' thought I,
'Thou art a league away, or more,
And now my weary feet are sore!
—Alas, our rest is never nigh,
But lies beyond us, By-and-By.'

Stave Fifteenth.

I.

Now as I went,
The sky was blent
With faint and fading streaks of red
(Loved of the lonesome whippoorwill;
For while the colours fade he sings,
And when they die, his voice is still).
My thoughts were such as twilight brings—
Of solemn, serious, sober things;
Till, as a flock of bats flew by
(The very blindest birds that be),
'Tell me, ye dim-eyed tribe,' quoth I,
'Is it by Nature's own decree
That Humans are as blind as ye?
Or if it be not Nature's plan,
Is it some scurvy trick of Fate
Which thus foredooms that every man
Shall always have an addled pate?'

II.

I cried, 'Egad!
The world is mad!
Each mortal is befooled to-day,

And to his sorrow
He learns to-morrow
How great a zany he has been—
To be so archly taken in !'

III.

Now though the fowler's net
(According to the Holy Word)
Is ever vainly set
In sight of any bird,
Yet with a man not so,
For to his rue and woe,
Poor wretch, before he is aware,
The lime-twigs have him in a snare!

IV.

Man is a dog, and has his day ;
He is of Earth, and not divine ;
He is of Hell, or hardly higher ;
Indeed he is of Satan's swine,
And wallows in his Master's mire.

V.

A Man is blinder than a mole,—
For the wee delver in the clay,
With meagre sight
And doubtful light,
Is certain not to go astray ;
But lordly Man, who sees and knows,
And who, at every step he goes,
Thinks that his guiding-light is clearer,
And that his journey's end is nearer,
Goes ever errant on his way
And misses finally his goal!

VI.

Moreover, it most mournfully appears
That neither any ancient rune nor writing,
Nor beech-wood book of any Skald's inditing,
Nor prophecy of Vala, Norn or Van,
Can warn the inborn folly out of man,
Or make him wiser as he grows in years;
For whether he be young, or in his prime, or hoary,
His record always is the self-same story—
A never-varying foolish tale
Of hopes that flatter and that fail!

VII.

Yea, verily forsooth,
Not only in his youth,
Or while his judgement is jejune,
But in his mellow season
Of very ripest reason
He has his self-delusions still;
Which not the frosts of age can kill
Nor even nip or chill:
And so the grey buffoon
Keeps up his rigadoon,
As if his heart and mind and will
Had all been mildewed by the moon!
Indeed he is the mooncalf's twin:
He is an ape
In human shape;
For though he lacks the antic and the grin,
He ranks in Nature's heraldry
As Folly's very next of kin:
He was, and is, and is to be
A fool of very first degree:

L 2

VIII.

He may not wear the cap and bells,
Yet something gowkish in him tells
That in his bonnet is a bee!
　　His proud pretence
　　Of sober sense
Is pitiful indeed to see!
　　He is not *quite*
　　A Bedlamite,
Whose ravings cannot be restrained
　　Or pranks prevented
　　Save under lock and key,
But though not totally demented,
Yet he is richly rattle-brained,
And though he still is left to roam at large,
Yet never would the World permit him to go free,
Save that the World itself is just as mad as he!

IX.

His name is Fimbulfambi—fool indeed![1]
　　Not of the motley sort
　　Paid with a prince's pelf,
　　To make a merry parle
　　And furnish sport
　　For king and court
(A kind of folly which the great may need,
And which the wise may profitably heed);
　　But Man—plain man—the common carl,
Is a poor witling not acutely schooled,
Possessing neither worldly craft nor ken;
And so, instead of fooling other men,

---

[1] As 'fambi' is fool, so Fimbulfambi is 'the greatest of fools.'

He fools his simple self,
And is a fool who loves to be befooled !

X.

His lunacy, a thing innate,
Is not a craze that will abate
     .   Or soon be past,
But cheats him early, cheats him late,
     And cheats him to the last !

XI.

Fooled from the first beginning,
Fooled to the final end,
Waiting for luck, yet never winning,
Deceived alike by foe and friend,
Not knowing how to gather or to spend,
     To borrow or to lend,
He boggles, blunders and goes wrong
     His whole life long !
He trips and slips at every stage
From youngest youth to oldest age !

XII.

He thinks that he is canny and is clever,
And that he ranks among the cunning men :
     And so he may ;
     But this I say
—Yea, I declare, by all the heavenly powers !—
That Mortal Man from Adam's time to ours
Has been a fool, and so will be for ever !
He is a simpleton—a rantipole—
     A ninnyhammer, dense and dull—
     A stupid, oafish, silly soul—
     A jabbernowl—

Whom every flattering hope can gull
Or fair allurement can cajole:
A dolt, who down through all his days
Has some new maggot in his skull,
Some new delusion of a kind
To tickle and torment his mind,
　　　Until his tortured brain,
　　　Under the rack and strain,
Gives evidence—alas! too plain—
　　　That in all tribes and races,
　　　And in all times and places,
A universal strange insanity
Runs in the heads of all humanity!

XIII.

Thus in a morbid mood
I for a while pursued
My train of cynical reflections;
　　　And, musing half aloud,
　　　I, with a spirit proud,
　　　Spake in a sneering tone
Of other people's imperfections—
　　　Forgetful of my own.

XIV.

Then, with my hand against my breast,
To quell a rising heart-ache there,
I asked myself if, like the rest,
I too, in seeking for the Best,
　　　Was grasping at the Empty Air?
Did I too follow and obey
The beck of hopes that would betray?
What answer could I make? What could I say?

I said, Oh! woe is me!
The falser all such fancies be,
The more I feel their sorcery!

XV.

They cheat, they cozen, they beguile,
Yet I believe them all the while!
For oh! what cunning shapes they take!
What promises they make and break!
I parch with thirst—they give, to cool me,
The Cup of Tantalus, and fool me!
I faint with fasting—they provide
The Supper of the Barmecide!
I sleep—they shed upon my slumber
A shower of glories without number,
Whereof the brightest and the best
Are sure to prove the emptiest!
I wake—and to my dire confusion,
They tempt me with some fresh illusion,
Whereof the promise gladdens me,
The disappointment saddens me,
And the remembrance maddens me!

XVI.

I roam in Fields Elysian,
    Or in Saint Brandan's Isle,
Till Fancy, in derision,
    Informs me, with a smile,
That nothing but a vision
    Decoys me all the while!

XVII.

Sometimes these visions are so grand,
That all this solid North of mine—

This rocky strand,
These craggy cliffs and promontories,
These pine-clad capes—
Take more than mere terrestrial shapes;
They change to heavenly heights and glories;
As if the Vingolf[1] had been built agen
Upon its early plan,
With arches of immeasurable span
And pillars of a height untold;
Or as if Rind and Ran[2],
Throned on a mountain's brow,
Under a roof of blue and gold,
Were reigning still as in those times of old
When men were gods, and gods were men:
(And would that *I* were living then,
Or *they* were living now!)

XVIII.

—O Golden Year!
Thy dawn, I fear,
(Although we dream of it as nigh)
Is ever to be By-and-By.

Stave Sixteenth.

I.

In sleep I many a time have found
That jewelled Carcanet
Beyond all cost,
Which Freyia lost,—

---

[1] The Palace of the Goddesses.
[2] Rind is the Earth, and Ran the Sea.

That clasped her heavenly neck around,
But which she heedlessly unbound,
Till all the jewels were unset
And sank into the slimy ground—
    Not harmed, but hid away:
    For skalds there be, who say,
That still the Carcanet is whole,
And is the same which Loki stole;
    And that in Strelsa Bay
It shall be found some day[1].

II.

Moreover—call it fancy if you will—
These eyes of mine have seen on Gnita Heath
That other treasure far more precious still[2],
Which I have tugged for, and have grit my teeth
In trying to grub up, and bear away—
    Red gold indeed,
    Red as a glede—
Which madly I have hoped to count for mine,
    Yet never could succeed.
    Some say the gold
Now lies at twenty fathoms in the Rhine:
    But others hold
That it is lying on the Glommen shore,
    In plain and open sight
    And glittering in the light,
    Just as it did of yore—
Waiting till Sigurd[3] come agen, if so he may:

---

[1] Freyia's lost necklace was called Brisingamen.
[2] This mystical treasure on Gnita Heath was the gold which
Fafnir guarded till he was slain by Sigurd.
[3] Sigurd was Brunhilda's lover, who rode to her through the fire.

Or since he knows the'treasure to be curst,
He may not haste, and *I* shall find it first.

III.

I once imagined, in my fiery zeal,
That I could get my grip on Fortune's Wheel;
But just as I was reaching for the spokes,
The shining wheel proved but a glittering hoax.

IV.

I dreamed I built a Pillar, block on block,
And said, 'Now this is solidness indeed,
And safe to lean on in a time of need,'—
When, to my wonderment, my Pillared Rock
Changed all at once into a Broken Reed.

V.

I thought myself at sea in my kayák,
Not noting that the clouds were growing black,—
But when my boat of skins was struck abeam,
And when the roaring breakers were at hand,
And when my peril grew to be extreme,
I sat aghast—
For I had cast
An Anchor with a Rope of Sand.

VI.

I won a Laurel for my brow,
And proud I was to bind it there,
And felt it wondrous fine to wear,
But then the green illusive bay,
I know not why,
I know not how,
Began to disappear and die,

As when a fog-wreath melts away :
And so I have no Laurel now
—Although I hope my time is nigh
To wear another By-and-By.

Stave Seventeenth.

I.

I had a Love, and fondly pressed
The melting maiden to my breast,
And said, as happy lovers do
When passion thrills them through and through,
' Though every other hope I cherish
Should disappoint me and should perish,
Yet Love is lasting—Love is true.'
    But then I little knew
How Love, despite its vow and ring,
Could prove itself a fickle thing,
   Or how its pledge of faith
    Could be forsworn !

II.

But Love is mortal from its birth ;
It is the offspring of the Earth,
   And dies, like all things born !
   It is a mountain-wraith—
    A vapour of the morn !
It is a kiss and a caress—
And then a doubt and a distress,—
And then at last a nothingness !

III.

I liken Love to our Norwegian Spring—
　　　　Sweet while it yet is vernal,
　　　　But not to be eternal.
Is Love Eternity? Love is so brief
That it is shorter far than Time!
　　　　　　For Time is long,
　　　　But Love is for a day!
　　　　　　—Praised in a song,
　　It is outlasted by the rhyme!
Love? Name it to me nevermore—
　　　　My heart is sore!

IV.

　　So I will vary now my theme,
　　And turn me to another dream.

One night I felt the overwhelming power
Of heavy sleep. It was the midnight hour
When dreams are strongest (being new and fresh),
And cause the clammiest creeping of the flesh.
I saw the dim and fathomless abyss
That yawns between the other world and this,
　　Spanned by the Bridge of Al Sirát—
　　　　A wondrous bridge indeed!—
　　As slender as a spider's thread,
　　　　Yet crossed at lightning-speed
　　By spirits of the newly-dead!
I leapt upon it like an acrobat!
　　　　—At every step I took,
　　　　It violently shook,
And midway over the great gulf it broke!
Whereat, in sweat and anguish, I awoke!

And now at night I sleep and toss,
        Or wake and groan,
In dread of having yet to cross
        That chasm—and alone!

v.

The Sciolists may say,
'The world is nothing but a seeming,
And we who think we live, are dreaming—
     Dreaming in open day.'
But I reply,
The world is substance, and is real—
And not a mighty, mountainous heap
     Of emptiness and nought;
Nor a colossal fabric built in sleep,—
     All by our fancy wrought:
It is a thing, and not a thought.

VI.

The light is not the eye:
The star, the rose, the drop of dew—
     Each beauty that we view
Is quite exterior to our mind,
And would exist if we were blind.

VII.

Moreover, I make bold to say,
       That in our sleep
      (If it be sound and deep),
The brightest and most vivid of our dreams
(Those giving us our glimpses and our gleams
Of regions mystical and far away)
Are of a fabric not entirely planned
By any process which we understand;

Nor are their figures cunningly combined
In curious shapes and patterns—all designed
    Within our slumbering brain' alone ;
    They have a being of their own—
        A nature not akin to ours ;
For they have foreign elements and ultra powers—
Strange energies of a Supernal kind,
Remote from any motion of our mind :
They cast their spells and work their weird effects
As Puck, or Ariel, or some other sprite, directs.

VIII.

If otherwise, how can it be, I pray,
That visions seen in sleep are also seen elsewhere,
Even at mid-day, in the sun-illumined air ?—
Visions so visible and so enticing fair
That they have potency to grapple with a man,
To wreak their will upon him, and to act
As if their airiness were all compact
Of living substance ; or as if, in fact,
They were the ruling, mischief-making forces
That misdirect him in his worldly courses,
    Divinely guiding him in sleep by night,
      And then in open day
      Alluring him astray !

IX.

    What follow we but dreams indeed ?
Though, knowing them for dreams, why do we
    give them heed ?
We give them heed, for though they be but dreams,
Yet each is something other than it seems ;
It is an outward actual thing, as well—
Not a mere inward vision or a spell :

It is an evil genius, or a good:
It either is a comfort or a bane:
Nor can we shake it from us, if we would.
   —In spite of all that we can do,
   Its power upon us will remain.

X.

   But, on the other hand,
How can we prove, or take as true
(What never proof, indeed, can render plain)
That all the Universe is in our brain,
   And is a dream and nothing more?

XI.

   Are we to understand
That this huge Earth, with all its solid land,
   Deep down to its foundation-stone,
   Is but a dream alone?
Is it a fancied world wherein we dwell?
Are mortals born of fancied pangs of birth?
And when their days are ended, is their death
A merely fancied passing of their breath?

XII.

Such sophists surely do not reason well;
Their reasoning is a thousand miles amiss!
   For, tell me this:
If it be fancy merely—nought beside—
That when we hunger we have need of bread,
Why not imagine then that we are fed?
Why not imagine too that all our ailings,
Our pains, our aches, our faintings and our failings,
Our ills of mind and body, all are banished?
   That every sting, that every smart,
   Has been exorcized and has vanished?

If this can be, why then
Should any man of all the race of men
Be ever sick, but strong and well, instead?
Or why henceforth should there be headache in a
　　head,
　　　　Or heartache in a heart?

XIII.

Now Fancy is not all: but it is much!
It catches us as with an ogre's clutch;
　　　　Nor can we ever slip
　　　　From such a dragon's grip.
　　We boast that we are free,
　　　　But we are held in awe
　　By what we *think* we see,
　　　　As if in sooth we *saw*!
　　　　We are enthralled
By what are far too fondly called
　　Our fine imaginations,
　　Whose dazzling scintillations
Allure us oft to our mishap—
　　Like victims to a trap.
Our hopes are baits; our fancies, tempting gauds;
Our visions, make-believes and frauds;
　　　　They mystify,
　　　　They feign, they lie:

XIV.

　　And, worse than all,
They often in their ultimate intent
Are most malignant, and on mischief bent!
They strew our path with flowers, and on we go,
　　　　And little do we know
That they have dug meanwhile some hidden ditch,

Some pitfall, headlong into which,
Without a warning we are doomed to fall.

XV.

Their subtilty is deep and keen;
Their mischief cannot be foreseen:
I am too dull—I am too daft—
To penetrate their cunning craft:
I never dream of the deceit,
Till Jack-a-Lantern's tricksy fire
Has lured me to the bog and mire:
      And even then,
      In slough or fen,
So long as I can see the flicker,
My heart is sure to beat the quicker;
And on and on, through damp and chill,
With little wit, yet mighty will,
I follow, follow, follow still!

XVI.

Oh blessed, blessed, blessed thrice,
Are all such visions while they last!
I follow, follow, follow fast—
For they will vanish in a trice,
Ere even the pursuit be past!
But oh! they are as fair and fleet
As those swift Birds of Paradise,
Which, being uncreate with feet,
Can never loiter nor alight,
And so must ever be in flight![1]

---

[1] The Swedish naturalist Linnaeus has gracefully perpetuated this superstition concerning the Bird of Paradise by bestowing on the pretty creature the name *Paradisea apoda*—the word apoda being Greek, and signifying 'without feet.'

M

XVII.

A hundred hopes, all in a day,
    Will come to me and haunt me,
    And cheer me and enchant me,
And promise nevermore to leave me ;
      Yet being restless things
      That cannot fold their wings,
The hundred all at once will fly away—
As if they came on purpose to deceive me,
And fled for nought except to vex and grieve me.

XVIII.

So, though I love their witchery well,
I am resolved to break the spell.

Must I be evermore the dupe
Of all the tricks of all the troupe ?
Shall I not shut and lock my door
Against this wild and rabble rout,
And do my best to bar them out ?
Shall I, whom they have cheated once,
    Still trust them as before,
And like a double, treble dunce,
Be doubly, trebly duped, and left to find,
    With disappointment sore,
My apples to be golden in the rind
    Yet ashen at the core ?

—I will be juggled with no more!

XIX.

Why should I grasp at fancied gains,
To have my labour for my pains ?—
Attempting, every day I live,
To gather Sunshine in a Sieve ?

XX.

Why should I sweat and groan,
Turning the ponderous stone
That grinds the grist of Frodi's Mill[1],
Whilst gods and men look on and laugh
To see me ever grinding still,
Producing nought but chaff?

XXI.

Why, like a naked Carib,
Or semi-clouted Arab,
Should I go plunge and dive,
And come up less than half alive,
And more than half distraught—
Having amid the eddy's whirls
In merest madness sought
Imaginary pearls?

XXII.

Why should I race
At breakneck pace,
With whip and spur, and onward press,
As if I rode a steeple-chase—
Yet never for a moment guess,
Until the gallop is concluded,
That I was all the while deluded,

---

[1] Frodi was a fabulous King of Denmark at the time when Caesar Augustus was Emperor of Rome. The peace which then prevailed among all the nations of the world was called in Iceland 'Frodi's peace.' For Frodi had a miracle-working mill (named Grotti) which ground out whatever Frodi wished—peace or war, gold or meal; and it even furnished the fine white salt for salting the sea.

And that the Cup I sought
Was but a thing of nought,
Existing only in my drunken thought?

XXIII.

Why should I swagger
With sword or dagger,
And boast and be defiant,
And valiantly my weapon draw
To kill some ogre or some giant
Who proves to be a Man of Straw?

XXIV.

Why should I range and roam
In hope to find the Pleasure Dome
Of Kubla Khan?
Or think that I can ever trace
The undiscoverable place
Where Alph the Sacred River ran?[1]

XXV.

Why should I go
To Roncéveaux,
To hear the blast of Roland's Horn,—
That sounds no more to mortal ear?

XXVI.

Why should I fancy I was born
To seek and find Ithuriel's Spear?

---

[1] Coleridge's celebrated lines which he composed during an opium-sleep were these—

    ' In Xanadu did Kubla Khan
    A stately pleasure-dome decree,—
    Where Alph the sacred river ran
    Through caverns measureless to man,
      Down to a sunless sea!'

XXVII.

Why should I hunt the Unicorn,
　　　　Or chase from crag to crag
　　　　Saint Hubert's Cross-crowned Stag,—
　　　　When no such living thing　　　　,
Has on the blessed Earth been seen
Since Oberon was himself the King
And had Titania for his Queen?

XXVIII.

Why should I try, with panting breast
　　　　And with fool-hardy pride,
To swim the Maelstrom, South or West,—
　　　　　　Or seek to stride,
　　　　　　And hope to guide
　　　　With rein or bridle-bit
Arion's Dolphin to the Silver Pit [1]—
Thence onward to the Islands of the Blest?

For be those islands West or South,
　　　　Or be they greenly bowered,
They lie within the Sea-Wolf's frothy mouth—
And whoso enters there must be devoured.

XXIX.

Why should I deem that Egypt's Sphinx
Will ever tell me what she thinks,—
Since all her fame for being wise
Comes of her making · no replies? [2]

---

[1] A deep cavern in the German Ocean.

[2] The Sphinx is here feminine, in conformity with common par-
lance : for Greek Art has diffused her image throughout the world as
a creature with female breasts : but the Sphinx of Egypt is without
these breasts, and is spoken of in that country as masculine.

XXX.

Why should I try, with mortal ears,
To hear the Music of the Spheres,—
Since God Himself has struck them dumb,
Forbidding them to whizz or hum?

XXXI.

Why should I hope to see, with mortal sight,
The Pillar of a Cloud by day
　　　And of a Flame by night,—
Since these no longer wait upon our way
　　　To guide our feet aright?

XXXII.

Why should I hunt the Holy Grail,
Foreknowing that my search must fail?—
For though I be not basely bad,
Yet who is good like Galahad,
　　　Or pure like Percivale?[1]

XXXIII.

　　Why should I bruise my bones
　　By sleeping on the stones
In Orkla or in Okakell,
　　In Strelsa or in Strevven,

---

[1] According to a Christian tradition, the Holy Grail, or Sangrael, or sacred cup from which Christ drank at the Last Supper, was brought to England by Joseph of Arimathea, and having been lost, was made an object of quest by a number of King Arthur's knights. But the knights, with two exceptions, were men of worldly lusts—which prevented their eyes from obtaining a vision of the cup. The two exceptions were Galahad and Percivale, who, on account of the sanctity of their lives, were each allowed a glimpse of the cup—but a glimpse only.

As Jacob once in Bethel slept,—
　　Expecting in my slumber
　　That Angels without number
Would step agen as once they stepped
With shining feet, and come and go
Upon a Ladder to and fro
　　Between the Earth and Heaven?

XXXIV.

—Away, ye idle hopes and dreams,
That have deceived me long enough!
Ye are of thin and flimsy stuff—
　　Yet strangely strong!

　　Ye far too long
Have bound me with your viewless chain!—
　　Ye now shall end your reign!

Who but a fool like me would longer delve and pant,
　　And toil and strain,
In hope of piling up in everlasting adamant
　　A tower or fane
On nothing firmer for foundations
Than day-dreams and hallucinations?

XXXV.

Oh that a man were skilled
So that his hands could build
Just what he wished—just what he willed!—
Till all his Fancy's beautiful creations
Should just as cunningly be wrought
In stony substance as in airy thought!

XXXVI.

If Hope could work its own fruition,
How boundless were a man's ambition!

But though to mortals Hope is sweet,
Yet Toil is hard, and Time is fleet,
And Life is short. So, lest I waste
My days and years—that hie in haste—
And lest by heedlessness or sloth
      (Or peradventure both)
I finally should fail to earn
The unknown good for which I yearn,
I hereby make a solemn oath,
That in a world of time and sense,
I, who must soon be summoned hence,
Will try to win, while yet I may,
No transient honour of a day
      Nor pleasure of an hour—
To wilt and wither like a flower:

XXXVII.

But I will seek some better boon
      Not perishing so soon—
Some earthly blessing that shall last
Till all my mortal course be past,
And which shall never once meanwhile,
      By trick or guile,
Transmute itself from good to ill
(As many an earthly blessing will);
But which, so long as I shall here remain,
Shall be to me a bliss without a bane,
      A peace without a pain,
A joy without a sorrow to attend it,
      Or shade to mar it,
      Or hurt to scar it,
Or mortal accident to end it:
A lifelong heritage for me to keep

With a possession safe and sure,
And a contentment calm and deep.

XXXVIII.

For oh, my Heart, if thou be pure,
      Thou must despise
      A lesser prize!
Thou must contemn a meaner good!
Thou must, with manly hardihood,
      Toil only to attain
      The very noblest gain,
Or both thy Life and Labour shall alike be vain

XXXIX.

      And so, O Soul of mine,
If such a prize is ever to be thine,
      Thou must abjure
All glittering shams, all showy cheats;
All flattering harmful self-deceits;
All the too plausible temptations
That are but dangers in disguise;
All the too-cunning calculations
      That circumvent
      Their own intent,
      And are the lies
      Wherewith the wise
Delude themselves before their very eyes;
      All tricks that none suspect,
      Deceiving the elect;
      All the pretended sweets
      That are not sweets at all
      (For they will turn to gall);
      All the high expectations
      That only rise to fall;

All the transparent, air-blown, hollow,
Yet spangled bubbles that men follow;
All empty pomp, all vain acclaim,
All the mere nothing of a name;
All pride of place, all the false glory
That glitters, yet is transitory;
All vanity of song and lyre,
   Of tongue and pen;
All worldly praise that men acquire
   To lose agen;
All riches with their flying wings;
And all the vain and valueless array
   Of visionary things,
Which, though ephemeral, feed the fire
Of never-satisfied desire.

XL.

Now many a mortal, if bereft
Of worldly trifles such as these,
Might think he had but little left
(Except his brimming cup of woe,
   Full to its overflow);
Yet willingly I let them go,
As pleasures that have ceased to please:
For somewhere in the world, by land or sea,
   There is for me
   (As well I know)
Some pearl of greater price remaining,
A thousandfold more worth the gaining.
   And I will spare
   No toil nor care
In learning *what* it is, and *where*:
For be it far, or be it nigh,
I hope to win it By-and-By.

Stave Eighteenth.

I.

The Sun had set in purple state,
And all the royal day, so splendid,
Was now beginning to be blended
    With dim and dusky hues—
The harbingers of dews.

The twilight came—to linger late;
    The Curfew Bell
    At Okakell
Would scarce for yet an hour or more
Begin to rumble out its roar;
It was a time to meditate:
So when I reached the graveyard-gate,
I raised the latch, and in I passed,
And sighed, and sat me down at last
Where many a pilgrimage had ended.

II.

    But though I sighed
    Yet I was hardly sad,
For as a Norsker I had always had
    (Even from early youth)
A tender and a loving pride
In those old crumble-tumble stones uncouth,
    Which slanted now a hundred ways,
    And which, with dates of ancient days,
Had made the churchyard famous far and wide.

There lay my long ancestral line,
    And there amongst the dead
    I oft had sat and read

The Sagas, human and divine:
Yea, there to crickets I had oft recited
   Some new-made lay of mine,
Which people in the thorps had slighted,
But which the nimble-footed insects heard
   And seemed to understand,—
For they would hop about me, quite delighted,
As if they had mistakenly inferred
That I was just another of their chirpy band.

III.

And now the fennel (herb of grace)
Gave out its odours at my feet—
(What other herb is half so sweet?)
And round me in the glimmering light
The tall and sacred asphodel
Stood here and there in yellow bloom;
While like a snowflake, cheery white,
The daisy dotted many a tomb.

IV.

Thought I, 'These ancient graves contain
Inhabitants more numerous far
Than all who live in every thorp
From Nanna's Heim to Hyndla Scar,
From Hyndla Scar to Appendorp,
   And thence to Peif
   And Gammal Geif.'

V.

I then remembered to have read
   How Zeno said,
To one who asked him 'What is Life?'
'Go put thy query to the dead!'

And thus I asked: 'O ye who dwell,
Each in your narrow silent cell,
Whether of marble or of brass,
Or of a rounded roof of grass,
Tell me, ye tenants of the ground,
What treasure-trove ye here have found?
If ye could answer from your clay,
What would your lips of ashes say?'[1]

VI.

Then while as yet I spake,
My knees began to shake,
For in a whisper, faint yet clear
(Born of my fancy and my fear,
And shrilly, like the soughing sound
Of many pines), the buried dead
From under every stone and mound,
With many voices, all as one,
Answered and said:

VII.

'O thou belated wandering wight,
Now that the cheerful day is done
This place is gruesome in the night,
For we are ghosts, and if we rise
We are a terror to men's eyes!
Besides, have thou a care!
This robe of thine is dripping wet;
A mortal mist is in the air;
Thou seemest strangely to forget

---

[1] Familiar colloquies between the living and the dead are frequent in the old Norsk poetry—for to the Norsk fancy the Supernatural (as its name implies) is only a superior form of the Natural.

That every day, at set of sun,
In this hot season of the year,
• This old and mouldy churchyard here
Is moist with every dead man's sweat—
    A dank and clammy dew;
Or rather, not a dew at all,
Since from the sky it does not fall,
But rises from the churchyard-mould,—
And, coming out of graves, is cold!
It now is rising, we perceive,
And since we do not wish thee ill,
We give thee warning—take thy leave!
For if the damp and charnel chill
Should chance to strike thee through and through,
O loiterer, it would work thy rue:
It is a poison—it will kill!'

VIII.

Whereat, upleaping from my seat
    (Which was the carven stone
    Of one whom I had known—
A comrade of my early days),
I looked about in mute amaze,
Expecting then and there to meet
His spectre in a winding-sheet;
But neither he nor other sprite
    In that undarkened night
    Was palpable to sight.
But there were noises round me in the air,
And ghostly voices said—or seemed to say—
    'Belated man, beware!
    If thou hast come to pray,
    Make short thy prayer!

—This is our second warning—now away!
Begone, lest thou repent thy further stay.'

IX.

Then, though I shook from top to toe,
I answered, 'Bid me not depart
Till, for the comfort of my heart,
Ye tell me what I wish to know—
For until then I will not go.'

X.

The ghosts, without a shriek or groan,
Or even gibber in their tone,
        This answer gave:
    'O carl of curious mind,
        What brings thee here
        To pry and peer
Into the secrets of the grave?
        What hopest thou to find?
        What mystery wouldst thou clear?

Now we, the buried dead, rejoice
To interchange with thee a voice—
So stay awhile, if so thou wilt;
But stop thy chattering teeth! be bold
        And of good cheer!
        If thou art free from guilt,
        Then why not free from fear?
A heart, if honest, will be brave,
        And should be self-controlled!
Command thy pulses—be serene,
        Speak—let thy wish be told!
It shall not be a bootless bene.'

XI.

My teeth then chattered all the more!
I stammered, yet I tried to say,
'Ye souls of mortals passed away,
I feel myself impure—unclean—
Unworthy thus to stand before
The disembodied and unseen!
And though with good intent I come,
I dare not speak, nor yet be dumb!'

XII.

Quoth they, 'It would have been a boon
If thou hadst brought with thee thy kit
To cheer us with a pleasant tune!
        We have no music now,
Except the swallow's shrilly twit,
Or shrieking of the coot and loon,
        Or from the mountain's brow
The plunging of the water-fall,
Or blast of horns that hunters blow;
But still the fiddle and the bow
Is what we love the best of all!

So bring us thine, some stilly night,
At rising of the harvest-moon,
                And if the light
                Be not too bright,
                And if thou play
        Some old and once familiar lay,
                We will arise unseen
And dance around thee on this hallowed green;
                And ere the dance be done,

Thou shalt have glimpses of us, one by one,—
Or all together—if without affright
Thou hast the hardihood to bear the sight.

XIII.

'Meanwhile, it now behoveth thee to know
That whoso with the dead would speak
Must rist the runes that long ago
Were first engraven
Upon the eagle's beak,
And on the nib of either raven,
And other runes, both writ and sung,
Which He whom men call Gangléree[1]
Composed for mortals while He hung
Upon the Meima-meider Tree[2].
Nine livelong days and nights hung He!
And from the branch where He was tied
He uttered runes until He died!

XIV.

'Alas, the living now indeed
Pay but a very slender heed
To these and other sacred things!
What mortal knows the runes, or how to rist them?
The World has lost them, and has never missed them!
It has disdainfully let go its hold
Of what it prized beyond all price of yore!
The fruit of Ígdrasyl is plucked no more!
And now no Norsker clings

---

[1] Gangléree was Odin.
[2] Another name for the world-tree Ígdrasyl, whose roots were in the lower regions, whose trunk was on earth, and whose branches were in Heaven.

To the old runic lore—
The lore of priests and kings—
The lore of Edda's bards and of the skalds of old !
The ancient faith is fading year by year—
A loss so sad that *we* lament it *here*,
Who in our graves are cold.'

xv.

Whereat I suddenly felt bold
(As when a fool grows instant proud),
And boastfully I said aloud,
'I *know* the runes which Gangléree
Composed while on the Great Ash Tree !
Their names I will recite,
And ye shall harken if I say them right :—
The Igg runes,
The Sig runes,
The Lim runes,
The Brim runes,—
The runes on graven shields,
For winning foughten fields,—
The runes on Gungner's point and Grani's breast
And Freyia's feather-crest,—
The runes on Bragi's tongue,
For help of singers while their song is sung,—
The runes on Harbard's leather sandal[1],
The runes on Vingthor's hammer-handle[2],
The runes upon the bridge's either end,
The runes upon the hand that grasps a friend,—
The runes the bear has on his paw,
The camel on his hump,
The tiger on his claw ;—

[1] Harbard was Odin, disguised as a ferryman.
[2] Vingthor and Asathor were different names for Thor.

XVI.

'The runes which every Norn
Wears on her finger-nail
(That Fate may thus prevail
Over each creature born,
Not only over Man
But over As and Van) ;—
The runes around the rim of Gjallerhorn,
    Predicting when the dreaded trump
    Shall sound the Resurrection Morn :—
Yea, and the runes of Ragnârok,—
    That awful day
When Heaven and Earth shall pass away ;—
The day when all the Gods shall die
    Save one alone ;—
And He is not of Odin's hall
    But the Great God of all,—
Who from His solitary Throne
Shall speak a word that shall create
A greener earth, a bluer sky ;—
And Who (for so the runes relate)
Is waiting till His time be nigh
To dwell with mortals By-and-By.'

Stave Nineteenth.

I.

Thus did I chatter with a bold loquacity,
Until the spectres chid my mad audacity.
    'Oh, nay, O ranting boaster, nay!
    Thou knowest not the runes !' quoth they ;

N 2

'To know a rune by name is nought—
The thing to fathom is the thought!
The runes are mystic, and their meaning lies
Beyond the guesses even of the wise:
And only we who wear the flesh no more
Can be the teachers of this mystic lore;
And being dead, we greatly grudge the giving
Of these our subtile secrets to the living.
    We seldom deign to make reply
    To questions from a passer-by:
    Yet now for thee we have a word .
    —If we are able to be heard:
    For dead men's voices are so weak
    That oft the living, we believe,
    Can hardly hear a word we speak.

II.

        'But on this quiet eve
          We now will try
To blow our dusty windpipes clear
And reach thee gently through the ear,
Lest we should fright thee through the eye.

So, first of all, O listener, lie
Full-length beneath this willow-tree,
And be as still as still can be,—
And while the dusk begins to darken
Bend down thine ear to us and hearken;
And deem thyself, in listening so,
A favoured mortal to receive
A message from the dead below.'

III.

So down among the graves I lay,
And though my terror was profound—

Beyond all former dread and fear—
Yet close against the mossy ground
I pressed my eager ear,
And held it there, so whist and near,
That I could catch the faintest sound;
And whilst the dusk fell darkly round.
I heard the dead distinctly say:

IV.

'O living man, we clods of clay
Were once like *thee*—we sought what *thou*
So ignorantly seekest now.
We spent a lifetime each, in quest
Of what in all the world was Best;
But as to what the Best might be,
No two among us could agree:
So each, according to his whim,
Pursued what seemed the Best to him.

V.

'Some sped the plough,
 And spent their thankless toil
 Upon the self-same soil
That hides them now:

Others, with wilder likings
 And souls more free,
Followed their sires the Vikings
 And ploughed the sea—
(To find at last their graves
Not here, but in its waves).

VI.

'Some dug for gold—
First for a little, then for more,

And with a growing greed
Heaped up a hundredfold
Beyond their use or need:

Others were poor indeed,
And all their worldly stock and store
Consisted of the rags they wore;
Though now the difference, once so vast,
Between the rich and poor is past,—
For here they now are both alike at last.

VII.

'Some (who were children) found their joys
In merely childish sports and toys:

Others, when they were young no more,
Were still as childish as before,
　　And spent their precious hours
　　In building lofty towers,
　　　Yet all of sand;
　　　Till every wall
　　　And pillar tall,
Having no strength whereby to stand,
Had nothing else to do but fall.

VIII.

'Some wished for Wisdom; others just desired
A fresh new Pleasure where an old one tired.

IX.

'Some strove for things of sounding name—
Like Pomp and Glory, Power and Fame:

Others for things thought little of—
Like Truth and Virtue, Faith and Love:
A few (not many) tried to live

Supported by an inward stay
(Drawn, as they boasted, from above),
Not caring what the world could give,
Nor what the world could take away.

X.

'But each, whatever was his aim,
Was doomed to miss it all the same:
It mattered not a jot or tittle
Whether we strove for much or little:
We always murmured at our lot;
        Our lives were spent
        In discontent;
We each desired—we knew not what;
We sought it, but we found it not—
For while we struggled, hoped and sighed,
Our days were ended, and we died.'

XI.

—As thus they spake, I thought they moaned,—
But it was I, who sighed and groaned;
For through my body crept a chill,
And yet I lay and listened still.

XII.

'The grass is wet,' quoth they, 'Arise!
Trace out the letters on this stone;
And if, despite the dusk, thine eyes
Have light enough whereby to read them,—
O pilgrim, ponder them and heed them.'

XIII.

Dim was the legend—time had half effaced it:
But when with patience finally I traced it,

The words were simple—they were these alone:
      'O passer by,
Hope as thou wilt, toil as thou must,
The end of all things is the dust,
      And thou must die.'

XIV.

I answered, 'This I know full well—
      Much to my dole:
What else, ye dead, have ye to tell?
      What of the Soul,   ·
And of its flight to Heaven or Hell?

XV.

'Vain is thy question,' they replied,
'For where those fabled countries be
      We *know* not,
And thither, though our ghosts are free,
      We *go* not:
      We still abide
      Here where we died;
Here is our last long home;
      Our mansions are these mounds;
      Here through the livelong day
      In quietude we stay,
And if at night we venture out,
Impelled by some desire to roam,
      We merely flit about
Through these familiar churchyard-grounds,
      Or softly stray,
      As spirits may,
Each to his own most cherished spot—
Perhaps to the belovèd cot

Where he was born, or where the tear
Fell finally upon his bier—
That farewell tribute which to *us*, the Dead,
    Is ever after dear,—
So dear, that in our grimy bed
We lose remembrance of it not,—
For it reminds us, lying here,
    How they—the tender-hearted—
    Who wept when we departed—
Shall each in turn, as time draws nigh,
Come here to join us By-and-By.'

Stave Twentieth.

I.

'But is there then,' demanded I,
'No Other World for those who die?'

II.

    Quoth they, 'Be not appalled!
Be not oppressed with any dark misgiving!
    The Other World, so-called,
Is just the world wherein you now are living!
It will not be another, but the same—
Not changed a whit from what it was before,
Not even altered in its ancient name:

    For on and on, and evermore—
    Down through the future as of yore—
    It shall be styled the same old Earth:
    Man has no Other World than here:
    This is his first—his final sphere.

The million other orbs that fly
With greater glitter through the sky
Are the illustrious dwelling-places
Of other and less mortal races,
    And not reserved for man,
    Whose modest globe (a star
    Less huge than others are)
Has merely just sufficient room
To be his dwelling and his tomb!

Some call it under curse and ban,
But grievously they misconceive it;
    For truly be it said:
The Earth, by Nature's kindly grace,
Is such a green and pleasant place,
That both the Living and the Dead
Must equally be loth to leave it.'

III.

'To whom then shall we pray,' asked I,
'If we are not to look on high?'

IV.

Said they, 'O mortal, Prayer
    Is but an empty cry,
    An unrewarded sigh,
    An idle breath of air,
    A futile vain device
Which men in misery and despair
    Imagine will suffice
To reach the Gods above the sky,
    Who, listening there,
Will of their pity not deny
But grant the ever-foolish plea

(For foolish it must ever be).
And though thou feel,
Whilst thou art in the act to kneel,
That prayer is something strangely sweet,
Think not, O man, to lure and cheat
The most high Gods by bowing at their feet!'

v.

'They never can be duped and wheedled so!
And though indeed a bended knee
Is what the Gods delight to see,
Betokening reverence to their deity,
Yet well they know
That when the mind of man is overwrought
With too much sorrow, too much care and thought,
The suppliant begs for what he never ought;
And so the Gods must turn away,
And answer Nay:
And every mortal therefore should be taught
That though he kneel and pray
For seven (or seventy) times a day,
Yet vain will be his plea or hope
If it transcend
The limit of the life whose scope
Hath here an end.'

VI.

'Then blessèd be the Earth,' I cried,
'And blessèd, more and more,
Be this best piece of it—my joy—my pride—
My darling native shore!—
Which now is stirred with vague alarms.
—Ye spirits, tell me, Is the hour at hand

When every Norsker must be called to stand
    For Freedom and the Fatherland?
And tell me, Must the peasants quit their farms
    And spring to arms?
And tell me, Shall the Golden Lion win?'

VII.

The dead replied:
    'We who have died
Are keepers of the peace.
    We say to thee, ·
And to thy brethren, Keep it Ye!
    Wake not the trumpet's din!
God has His day for wars to cease—
    Which is, ere they begin!

Your farms are not for battle-fields—
    The land is to be free ·
Without the help of swords and shields;
    Freed by a nobler strife
Than wound for wound, and life for life!
The crime on Earth which Heaven the most abhors
Is blood of brothers, shed in civil feud!
    Let not your fields be thus imbrued!
      Let no such blood be shed!
      Disturb ye not the dead
      By such unholy wars!'

VIII.

The spectres of a sudden hushed their strain,
And seemed to shudder with prophetic pain.
    'Speak on,' I said,
    'And tell me more—

If not of Freedom's rise (or fall),
          Or of the Country's call—
Speak of yourselves, ye hallowed dead!
          Speak, I implore!
I marvel that ye speak at all!
Speak, though ye threaten and appal!
Oh, say, ye in the darkness there,
          Down in the damp and cold,
          Out of the light and air,
          How do ye fare?
Speak! let the truth be told!'

IX.

          Then, to my glad surprise
(For I had now been growing bold,
Or not so paralyzed with fear),
They spake more freely than before,
And said, 'Though shut may seem the door
Of this our habitation here,—
          Though darkness be our home,—
          Though dust be in our eyes,—
          Yet is our sight as clear
As if we gazed from Freyia's dome
          In heavenly Fensalir[1]:
For upward through our graves of green,
          With vision keen
We peer into the throbbing breast
Of every pilgrim who draws near
          Or sits awhile to rest.
          And so, O vagabond, we peep
          With scrutiny so deep

[1] The abode of the goddess Freyia.

Into thine own and inmost heart
That we can see and search its very core;
And often have we seen and searched it heretofore!
 If thou demand a proof—a test—
  Be this the sign:

X.

  'This robe of thine,
 Though of a pattern odd and queer,
  Is far from making thee appear
A stranger in this ancient burial-place;
  Here lie the fathers of thy race;
Here have thy field-mates slept for many a year;
  Thou knowest every stone.
 Think not, because of thy disguise,
 To come and pass not plainly seen,
   Nor truly known;
 For were thy gown the gaberdine
That garmented the Wandering Jew,
It could not cloak thee from our view!
  We know thee well enough,
  And well we love thee, too:

XI.

'Thou art the Bard of Nanna's Heim,
  Whose rhyming wit
  And rosined kit
Full often gave us pleasant sport
Ere yet our frolics were cut short!
  So though thy voice be rough,
  And though thy rhymes be hard,
And though they pass for rustic stuff
Not worthy of the world's regard,

Yet since thou often dost rehearse
Our names and virtues in thy verse;
  And since a minstrel's mind,
However low his lot may be,
Receives the help of Gangléree
And Bragi and the Sisters Three,
And so is rendered quick to learn,—
  We therefore are inclined
To teach thee what thyself in turn
Shalt teach thy fellows; heed us, then.—

XII.·

'Whilst yet we lived with living men
We always had, like thee, a dread
Of being gathered to the dead;
The boldest of us felt a fear
At lying in a lodgement here:

But to our sweet delight and wonder,
Here in the turf that we are under,
Housed close together, yet asunder,
We find, each in his narrow space,
A boon which not in all the round
Of God's wide footstool has a place,
Save only in the grave's own blessed bound.

  For life bestows upon the living
  No gift which they may gauge or measure
    Or hoard or treasure,
So worthy of a human heart's thanksgiving
  As is the final gift instead
  Which Death bestows upon the Dead!

XIII.

'The Earth to mortal man is fourfold blest :
Blest in his birth, though he be born to grief;
Blest in his term of life, for this is brief;
Blest in his death, which is his sweet relief;
And finally, for ever, and in chief,   .
Blest as the place of his Eternal Rest—
And this, of all his blessings, is the best !

XIV.

'It is a boon unknown
Save to the dead alone !
Here, underneath this hallowed sward,
We find our last and chief reward !
No prize for which in life we strove
Equals its *after* treasure-trove :
But what it is that we have found
Cannot be guessed above the ground ;
Nor shall we blab it. So, farewell—
Depart—and tease us not to tell
What never yet the dead have told,
Albeit questioned from of old !

XV.

'Go, mortal, till the happy day
When thou shalt hither come to stay !
—That day, with its immortal cheer,
Will soon be here !

XVI.

'Meanwhile, O humble poet, if it fret thee
To find the Earth not ringing with thy name,
And if the Living slight thee and forget thee,

Yet never mind—keep singing all the same!
There is for thee a laurel not to wither!
For we, the Dead, shall keep alive thy fame;
And when thou finally returnest hither,
We shall salute thee with thy just acclaim!
Now go—this warning is the last—begone!'

XVII.

But willingly would I have stayed till dawn,
To put a hundred questions to the ghosts
As to those dim illimitable coasts,
Those misty Meadow-banks of Asphodel
   Which, be they Heaven or Hell,
   Must still to me remain
   (Until I tread that shore)
The same unsolved enigma as before!

XVIII.

For oh! though golden was the chance I had
To ask the spooks to make the mystery plain,
  Yet I was such a stupid cad
   That my bewildered brain
  Denied me. at the moment what to say;
  And even to this very day
   I still deplore
That with an opportunity so great
My laggard wit should have arrived too late.

XIX.

So, like the sudden snapping of a thread,
My one and only parley with the dead
   Came to a close;
   And I arose,

o

Shook from my gown some glittering drops of dew,
Glanced up at Freyia's yet undarkened dome
(That now began to show a star or two),
Took up my wallet and my staff anew,
And was about to hie me to my home
             (Which now was nigh);
When, with a sudden clash above my head,
      The Bell of Bobo Tower
      Swung out with all its power!

XX.

The bell hangs high,
    Yet it was hit so hard
That all the burial-ground beneath was jarred!

This is the only Curfew Bell
    In all the Ampt of Okakell,
And twenty thorps can hear it well.

And now it rang,
    With bang and clang,
In signal of the Curfew Hour
(A custom which in Nanna's Heim
Was fixed in mediaeval time
    By Eric[1] and his Danes,
    And where it still remains).

XXI.

Right well I knew the iron tongue,
And oft had climbed to where it hung.
It never woke my fear before,
But now I shuddered at its roar;

---

[1] Eric was called the Blood-Axe.

For now I thought how oft the bell had rung
With slower hammer and more solemn chime,
    Whilst all the gathered mourners of the Ampt,
        Each with uncovered head, ·
    Had through the same old churchyard tramped,
        Bearing with measured tread   ·
Some neighbour from his flowery bier
        Down to his grassy bed.

XXII.

I stood and listened in the gloom,
Until the echoes of the boom
All seemed to warn me as they rolled
That *I* should be the next for whom
The knell of requiem would be knolled!
I shivered with an icy cold!
The mortal mist was rising fast!
It froze me stiff—I stood aghast—
My pulses stopped—I held my breath!
'The Crown of Life,' said I, 'is Death!
It may be far—it may be nigh—
But I shall win it By-and-By.'

———◆◆———

PONCE DE LEON'S FOUNT OF YOUTH.

'These are not natural events.'—*Tempest.*

A NEW VERSION.

THIS mad and merry tale, my gentle friends,
　　Is told so often, that you call it trite;
But you shall find, before my ballad ends,
　　That former bards have never told aright
The droll adventures of the hoary-headed Knight.

An ancient city, built of ocean shells[1],
　　Is called his monument, yet lacks his name;
And now he needs a chronicle that tells
　　His queer exploits, and celebrates his fame,
Yet makes him not a butt of ridicule and shame.

So sit ye down, and though the world has laughed,
　　With mirth renewed, for thrice a hundred years,
And called the hero of the story daft,
　　And mocked him as a lout with ass's ears,—
Yet listen to my lay, and spare your jibes and jeers.

---

[1] St. Augustine is the oldest city in the United States, and its
finest edifices are not of stone but of coquina.

II.

You know that in a tiny Floating Isle,
  That once lay anchored off San Salvador[1],
A Magic Fountain bubbled for a while,
  Which, though perhaps it sparkles now no more,
Yet wrought a strange enchantment in the days of yore.

It gave to wrinkled age the bloom of youth,—
  Nor can the miracle be now denied,
For Pope de' Medici[2], who knew its truth,
  Took pains to have the fountain certified,
And would himself have drunk the waters, but he died.

The oldest cripples, half a century lame,
  Who just could hobble to the fountain's brink—
No matter who they were or whence they came—
  Were in a jiffy (or as quick as wink)
Transformed to youth and vigour by a single drink.

III.

This Magic Well, this fountain of delight,
  Was guarded by a witch—a griesly crone
Who in a cave of coral (pink and white,
  And paved with madrepores) had dwelt alone
Till she was now the oldest Sibyl ever known.

---

[1] Up to the present time, five different islands have claimed to be the San Salvador of Columbus : that is to say, Turk's Island, according to Navarette ; Cat Island, according to Irving and Humboldt ; Mayaguana, according to Varnhagen ; Watling, according to Peschel and Major ; and Samana, according to Fox. A re-examination of these various claims was lately made by Lieut. J. B. Murdoch, of the United States Navy, who seems to prove (almost conclusively) that the Landfall of Columbus was at Watling. If this decision stands without reversal, Watling's Island (so-called after the old buccaneer, John Watling) should change its name, and be hereafter charted as the real Guanahani or San Salvador.   [2] Leo X.

But though this ancient warder of the well
   Had never drunk of it, to make her young—
Yet every root around it felt its spell,
   And never-fading blooms above it hung,
Nor could the mosses wither which it flowed among.

IV.

This fairest spot on all the ocean's face
   Was known as Bimini, a Carib word
That signified the most enchanting place
   Whereof the cannibals had ever heard—
An earthly Paradise for man and beast and bird[1].

V.

The isle had once been anchored, I have said;
   But nought could hold it fast against the tide;
It slipped its moorings and away it sped;
   And seldom after was it ever spied,
But wandered undetected in the ocean wide.

---

[1] The first appearance of Bimini, by name, on any map, was on a rough sketch-map made in 1511 by Queen Isabella's secretary, Peter Martyr, who was a personal friend of Columbus, and who chanced to be in Barcelona when the Admiral arrived at that town on returning from his first voyage. Columbus and Ponce de Leon, among the wonders which they told Peter Martyr, spoke of an island which they had not seen but of which they had heard,—containing a fountain which (according to the Caribs) could make old men young. This story so fascinated Peter Martyr that he wrote of it to the Pope, argued its credibility, and afterward drew a map showing where the wonderful fountain might probably be found. This map has recently been reproduced in *facsimile*—in the admirable series of early West Indian documents edited by Justin Winsor of Harvard University.

So though it was the Eden of the Sea,—
  Yet as to where this grove of beauty lay,
The braggart Indian bards of Caribee,
  In boasting of the Fount, could never say;
And strangers, sailing thither, had to guess their way.

VI.

And here begins the tale I wish to tell;
  Not the old empty story told before,
Of how the seeker never found the well,
  But how he found it, and how furthermore . . .
Yet wait and listen . . . there is wonderment in store [1].

VII.

Old Ponce de Leon—with some younger men,
  To whom, at first, his plan was far from plain—
Sailed in his caravel from Boriquenne [2],
  In faith of finding in the Spanish Main
This lost yet loveliest link of the Lucayan Chain [3].

---

[1] During the first half of the nineteenth century, millions of American school-children (the author of this ballad being one of them) were strictly taught that Ponce de Leon discovered Florida on Easter Sunday, March 27, 1512, and that he gave the country its floral name because Easter lilies were then and there in beautiful bloom. But this sacred date, with its sweet and flowery adornment, must in these later and *fin-de-siècle* days be extirpated from our historic annals : for we are now informed by Mr. Fox—with his myth-destroying mathematics !—that Easter Sunday in the year 1512 did not fall on the 27th of March ! Thus it is that history is written—and re-written—and then *un*-written ! This collapse of the old chronology has left the present balladist free to deduce a few new dates from Circumstantial Evidence; to evolve several new incidents from Inner Consciousness ; and to give the tale a new moral for the sake of Poetic Justice.

[2] Now Porto Rico.

[3] The Lucayas are generally styled in English the Bahamas.

The grim old Rover now was very rich,
  And had an Indian province for his own,
But also had a sharp sciatic twitch,
  With a lumbago such as made him groan;
Nor had he any hope of cure, save one alone.

This only hope, though out of Nature's range,
  Was yet within the power of Nature's Lord;
And Ponce had never doubted nor thought strange
  That his evanished youth could be restored
By just a sip of water from the Sibyl's gourd.

VIII.

'Indeed, our Pontiff, ere he passed away'
  (So Ponce reflected with a pious shrug),
'Tried every nostrum which a Christian may,
  Yet found no benefit from any drug,
And begged for water from the Jordan in a jug.

'And therefore Pilgrims from the Holy Land
  Devoutly carried, on their journey home,
Each in a little bottle in his hand
  (To be a present to the Pope of Rome)
That sacred double carbonate of lime and loam.

'But Jordan-water, in a jug or jar,
  When borne a thousand miles by man or horse,
A summer long, or often longer far,
  Must lack' (thought Ponce) 'the freshness and the
      force
Of *my* perennial fountain, tasted at its source.

'So *I*—like Jason of the Golden Fleece,
  Who scoured the Orient till he snatched his prize—

Shall scour the Occident, nor shall I cease
  Till I discover where the Island lies,
And see the Fount of Youth gush up before my eyes.

IX.

'For what to me is all my high degree,
  Or what my buccaneering and its gains,
Or what my lordship of the Carib Sea,
  If I be doomed through all the winter-rains
To twitch and writhe and wriggle with rheumatic pains?

'So, O ye breezes, louder be your blast!
  And, O ye billows, higher be ye rolled!
Till I on that enchanted coast be cast
  Where these, my silver hairs, shall turn to gold,
And this, my rack of bones, shall be no longer old!'

X.

Thus mused this very venerable chief,
  This viceroy over half a zone and clime,
This grim, colossal and illustrious thief,
  This best old bandit of that good old time,
Who never dreamed that buccaneering was a crime.

The Greeks were once highwaymen of the seas;
  The Romans pillaged in the selfsame way;
The great Columbus also, if you please,
  Was first a pirate (so the Sagas say);
And Ponce was of the selfsame honoured guild as they.

XI.

—Now as the Heavens are high above the Earth,
  A gifted soul outranks a common man;

And Ponce de Leon, though of lowly birth,
 Aspired, as only lofty genius can,
To win the foremost name in Glory's very van.

He argued—'I possess unbounded wealth;
 I own an Ocean—or at least the Shore;
I need but Life and Time, but Youth and Health!
 If *these* were mine, I could accomplish more
Than any mortal ever dared attempt before.'

As thus he reasoned with his agèd brain,
 That teemed with memories of his youthful years
(Those gallant years which he had spent in Spain,
 And which were full of glorious souvenirs [1])—
'Thank God, I shall be young agen!' said he, with
  tears.

XII.

—Now you may say that Ponce was self-deceived—
 That crazy hopes like his were doomed to fail—
That Youth, if lost, can never be retrieved;
 Yet these are cavils that will not avail
When once you know the sequel of this truthful tale.

Meanwhile—oh pooh not at my lengthening lay,
 Nor call it fashioned on a tedious plan;
For as to Ponce, I undertake to say,
 That never since the race of men began
Was any other mortal half so strange a man!

---

[1] As a young soldier, Ponce de Leon had served against the Moors,
and had witnessed their final overthrow at Granada.

Strange was the blazing twinkle of his eye!
Strange was his skin of freckled ormolu!
Strange was his torrid temper, hot and high!
And strangest was his project to renew
His long-lost Youth, when now his years were Eighty-
Two!

XIII.

Behold my Hero, with his scarlet plume,
His grim moustachios—which he fiercely twirled,
And his tobago-reed [1], whose novel fume
In ever-widening circles since has curled
In one festoon of fragrance round the rolling world!

And though his limbs were now no longer spry,
And though he had upon his scrawny neck
A wen that made him hang his head awry,
Yet never captain paced a quarter-deck
Who carried greater terror in his nod and beck.

---

[1] Though this was the Carib original of the now universal tobacco-pipe, yet strictly speaking Ponce's tobago-reed was not a pipe at all. It had no bowl. It was a long and tapering stalk, hollowed out by expelling the pith; and it terminated at the smaller end in twin off-shoots, or forks, both of which were cut off short, within an inch of their junction, forming by their bifurcation the two prongs of the letter Y. The main stalk—that is to say, the stem of the Y—was half a man's length, or more. A handful of the dried weed was put into a dish or shell, or into a small heap on the ground, and set on fire; emitting a heavy smoke. Into this smoke the single end of the stalk was thrust by the expectant smoker; who, sitting to windward of the fume, carefully inserted the two prongs—not into his mouth—but into his nose—a prong in each nostril. If his inhalation was vigorous, he soon had his brain full of fumes—pungent and seductive. In fact the Spaniards found them intoxicating.

He wore between his pistol and his dirk
　A carven crucifix (of cunning art),
Which oft he kissed—and, pensive as a Turk,
　He oft within his wooden tower apart
Sat with a gold Saint Mary held against his heart.

XIV.

Of all the sailors who have ever sailed,
　Since first the Earth had vessels or a sea,
Old Ponce, so old that now he ached and ailed
　With metatarsal gout from toe to knee,
Is the immortal Ancient Mariner for me!

And this is why I bravely volunteer
　(With proud ambition in this breast of mine)
To vindicate his seeming mad career,
　In happy hope to make his wisdom shine
(And mine with his) from Line to Pole, and Pole to Line.

XV.

His caravel was called 'The Flying Horse'
　(Or Hippogriff), and dragon's wings she had,
And sharp she was of beak, and cleft her course
　As keenly as a herring or a shad,
And foamed about the mouth—like Ponce when he
　　was mad.

This little ship of nine-and-ninety tons,
　Though now she seems perhaps a trifle small,
Yet carried culverins and other guns,
　With kegs of powder and relays of ball,
Together also with a coracle or yawl;

Or I should rather say a birch canoe,
  Or wicker wherry of the Carib sort—
A tiny boat, not big enough for two,
  Which Ponce could paddle, seated on a thwart,
And go alone in, when he wished to make a port.

XVI.

For with his mighty secret on his mind,
  Which his companions were forbid to share,
His quest was of a sly and stealthy kind,
  Requiring him to go a solitaire,
And much as if he sought the nest-egg of a mare.

XVII.

Up from the ocean many a sunken hill
  Arose to greet him with a sunny smile,
And many a coast more flowery than Seville
  Perfumed the air at sea for many a mile,
As on, from day to day, he cruised from isle to isle.

At every isle he landed all alone,
  And dragged his wherry up the grinding shore,
And hunted for the Cavern of the Crone,
  In hope to bribe or bully or implore
The wrinkled-visaged Witch to let him drink galore.

XVIII.

Those islands then were like those islands now—
  The most sequestered on this earthly ball;
And as for multitude, I dare avow
  They were a thousand[1] (counting great and small);
And Ponce was bent on touching at them all;—

---

[1] They outnumber a thousand; and except the few of habitable
size, they are mostly wild and virgin to this day; nor are springs of
fresh-water, even in the greenest of them, easy for ships' crews to find.

Or bent at least on taking each in turn,
  Till he should find the guerdon of his quest—
Despite his daily fresh chagrin to learn
  (If learn he did, although he mostly guessed)
That the Enchanted Isle lay further to the West.

XIX.

It was before the time of telescopes,
  And Ponce de Leon had no optic glass,
But trusted to his eyes—and to his hopes,
  And not a spot of greenness did he pass
Without a scrutiny of every tuft of grass.

And since such Yuccas he had never seen—
  No, not in any verdant vale in Spain—
He asked himself, 'What gives them such a green?
  It cannot certainly be common rain—
It is immortal water trickling through the plain!'

XX.

So, though the sunshine smote him nearly blind,
  He wrapped his head with leaves to shade the gleam,
And followed every brook that he could find,
  And dipped his calabash in every stream—
In hope of chancing on the fountain of his dream.

XXI.

A calabash, as you perhaps remember,
  Will hold a gallon measure, called a Kong;
And day by day, from April to September,
  The venerable hero of my song
Was kept at water-bibbing as he went along.

It was a novel drink to him at first
  (Not swallowed since his green and salad days),
Yet now he swigged it till he feared to burst, ·
  Or else to boil—for in the torrid rays
He felt himself a skillet in a kitchen-blaze.

XXII.

But though his face was burnt to triple bronze,
  And though his lips were blistered by the heat,
Yet this indomitable don of dons
  Went boldly forward on his scabby feet,
In spite of savages whom he might chance to meet.

But luckily, in those Lucayan glades,
  The human creatures whom he met were few—
And mostly naked—being Carib maids,
  Who modestly, when Ponce appeared in view,
Ran off and hid themselves—as frightened children do.

Meanwhile, no man of all the caravel,
  Save only Ponce himself (whose head was hoar),
Had leave to land; and this was wise and well:
  Great are the perils of the sea!—but more,
A thousandfold, are the temptations of the shore[1]!

XXIII.

The Captain's lonely landings grew mysterious,
  And daily puzzled his bewildered crew,

---

[1] The gentle character of the natives whom Columbus found in these islands was set forth by him in quaint words in a letter to Ferdinand and Isabella, saying, 'Their conversation is the sweetest imaginable; they are always smiling; and so gentle and affectionate are they that I swear to your Highnesses there is not a better people in the world.'

Who dared not ask a leader so imperious
  What secret enterprise he had in view;
Nor could their wit discover, for they lacked a clue.

They argued noisily, with shallow minds,
  That he was baffled in a quest of gold,—
For every day, with oaths of forty kinds,
  He cursed the weather, were it hot or cold,
And cursed his gout, and cursed himself for growing old!

XXIV.

In growing old, De Leon feared a foe
  More grim and ancient than himself by far—
A mystic enemy, whose subtle blow
  Was not from tomahawk or flint or spar,
But from the Unseen Scythe that leaves a sadder scar.

Yet the scarred Captain to himself would say,
  'Not long the Swinger of the Scythe shall wreak
His vengeance on me in this slashing way,—
  For not a seam shall scarify my cheek
When once I find the healing fountain that I seek.

'And find it, by Saint Tibb! I must and will!
  How can a fountain keep from being found?
Its living springs must have a running rill
  That soon or late shall burst above the ground,
And spill the sparkling waters everywhere around.

'Or if the runnel never breaks the sod,
  But hides and burrows where no eye can see,
Can I not cut me a divining-rod?
  Will not a twig from a Witch-hazel tree
Suffice to lead me where the lurking waters be?

'And I will gulp them till my wrinkled skin,
   That now is rougher than a hedgehog's hide,
Shall be as smooth upon my brow and chin
   As when I started in my youth and pride
With old Columbus for the planet's hither side!

XXV.

'And *my* discovery shall by far outshine
   The else unequalled glory of his own;
For such a wonder-working well as mine—
   Creating man anew in flesh and bone—
Shall be a shrine of pilgrimage from every zone.

XXVI.

'The Floating Isle shall then no more go free,
   For I will hitch it with a copper chain,
And moor it so securely in the sea,
   That while the Heavens shall last it shall remain,
To be an Earthly Harbour free from death and pain!

'And I will prick it on an ocean-chart,—
   That to the Fount of Youth all agèd men
May steer their course, and may with hope and heart
   Bear thither—each his threescore years and ten—
There to throw off his burden and be young agen.

XXVII.

'And, oh! heigho! when all the old are young—
   When not a head in all the world is grey—
The Scythe which Father Time so long hath swung
   He then shall whet no more, but fling away,
And be himself a Child, for ever and a day!

P

'Then Love and Age (now Ghibelline and Guelph)
   No longer shall be constantly at feud,
For Love shall keep as young as Cupid's self,
   And frosty Dons shall have their May renewed,
And old Duennas shall re-bloom and be re-wooed!

'Meanwhile, though good Queen Isabel is dead,
   And though King Ferdinand is sick to die [1]
Yet *I* shall never make the grave my bed,
   Nor ever bid the merry world good-bye;
For Death shall never hit me, though his arrows fly.'

XXVIII.

Thus spake De Leon, gabbling to the sea;
   And though no boisterous wave could be so rude,
And no complaining wind so gruff as he,
   Yet now his mind was in a halcyon mood,
And hopefully he ploughed the salty solitude.

XXIX.

It was the season of those steady gales
   That never change their course the summer through
But hum their music to the swelling sails
   And rush the vessel through the briny blue,
And challenge the delighted Dolphins to pursue.

And Ponce, who knew that where the Dolphins dive
   The ship is near a hospitable shore,
Wished that old Christopher were still alive
   To hail those happy harbingers once more
That welcomed the World-Finder to San Salvador.

---

[1] The queen died in 1504; the king, twelve years later.

XXX.

'Alas for Christopher! But by the Rood!
  I swear,' cried Ponce, 'I will not die as he—
The victim of a King's ingratitude—
  .Old and in chains! I will be young and free!,
And as for Kings, let all such vermin cease to be!

XXXI.

And Ponce, in raving thus, was not a fool,
  But proved himself prophetically wise;
For Kings have had their day; and kingly rule
  (A curse to nations) hides its head and dies ˙
Heaven-blasted in a Western World of freer skies.

And I, as Ponce's bard, predict a time
  When not in any hemisphere or zone,
Or coast or isle, or habitable clime,
  Will there be any King on any Throne;
For all the spacious planet shall be Freedom's own!

XXXII.

But to my tale!—which seems to lag and loiter,
  And limp as languidly as Ponce indeed;
Yet as my Hero had both gout and goitre,
  I beg that his adventures may proceed
Without the hurry of uncomfortable speed.

XXXIII.

Ponce was himself impatient—heroes *are*;
  And so, one evening, while his crew encored,
He thrummed like mad upon his old guitar
  In honour of a maid whom he adored,—·
Till as he thrummed, he cracked and crashed the
    finger-board.

His savage breast was by the music tamed :
  And at the breakage, with a rueful ken,
He gazed till he grew sheepish and ashamed,
  And swore to touch no mandolin agen
Till he could twang it as the youngest man of men.

XXXIV.

The maid whom Ponce adored was in her teens,
  And Ponce desired to be as young as she
(Or but a trifle older), as the means
  Of winning her reluctant hand : so he—
From Eighty-Two—resolved to change to Twenty-
    Three !

And I commend him for his keen discretion :
  He chose an age for which—I frankly say—
I entertain so fond a prepossession,
  That three-and-twenty—could I have my way—
Is just where I would like to stop and always stay.

It is the age when man is at his best,—
  When fancy still is young and wit is bright,
When there are fewest sorrows in the breast,
  When life is easy, and its burden light,
And when it is a pleasure still to love and fight.

XXXV.

But this is empty talk—mere idle chatter !
  And much I marvel why a bard is prone,
In treating of a high historic matter,
  To introduce digressions of his own
Where Truth would much more beautifully stand alone.

XXXVI.

Now when you read of mediaeval travel
  That tells of monsters wonderful to see,
You shrug your shoulders and you doubt and cavil,
  And for an explanation or a key
You hint that in the author's bonnet is a bee.

And so I dare not undertake to tell
  What living marvels old De Leon saw,—
Creatures of curious wing or fin or shell,—
  Or with what goose-flesh and hair-raising awe
He heard the horrid screeching of the big macaw;

Or how he shied at meeting the opossum,
  Or marvelled at the spider caught by flies,
Or fled the snake whose crest is like a blossom,
  Or trembled at mosquitoes of a size
That made him doubt the evidence of both his eyes.

XXXVII.

All this was chronicled by Peter Martyr,
  And all confirmed (as probably you know)
By Kubla Khan, the celebrated Tartar[1];
  But I omit it as too dull and slow,
For I must follow Ponce as fast as I can go.

XXXVIII.

More wary than the Vikings of the North
  (For he was tempting a more treacherous sea)
Old Ponce, the Sea-Wolf, watchfully went forth,
  And rolled his eyes to windward and to lee,
And sighted each new island with a gloating glee.

---

[1] Of Xanadu, according to Coleridge.

XXXIX.

Ahd not by day alone his sails were set,
    For then the Ocean's lofty roof at night
Was hung with all the lamps that stud it yet,
    And also with those Pleiads once so bright,
That twinkled long ago, but now are lost to sight.

Indeed the Firmament, though lovely still,
    Was fairer at the first (the Fathers say);
For sin has reached so far and wrought such ill,
    That now the stars burn with a lessening ray,
And Nature everywhere is in a slow decay.

XL.

My Rover roved through weeks of sun and rain,
    Of fog and mist, of hope and hope deferred,
Till he began to think his quest in vain—
    When suddenly the old Hidalgo heard
(One eve at dusk) the chirp of a celestial bird.

For unto troubled men, in times remote,
    When faith was simple and when doubt was rare,
There sang a Bird Unseen—whose heavenly note
    (Heard in the heart, inaudible elsewhere)
Gave to the startled listener hope amid despair.

Clear as the carol of a piping thrush,
    Loud as the lark's alarum at the morn,
Sweet as the trill that in the midnight's hush
    Is warbled from the breast against the thorn,—
So came the note to Ponce, to comfort and to warn.

XLI.

He listened till he wept.   His heart, though hard,
  Had at its core a soft and tender spot;
And heavenly things he held in high regard:
  For Ponce was what a pirate oft is not—
The Holy Mother Church's faithful son, God wot!

He now betook him to his castled poop,
  And knelt and told his beads till he was tired,
And till his back was bent with such a stoop
  That when he straightened up his face perspired,
And youth appeared the blessing most to be desired.

XLII.

Trusting the viewless bird as if in sight,
  He steered his vessel by the flying sound,—
Not veering to the left nor to the right;
  And though a hundred rocks shot up around,
Yet safer pilotage no vessel ever found.

XLIII.

The moon was gibbous, yellowing half the sea;
  And Ponce, in peering for a place to land,
Espied a solitary coco-tree
  Which, with a nodding tuft, appeared to stand
To bid him welcome to that weird and lonely strand.

In confidence that now his goal was near,
  He furled his fluttering canvas in its brails,
And clutched, with both his hands, from ear to ear,
  His frosty beard—which glistered like his sails,
And sparkled whilst he combed it with his finger-nails.

XLIV.

Casting his anchor by a beetling cliff
　That glassed its double in a clear lagoon,
He saw, on gliding shoreward in his skiff,
　The solemn Sibyl gazing at the moon ;
And piteously he begged of her the precious boon.

She listened patiently, yet with a frown,
　And sat and clasped her hands and bowed her head,
And bent her eyelids sorrowfully down,
　And sighed like one whose tears had all been shed
And who could weep no longer, but who moaned instead.

XLV.

'O fool!' quoth she, 'this youth-renewing draught
　Is one that *I*, though I am old like thee,
And though I keep the Fount, have never quaffed :
　And *thou*—ere quaffing it—be warned by me,
That to be old—then young—defieth God's decree !

'For hath not Heaven appointed unto man
　That though his days be evil, they be few?
Is life not wisely bounded by a span ?
　O thou who rashly wouldst thy youth renew,
Drink not the dangerous cup, lest it should work thy
　　rue !'

XLVI.

'Thou hag!' De Leon thundered in a rage,
　'Unseal the fount, nor thwart me in my will!
Give me the draught that rids the old of age!
　Dip me the cup so full that it shall spill!
And let me drink and drink till .I have drunk my fill.'

XLVII.

The crone replied with an uncanny voice,
  'I grudge thee not a draught—the fount is free;
The springs are triple—thou shalt have thy choice;
  Taste one or all, but pay me first my fee
For pointing out the different uses of the three.'

XLVIII.

He chinked his purse and answered, 'Be it thine—
  And thine be half of all that I possess—
Pearls from the river, rubies from the mine,
  And feathers of the Trogon[1] for thy dress;
For I am rich—a buccaneer, as I confess;

'Indeed I am a pirate of renown;
  But, by the Pyx! and as a man of truth,
I nevermore will plunder ship or town
  Except to share the swag with *thee*, forsooth,
If thou wilt give me in exchange the gift of youth!'

XLIX.

At first the Sibyl deigned him no reply,
  But pointed at him with her flaky hand,
And rattled from her throat so hoarse a cry,
  That Ponce imagined he was cursed and banned
For all his dreadful wickedness by sea and land.

But soon the Witch showed pity in her eyes;
  As if, in looking at the world so long,

---

[1] These brilliant feathers—carmine, green and gold—all lavishly intermixed—were used by the Montezumas in their royal head-gear.

She had observed how seldom men are wise,
  And how the wisest oft are in the wrong,
And how the weak are ever victims of the strong.

L.

Quoth she, 'I value not, O Privateer,
  Thy vaunted wealth, whatever its amount:
I ask thee only for thy listening ear
  Whilst I—without a largesse—shall recount
The separate magic virtues of the triple fount.

'The fount is triple: God Himself is so—
  For ever triune ; and by land and sea,
Alike in large and little, high and low,
  His works—of every order and degree—
Are founded on a mystic principle of three.

'This subtile trinity eludes the ken
  Of mortals of a carnal turn of mind,
And not the King of Spain, and all his men,
  If *they* (like thee) had landed here, could find
These waters, three in one, yet each of different kind.

LI.

'The first is sweet. And by an instant charm
  It gives thee back thy youthful form and face,
And puts the pith of youth into thine arm,
  While in thy heart, despite thy youthful grace,
Thy green old age must still retain its wonted place.

'The next is bitter. Virtue in it lies
  To make thee young agen in heart alone,
While still the feet of crows shall tread thine eyes ;
  Nor shalt thou be exempt in flesh or bone
From any of the twinges to which age is prone.

'The third, more wholesome than the other two,
    Is tasteless.   Most benignly hath it sprung
To antidote what both the others do :—
    For this is able, if it touch the tongue,
To cure the old of vainly wishing to be young.'

LII.

'Give me the first !' cried Ponce, with mad delight,
    'Let me be young in body, old in mind !
For Strength and Wisdom, if the twain unite,
    Must make the man in whom they are combined
The one most lucky mortal among all mankind.'

LIII.

He drank the first,—and never thrill so sweet
    Went palpitating through his veins before !
It tingled to his fingers and his feet !
    And all at once his hair—from being hoar—
Was turned to golden red, and he was young once more

And with his youth came all his prowess back,
    With more than common stalwartness of limb,
And fists already doubled—as to whack
    Imaginary knaves assaulting him !—
And soldier-like he stood, erect and tall and slim !

And neither when he fought his youthful fight
    That freed Granáda from the Moors at last [1],

---

[1] The fall of Granáda was on January 2, 1492 ; and on August 3
of the same year, Christopher Columbus set sail with his fleet from
Palos in search of the new continent—having on board his own ship
(according to tradition) the youthful Ponce de Leon as a ' cabin-boy.'

Nor when the New World hove upon his sight
  Whilst he was watching from the Admiral's mast,
Had Ponce de Leon's pulses jumped and thumped so
    fast!

LIV.

But though he now was young in flesh and frame,
  He felt no youthful passion or desire—
No tender wish for love—no thirst for fame—
  No glowing fancy—no poetic fire—
No lofty hope that lured his spirit to aspire.

The new-made giant felt within himself
  A young man's blood, heating an old man's brain,
Kindling the greeds of Age (its love of Pelf,
  Its lust of Power)—those itching fevers twain
That drove the doughty captain all at once insane.

And like a bull when first the Picador[1]
  Has of a sudden jabbed him with a prick,
The old Freebooter bellowed with a roar,
  And pawed the ground and gave a lively kick,
And grew infuriate with the spirit of Old Nick!

LV.

What would he do with his athletic rage,
  Too fierce to guide, too fiery to repress?
The old in their behaviour should be sage:
  But Ponce, whose brain was under burning stress,
Now planned a daring scheme of loot and lawlessness.

---

[1] At a bull-fight, the function of the Picador is this: Bounding into the ring on horseback, holding a lance under his right arm, he receives the bull's charge by thrusting the lance to the right and at the same moment turning the horse to the left.

He paddled to his ship with foaming speed,
  And sprang upon his deck, and called his men,
And thundered to them, 'Follow where I lead!'
  And drew his sword and slashed the air, as when,
In bygone years, he hewed his way to Boriquenne.

LVI.

The crew sat huddled round a cask of sherry,
  Which in his absence they had gimlet-holed,
And now, with skulls for drinking-cups, were merry,
  And did not recognize their Leader old,
But took him for an Urchin who had thither strolled.

LVII.

'Up with the anchor! Up with every sail!'
  Cried the mad Captain to the marvelling crew;
'Up and away, and whistle for a gale!
  And scuttle every ship that heaves in view!
For we are gallant pirates, honest men and true!'

LVIII.

'Pretentious Boy!' quoth they, 'Durst thou comman
  That we shall weigh our anchor, set our sail,
And leave our agèd Leader on the land?
  Beware, young rogue, lest over yonder rail
We fling thee to a shark, like Jonah to the whale.'

LIX.

'*I* am your Leader!' cried their ancient lord
  (Who felt his dignity of age the same,
Or even greater, with his strength restored,
  Than when of late his gout had made him lame)
'I am a Lion now, in nerve as well as name!

'And, by my beard!—this lion's mane of mine—
   I swear, ye rebels—for my wrath is hot—
That I will cut and cleave, from crown to chine,
   Each calf among ye—now and on the spot—
If when I give an order ye obey it not!'

LX.

'Thy beard, O Boy?' cried they. 'Now, by the Mass,
   What sign of beard is on thy peach-bloom face?
O beardless Youth, thy empty head is crass!
   Paddle thyself ashore—paddle apace—
Paddle De Leon's skiff back to its landing-place!

'For by thy false pretences we perceive
   That thou hast borrowed with a cunning guile
De Leon's skiff without De Leon's leave;
   And he may miss it in a little while!—
Now old De Leon is a dangerous man to rile!'

LXI.

'*I* am De Leon, changed from age to youth!'
   He vainly cried. Whereat they mocked the more,
And bade him 'Go and cut his wisdom tooth!'—
   And as he hurried off with boat and oar,
They pelted him with missiles half-way to the shore.

LXII.

Sticks, bolts, and bottles hit his head and back!
   His metamorphosed body was so bruised,
And his re-marrowed bones so full of wrack,
   And both his bran-new shoulders so contused,
That never had a Christian been so badly used!

LXIII.

Piqued that his leadership was thrust aside,
　Miffed that his dignity was set at nought,
Stung in his person, smarting in his pride,
　He hurried to the Crone, and said, distraught, ·
'The cup thou gavest me hath my confusion wrought:

'My crew, who see no more my wrinkled brow,
　Mistake me for a young and smooth-checked lad!
O Beldame, dip thy second bowl!—for now,
　Though Youth is what I wish for—yet, egad!
I want it with the same old shaggy face I had!'

LXIV.

The Sibyl dipped her shell a second time,
　And gave him from an effervescing spring
A draught that pricked him in his chyle and chyme
　As if a hundred hornets on the wing
Had each flown down his gullet with a separate sting.

LXV.

His chin at once grew winter-clad with beard:
　But now so young a heart bethumped his breast,
That when among his crew he reappeared,
　He styled their recent prank a youthful jest,
And ordered them to dance—*he* dancing with the rest.

'Dance one and all!' he cried—'Dance for your lives!
　Dance till the moon goes down! Then swim ashore
And coax the Carib maids to be your wives,
　And back to Boriquenne return no more!'
Whereat the tipsy tars set up a jovial roar.

The moon sank smiling at a sight so queer,
  And merrily the stars winked at the view;
While Ponce, who had not danced for many a year,
  Now boasted of a leg as good as new,
And undertook to foot a whole fandango through.

LXVI.

You know that such a wild and whirling dance
  Stirs up the liver in a lively style:
And Ponce—too elderly to skip and prance—
  Had pirouetted but a little while
Before he felt a queasy qualminess of bile.

The fierce fandango overtaxed his age:
  So on the slippery deck he tumbled down,
And rolled in helplessness and howled with rage,
  And winced with cramps and cricks from sole to crown,
And muttered, 'Heave me overboard, and let me
    drown!'

LXVII.

'Old Man,' they cried, 'thy wits are wild as *his*—
  That beardless Boy's—who claimed this beard of thine,
And made his cutlass dangerously whizz,
  And spake of cleaving us from crown to chine—
Till we had half a mind to souse him in the brine.'

LXVIII.

Quoth he, 'The mighty lad of bone and brawn
  Who paddled hither and cried "Ship ahoy!"
And leapt on deck, and with his cutlass drawn
  Gave word to kill, to burn, and to destroy,
Was certainly a Devil's Imp, and not a boy.

'So I command ye—*I*, your Captain Ponce—
  Haul up the Imp and swing him at the fore,
Or fetch a marlinspike and crack his sconce,
  For *I* am *he*—and lest I suffer more,
O comrades, hang me, brain me, drown me—I implore!'

LXIX.

'Old Ponce is in the doldrums!' cried the crew,
  'Give him his customary glass of grog—
Which never yet has failed to bring him to':
  But Ponce declined it! and they stood agog!—
And back he paddled shoreward through a friendly fog.

LXX.

Reeking with sweat from toiling with his oar,
  Gasping for breath, and groaning with a wheeze,
He dragged his wherry up the gritty shore
  And sought the bower of ever-blooming trees,
And dropped before the Sibyl on his bended knees.

LXXI.

'O fill for me,' he cried, 'thy final bowl,
  And let it countercharm, if so it can,
These cruel changes in my flesh and soul—
  For Youth and Age are not, by Nature's plan,
Put both at once together in the selfsame man.'

LXXII.

Cold was the draft, as if from Lethé's river,
  And his teeth chattered at the goblet's brim,
And through his body shiver after shiver
  Crept like a palsy, and his face grew grim,
And all his gout came twitching back through every limb.

Q

LXXIII.

'Yes, I am now myself agen,' thought he,
 * And for assurance, slapped his shaky thighs,
And felt like one who, from a heavy spree,
   Recovers with a mortified surprise,
Resolving to be henceforth virtuous and wise.

LXXIV.

Then the old Lion, in the misty night,
   Just as the fire-flies fled before the morn,
Took leave for ever of the haggard Sprite,
   Who slyly laughed, and said with kindly scorn,
'Another fool like thee shall nevermore be born.'

LXXV.

He found his crew asleep—whom he awoke
   By touching off a loaded culverin :
And some believed the noise a thunderstroke,
   While others fancied, from the deafening din,
That Gabriel's Trump had blown for Judgement to
      begin.

LXXVI.

The bluff old Captain, setting sail agen,
   Proved his identity beyond a doubt ;
For in his homeward run to Boriquenne
   He daily took his grog, and cursed his gout,
And let his pent-up hurricanes of temper out.

LXXVII.

Landing in Boriquenne, with head as hoary
   As when he started on his crazy quest,
Old Ponce at first resolved to keep his story
   A secret in his solitary breast—
But age is garrulous, and he at last confessed.

And having told his tale, he burnt his Chart [1]
So that the Fount could nevermore be found:
Lest other hoary-headed fools should start—
  (For there be many such, the world around!)—
Who might upon the coral-reefs be dashed and drowned.

LXXVIII.

Meanwhile in Boriquenne there had occurred
  A gay event that gladdened all the isle—
A joy whereat De Leon so demurred,
  That when he heard of it he wept awhile,
Nor was he ever afterward beheld to smile.

The darling Damozel whom Ponce adored—
  And whom he hoped, on his return, to wed—
Had in his absence married a young Lord:
  But Ponce forgave them both, and nobly said,
'Be ye my children now—my heirs when I am dead.'

LXXIX.

The rainy season came and drenched the town,
  And brought a mildew, followed by the Grip;
And Ponce, who mortally was stricken down,
  Called for his grog, and took a final nip,
And thus addressed his comrades with a quivering lip:

'This Life of ours on Earth is long enough,
  And Death is welcome—thanks to Him by whom
Our mortal frame is formed of fragile stuff,

---

[1] But though he burnt his chart, he did not destroy his diary. This diary was for a time in the possession of the celebrated Spanish historian Herrera. We have Herrera's own word for it. Some searcher of archives will probably bring the lost document to light. The luck of finding it ought to fall to Mr. Henry Harrisse, as a reward for his diligence in searching through half the archives of Europe for Columbian Antiquities.

Here to decay, and by a happy doom
To rise to Immortality beyond the Tomb.'

So spake De Leon on his dying bed,
  And raised his hand, and pointed to the sky,
And smiling on the bride and bridegroom, said,
  'When you are old, come join me by and by
Around the Fountain of Eternal Youth on High!'

LXXX.

His face was beautiful in death (they say);
  And now his statue should in gold be cast
To teach a world of Living Fools to-day
  How he, the Greatest Fool of ages past,
Could yet outlive his folly and be wise at last.

LXXXI.

Meanwhile, although this Lay of mine of course
  May leave a doubt not easy to dispel,
Yet if you ask from what authentic source
  I take the tale which I have tried to tell—
Dear friends, the Truth is from the Bottom of the Well [1].

---

[1] Dismissing this extravaganza, and reverting to sober history, the balladist begs to add that the Bibliothèque National of Paris (the largest Library in the world) contains no book or manuscript that confers an indisputable date of birth on Ponce de Leon. Nor is the tradition tenable that Ponce was the 'cabin-boy' of the *Santa Maria* in 1492. But the modern authorities all concur in saying that De Leon sailed with Columbus on the Admiral's second voyage, which was in 1493; that twenty years later, Ponce (having meanwhile grown old) undertook his expedition to the Fountain of Youth, but discovered Florida instead, on Easter Sunday, 1513; and that the venerable buccaneer died, in green old age, in 1521. His last illness was painfully aggravated by 'blood-poisoning,' occasioned by the prick of an envenomed arrow that hit him during one of his skirmishes with the hostile Caribs.

THE FOOLISH PRAYER.

..

A DACIAN shepherd—humblest of his race—
Espoused the lowliest of the maids of Thrace.

The pair were poorer than their barren wild,
Till Hope enriched them with a promised child.

At last, between a midnight and a morn,
Beneath their roof of straw, their son was born.

Ecstatic slumber followed childbirth pain,
And heavenly phantoms filled the mother's brain.

II.

'Ye are the Gods!' the happy sleeper cried—
'What errand brings ye to the cradle-side?'

III.

The bright Olympians said, 'We come to Earth
With bounties for thy babe, to bless his birth:

'His birth is humble—what shall we bestow?
What boon, as modest as his lot is low?—

'Thyself, O Mother, for thy child shalt choose:
Ask what thou wilt, and we will not refuse.'

IV.

Quoth she, 'What though he be of humble birth,
He is the fairest babe on all the Earth!

'So grant him Wisdom, Virtue, and Renown!
Make him a Prince, and let him wear a crown!

'Make him a Hero—bravest of the brave—
Loved by a people whom his sword shall save!

'Make him a Bard—whose spirit-stirring strain
Shall charm the weary to forget their pain!

'Make him the noblest man of all who live,
Endowed with all the gifts the Gods can give!'

V.

Thus prayed the Mother—to whose simple mind
Her son appeared the chief of mortal kind.

VI.

The Gods, who love to hear a mother's prayer,
Begrudged no bounty to a babe so fair.

Said Jove, 'I give my sceptre to his hand,
And he shall be a Prince to rule the land.'

Said fiery Mars, 'I give my sword and shield,
And he shall conquer on the battle-field.'

Said bright Apollo, 'He shall have my lyre,
And move the souls of men at his desire.'

VII.

The other Gods each gave the sleeping child
So bright a boon, that in his sleep he smiled.

Around him lay his treasures—sceptre, sword,
Lyre—every gift the mother had implored;

Never to any of the sons of men
Had the Gods given such bounties until then!

Lest in the dowry there should be a lack,
They gave their All, and went impoverished back!

VIII.

But ere the Gods had reached their heavenly gates,
Down to the hovel flew the Triple Fates.

Around the Babe they crouched—uncanny, old,
Wan-visaged, wrinkled, direful to behold!

The slumbering mother, with a cringe of fear,
Divined what awful presences were near!

And in her sleep she wildly flung her arm
Across her child, to shelter him from harm.

The weak white barrier little could avail
Against the Powers whereat the Heavens turn pale.

The Fates—more sovereign than the Gods in sway—
Snatched from the Babe each precious gift away.

IX.

'The lavish Gods,' cried they, 'are rash to trust
Such treasures to a creature of the dust!

'What need hath *he* of Sceptre, Sword, or Lyre?
The son shall be a Shepherd—like his sire!

'We give him what is best—a Shepherd's Crook,
To lead his flock beside the meadow-brook.

'We give him toil and hardship—pang and throe,
Hunger and heart-break—poverty and woe!

'These are our gifts, O Mother, for thy son—
And for thyself, we cut the thread we spun.'

X.

•Then on the barley-straw that was her bed,
The mother's dream was ended. She was dead!

XI.

Her hopes died with her, and her fears came true:
Her son to manhood, and to sorrow, grew:

No Prince was he, no Hero, and no Bard;
No proud possessor of the World's regard:

He lived a Shepherd three-score years and ten,
And was the humblest of the sons of men.

At last, between a midnight and a morn,
He died beneath the roof where he was born.

XII.

The Gods—and at their heels the Fates—once more
Came down and entered at the hovel door.

'Ye Fates,' inquired the Gods, 'repent ye not
That ye condemned him to so poor a lot?

'Must *we*, the Gods of Heaven, henceforth forbear
To answer bounteously a Mother's Prayer?'

XIII.

The Fates replied, 'Chide not what we have done:
No mother prayeth wisely for her son.

'Her heart, through over-fondness, is beguiled
To beg all gifts and graces for her child.

'So *we*, the Fates, have in our wisdom willed
That prayers, when foolish, shall go unfulfilled.'

MOTHER CYDIPPÉ AND HER TWINS.

B.C. 400.

THERE had been newly wrought in Argos[1] old
    The Goddess Hera's image[2], armed and mailed—
A triple work of ivory, bronze and gold,
    And ere it yet was finished and unveiled
The statue thundered!—while the workmen quaked
      and quailed.

The sun was shining; not a single cloud
    Lay round the mountain-top nor on the sea;
And yet the thunder-peal was long and loud,
    And hushed the singing-birds on every tree,
And terrified the timid lambs on every lea.

II.

Though Hera's shrine was new, yet Hera's fane
    Had stood in Argos for a thousand years:
And always when the priests had prayed for rain,
    The answering showers that swelled the barley-ears
Were named by grateful peasants, Hera's pitying tears.

For Hera, by her right as Queen of Heaven,
    Could borrow Zeus's thunder when she would,
And strip it of its forked and fiery levin,
    And use it gently for the people's good,
Although her mighty voice was oft misunderstood.

---

[1] Argos was the most ancient city of Greece.
[2] Hera was the Greek name for Juno.

There was at times such terror in its tones,
 . That men who never feared a battle's shock
Would feel the marrow freezing in their bones,
　And stand and shiver till their knees would knock—
For Hera's thunderbolt could rive the hardest rock.

Her least displeasure made a world afraid;
　And yet she had a tender heart forsooth,
And was the Goddess to whom mothers prayed
　Who needed guidance for their sons in youth
To keep them in the ways of innocence and truth.

III.

Now when the rumour ran the region round
　That Hera's image had a living voice,
The vineyard-pruners, with a faith profound,
　Said, as they pruned their vines, 'Let us rejoice!
It is a promise that our vintage will be choice.'

Said others, 'Nay, some greater blessing still
　Awaits us from the Goddess Hera's hand,
For have we not, upon her holy hill,
　Upreared to her a monument so grand
That not another like it is in all the land?'

Impatient for the day that had been set
　For the unveiling of the finished shrine,
They all declared, 'Some clearer message yet—
　Some more intelligible word or sign—
Will then be thundered by those carven lips divine.'

IV.

So Hera, with her temple and her priests,
  And with her sacred town above the sea,
And with her thousand years of annual feasts,
  Had never yet, in any like degree,
Been honoured and adored as she was now to be.

V.

To get to Hera's feast (which none might miss
  Save to be punished by her vengeful frown)
Ten thousand Argives, from all Argolis,
  Would have to clamber up to Argos town,
Where stood the new-made image on the mountain's
    crown.

It was no easy hill for folk to climb;
  The height was giddy and the heat severe:
For Hera's feast came always at a time
  Which people dreaded as the day drew near—
The very longest, hottest day of all the year[1].

The young, the strong, the lover and his maid
  Might go afoot, close at each other's side,
With branches borne above their heads for shade;
  But all the old and feeble must provide
Some beast of burden, for they had a need to ride.

So every horse, and mule, and ox, and ass
  In all the valley, on that sacred day,
Must trudge to Argos by the mountain-pass
  Bestrid of twain or trine—or must convey
A crowd of ten or twenty on a cart or dray.

---

[1] The month of June is named after Juno, or Hera.

VI.

Hundreds had started on that festal morn;
    Hundreds were starting; hundreds were to start:
Yet one lone woman, wistful and forlorn,
    Must stay behind, and lose her precious part
Of that high sacrament, dear to a mother's heart.

VII.

This was Cydippé—in whose wattled cot,
    A league from Argos, on the marshy moor,
Her boys beheld her weeping at her lot;
    For she was widowed, crippled, old and poor,
With now another hardship harder to endure.

Which was, that this all-hallowed day should dawn,
    Yet in her empty byre no beast be found
Whereby her feeble body could be drawn
    Across the moor and up the hilly ground
To Hera's feast, to see the thunderous Goddess
    crowned.

Cydippé, who had served in Hera's fane,
    A priestess ere she was a warrior's bride,
Wished, as the widow of that warrior slain
    (And must a wish so pious be denied?)
To kneel within the fane once more before she died.

VIII.

Cydippé's sons—her tall and blue-eyed twins,
    Scarce old enough to know a grief or care—
Too young as yet for down upon their chins,
    Showed in their boyishness a manly air,
As if their father's soul had fixed its lodgement there.

'Our mother's heart,' said they, 'will surely break,
  If on this crowning day of all the year
She goes not up to Argos—there to make
  Her offering to the deity austere
Whom godly Greeks adore with equal love and fear.'

So whilst the widow sat apart and sighed,
  Her boys (in whispers) taxed each other's wit
How up the Holy Mountain she might ride;
  And on a happy plan they chanced to hit
That needed neither beast nor bridle, rein nor bit.

IX.

'But ere we tell our mother our design
  We first will go and beg of her,' quoth they,
'The mortal boon that is the most Divine—
  A mother's blessing—which, the Sibyls say,
Once given on Earth, not Heaven itself can take away.'

X.

They knelt before her, one at either knee,
  And she, in silence, laid on either head
A wrinkled hand, and blessed them tenderly,
  Dropping a tear in memory of the dead:
Then, giving to the living each a kiss, she said:

'Go ye, my lads, and leave me here behind;
  I am too old to climb so high a hill:
Go ye and pray the Goddess to be kind
  To her old servant who would serve her still
Except for lack of strength, and not for lack of will.'

XI.

Cried they, 'Thou too shalt go, despite thy years;
    For *we* are strong, and Love makes Labour light;
And we will yoke ourselves like coupled steers,
    And pull and tug with all our main and might,
And wheel thee to the very top of Argos height.'

XII.

A sudden rapture lit Cydippé's face
    To see her sons show such a filial care:
To whom she said, 'The Goddess of all grace
    Will surely, with a boon exceeding rare,
Reward ye both, in answer to a mother's prayer.

XIII.

Up sprang the boys, and, turning on their heels,
    Skipped to the byre, and rigged and trundled thence—
Complete with axle and a pair of wheels—
    A battle-car, which, like a thing of sense,
Groaned, and a cloud of dust rose from it thick and
        dense:

And off flew fowls—for fowls had built their nests
    In that old vehicle for twenty years;
And now the terror in their fluttering breasts
    Burst forth in that half-cackle which one hears
Shrilling along a barnyard when a hawk appears.

XIV.

The Chariot was the ponderous battle-car
    From which Cydippé's lord had long ago

(A Doric warrior in the Spartan war[1])
  Hurled many a fatal javelin at the foe,
Till by a Spartan spear he was himself laid low.

(For merciless had been that civil feud,
  That long and useless internecine strife,
Which brought Cydippé to her widowhood
  Ere she had hardly been a year a wife,
And doomed her to a hut of poverty for life.)

XV.

Into the creaking car, in skittish fear,
  The widow clambered with unsteady feet,
Bid by her boys to be their charioteer;
  Whilst *they*, in mirth, kept up a gay conceit
Of prancing like a pair of battle-steeds from Crete.

XVI.

The lads across their shoulders slung a beam
  Cut from a cornel-tree, a sapling tough,
And equal to the strain; nor did they deem
  The yoke too galling, or the road too rough,
In serving her whom they could never serve enough.

A league they dragged her through the level plain,
  Still laughing at their labour as a jest;
But soon their mirth was sobered into pain,
  As each, with tightening lips and panting breast,
Tugged in fierce silence up the mountain's flinty crest.

---

[1] This was the civil war that culminated in the famous battle of Mantineia, in which the Argives were defeated by the Spartans, B.C. 418.

XVII.

Great was the wonderment on Argos height,
  And loud the cheer that from the people broke
When old Cydippé slowly wheeled in sight,
  Drawn by her twins, coupled beneath their yoke;
And thus the kneeling matron to the Goddess spoke:

' Not for myself, who bow to thee agen,
  Crave I a blessing, being doubly blest,—
But oh, of all the gifts of Heaven to men,
  Grant to these boys of mine, at my behest,
Whatever boon is for their tender youth the best.'

XVIII.

Now on that sultry night, on beds of straw,
  Ten thousand Argives slept on Argos hill;
But not Cydippé, who, with holy awe,
  Sat up and watched; for when the camp grew still
She hoped for some new token of the Heavenly will.

XIX.

At last, a crash of thunder rent the air!
  Whereat Cydippé, with a smothered cry,
Said, ' It is midnight. Hera hears my prayer!
  She is herself a mother, and draws nigh
To tell me that a mother's prayer is heard on high.'

XX.

Cydippé, wondering if the thunderstroke
  Had roused her sleeping twins, on tiptoe stepped
To where they lay, to see if they awoke.
  —Little she guessed, as back agen she crept,
That Hera's thunderbolt had slain them while they
    slept !

Cydippé in the morning called them not:
  'Nay, let them slumber long,' she softly said;
'Their toil of yesterday was hard and hot.'
  But when at last she hobbled to their bed,
The horror-stricken mother found her darlings 'dead.

XXI.

On all the town of Argos fell a gloom,
  'And people cavilled that so good a dame
Should lose such noble boys by such a doom,
  And said, 'The cruel Goddess is to blame!'
And for her murderous bolt they cursed her holy name.

And some made threats to overthrow her shrine
  And fling her image headlong down the hill!
'Is *she*,' they cried, 'a Goddess? *She* divine
  Who thus can find it in her heart to kill
Such innocents, who never wrought or thought an ill?'

XXII.

But the sad mother of those lumps of clay
  Laid once agen a hand on either head,
And kissed her darlings in the same old way
  (As if to *her* indeed they were not dead),
And lifting up to Heaven her broken voice, she said:

'O thou dread Goddess, whom I still adore,
  I think not of thy wrath, but of thy ruth;
For every childless mother evermore,
  Through all the world, *shall know by me* the truth,
That children, to be blest the most, must die in youth.'

R

THE MEADOW OF ASPHODEL.

I.

I TOSSED in a fever on my bed
And railed at life; till I even said,
'I would to the Gods that I were dead!'

I slept and dreamed of the Vale below,
Where Lethé's waters are feigned to flow,
And whither the dead are doomed to go.

I heard in my dream a brazen sound,
The toll of a bell! I gazed around
At mourners bearing me to my mound!

And under my mound, alive and well,
I sank to the place that some call Hell,
And others the Meadow of Asphodel;

And others Tophet; and others still
Elysium, Tartarus, Odin's Hill,
Or Pluto's Valley—or what they will,

According as in their oaths or prayers,
Or hopes or terrors, or griefs or cares,
They speak of it as a bourne of theirs.

II.

—The filmy populace of the place
Approached and felt of my hands and face,
And folded me in a chill embrace.

'O child of the cheerful world,' quoth they,
'How durst thou venture to grope and stray,
So far from the blessed light of day?

'What augury doth the sign denote,
That hither from yonder shore remote
Thou comest, yet not in Charon's boat?

'If thou be Mercury in disguise,
Uplift thy wand and bid us arise,
And lead us back to the shining skies!

'The shining skies! Are they still as blue
As once they were to our mortal view,
Ere Death with his arrow wrought our rue?

'The Sun! Doth he daily rise and set?
The Stars! Do they nightly twinkle yet?
O tell us! for we forget, forget!

'And how does the beautiful Earth now seem?
For we—the quaffers of Lethé's stream—
Forget, as one forgetteth a dream!'

III.

—I answered and said, 'Ye spirits fair,
No wand of Mercury do I bear
To lead ye back to the upper air.

'The Earth is just as. it was before;
But I, with a heart grown sick and sore,
Have done with the Earth for evermore!

'To live . . . is hardly a boon at best;
And, weary of life, I long for rest,
And come to tarry among the blest :—

'Among the blest—who have flung aside
The sword, the shield, and the victor's pride,
To rest from the battle and here abide.'

IV.

—'Thou fool!' said Voices of hollow sound,
'Thou comest where rest is never found—
For who is at rest beneath the ground?

'What ghost hath ever a quiet mind?
And what is death but to look behind
And yearn to be back among mankind?

'For here, in this dusky realm below,
We wander bodiless to and fro,
And suffer a strange and novel woe:

'We have a passion that hath no name,
And only the dead can feel its flame—
Desire for the Life from whence we came;

'Desire for the World that once was ours;
Desire for its sunshine and its flowers;
Desire for its temples and its towers:

'Desire in vain! for the dead are dead,
And *what* remaineth, when life is fled,
Save only *desire* of life instead?

'O thou who art warm, whilst *we* are cold,
We fain would live as we lived of old—
With babes to fondle, and flocks to fold,

'And fruits to gather, and sheaves to bind,
And songs to sing, and the merry mind
Which here in the mist we never find!

'We sigh for morn and the mountain-height;
We sigh for eve and the ingle-light;
We sigh for the bliss of sleep at night:

'We long for toil, with its tug and strain;
We long for joy, and even for pain;
We long for love, but we long in vain!

'For spirits can neither smile nor weep,
Nor wearily toil nor sweetly sleep,
But only an endless vigil keep—

'An endless vigil, whose baffled ken
Keeps looking up to the Earth agen,
And longing to live with living men.'

V.

—Then greatly I marvelled thus to learn
That out of the dust of tomb and urn
The dead would fain into life return.

'Is death no blessing at all?' I cried;
And some said 'Never!' and all replied,
'O would to the Gods we had not died!

'The living have feigned us dwelling here
In gardens of more than Eden's cheer;
But hardly a desert is half so drear.

'Our dim eternity is not worth
A single day on the shining Earth—
With music and dancing, wine and mirth!

'Go back, O mortal, nor turn thy face
From light and life and the pleasant place
Where dwell the living of all thy race.'

VI.

—Bewildered, I sat me down to think;
I thirsted, and stooped to Lethé's brink,
But shivered and felt afraid to drink:

I hungered, and hunted round and round
For fig or melon, on tree or ground;
But apples of dust were all I found.

And all the meadow was grey and bare,
And not a lamb was shepherded there,
And not a blossom embalmed the air.

'Are these th' Elysian Fields?' said I,—
'Then better, I think, are Earth and Sky,
And better for me to live than die!'

VII.

—Then crowded around me every ghost
From all the corners of Pluto's coast,
Till I was girt with a countless host.

And then they said with a mighty moan,
'O child of folly, yet wiser grown,
Go back—till a shroud for thee be sewn!

'Thy tally of days must be complete
Ere thou have right to thy winding-sheet:
Go back and endure thy fever-heat!

'Go back, whatever thy pain or ache;
Go back, however thy heart may break;
Go back, for thy spirit's future sake.

'Go back to thy life, and live it through!
Thy days are evil, and yet are few;
Thou soon shalt hither return anew.'

VIII.

—Whereat, like a flock of swans in flight,
The phantoms rippled their robes of white,
And said, 'Farewell!' and were out of sight.

My dream was ended—my fever spent—
And forth to my toil I gaily went:
And life was sweet, and my heart content.

And far be the day when toll of bell
Shall herald my ghost to Heaven or Hell
Or doleful Meadow of Asphodel!

QUEEN HORTENSE'S STRANGE NARRATIVE.

Hortense Beauharnais, after her many misfortunes, including her loss of the Crown of Holland, relates to her friends at Malmaison[1] the following incident:—

I.

A PILGRIM on the Rhine, I wished a chance
    Of searching the Cathedral of Cologne,
To find the shrine of Marie, Queen of France[2],
    Whose Buried Heart (that once was Sorrow's own!)
    Lies there at peace beneath a nameless stone.

The stone is nameless, for the tramping feet
    Of generations, crowding to the Mass,
Have wrought the slow effacement, now complete,
    Of all the old inscription, though of brass;
    And now the slab is known to none who pass.

II.

Thus was I told. 'But nay,' thought I, 'some trace
    Must surely still be left to mark the spot:
For how could she who held so high a place
    Be doomed to leave so proud a heart to rot
    Within a tomb that is remembered not?'

----

[1] The once pretty château of Malmaison (in the neighbourhood of Paris) was the favourite country-seat of Napoleon I and Josephine, but is now shabby and dilapidated, and is used as a land-office for selling off Josephine's famous flower-garden 'in lots, to suit purchasers.'

[2] Marie de Medicis, wife of King Henry IV of France.

To seek this tomb until it should be found
• Appeared to me a feasible design,
And I was sure that if I rummaged round,
　Though other pilgrims long had missed the shrine,
　The luck to find it might at last be mine.

I said, 'I will array me as a nun
　(To hide my queenhood from all spying eyes),
And after vespers, ere the day be done,
　Will steal into the church in my disguise,
　In hope to kneel where that dear relic lies.'

III.

Queen, exile, beggar, and sad widowed wife,
　Her Living Heart—now but a lump of clay—
Had known each throbbing joy and grief of life,—
　All that the world could give or take away:
　And I at such a shrine had need to pray.

I too had had my rise and overthrow;
　I too had had my glory and my shame;
I too had thrilled to all a heart could know
　Of pride, and wounded love, and blasted fame,
　And burning hopes that perished in their flame!

IV.

Discrowned, I sought the royal nameless shrine
　That mocked the vanity of rank and birth,—
There, of the Buried Heart, to ask with mine
　What now a world of empires would be worth
　To such a wee and shrivelled scrap of earth?

V.

In all the awful Temple, vast and still,
  No fellow human creature did I meet:
And all alone I wandered at my will,
  In solitude so hallowed and so sweet,
  That Heaven itself seemed shrined in that retreat!

At first the sun was shining (and his ray
  Had been of summer's very brightest glare),
And even while he sank and slipped away
  He filled the temple with a light so fair,
  That I imagined God Himself was there!

Uprose the moon—whose beams, with many a stain
  Of crimson, purple, scarlet and faint gold,
Came flaming down through many a fiery pane,
  Kindling the haloes of the Saints of old,
  And burnishing the tombs that held their mould.

VI.

I searched where every slanting piebald ray
  Slid in its splendour to the stony floor,
In faith of finding—not yet worn away—
  Some tell-tale letter, carven there of yore,
  Above the bleeding Heart that bled no more.

Then finding none, I whispered with a sigh,
  'Oh for a Witch's Wand (if such there be)
Or Rod of Magic to be guided by,
  And pointed to the spot I wish to see!'
  —Whereat a sudden fancy came to me:

Thought I, 'This living, suffering heart of mine,
. As here I wander sorrowing through the fane,
Will of itself divine the hidden shrine—
    For at the spot where Marie's heart hath lain,
    My own, on meeting hers, will jump with pain.

'One heart must know another, if the two
    Have each been agonized, and both have bled;
A secret sympathy—from common rue—
    Must knit the twain as with a magic thread,
    Though one be living and the other dead.'

VII.

This hope so soothed the dolour in my breast,
    So softened what had there become so sore,
So cheered me with the promise of a rest
    From what was gnawing at my bosom's core,—
    That on I went, more eager than before.

On, on I went, where many a sleeper slept—
    On, on, through pillared aisle and paven choir;
And ever, as from stone to stone I stepped,
    I felt with awe that I was drawing nigher
    The hidden holy shrine of my desire.

I walked the length of all the moonlit nave,
    With stifled breathing and with stealthy feet;
And all was soundless as the silent grave:
    When, of a sudden—was it Fancy's cheat?—
    I heard the Buried Heart begin to beat!

VIII.

It was the saddest sound I ever heard!
    Sadder than any mortal sigh or moan!

Sadder than any woe of spoken word!
  I could not trace it to a special stone,
  Nor could I note the tomb that was its own.

IX.

With shame I say, I was afraid to stay
  In such a strangely-haunted solitude;
And turning on my heels I stole away;
    But all at once the beating was renewed,
    For while I fled, the panting Heart pursued.

It panted like a living thing distressed,
  And then it paused a moment and stood still,
Till, as I listened, I became oppressed
    As by a spell—and many a creeping chill
    Passed through me with a palpitating thrill.

X.

I thought to see it take a spectral shape—
  Some ghastly form in which a soul appears
That from the grave hath made a sad escape;
    But though I saw it not, yet in mine ears
    It throbbed, and filled me with unearthly fears.

XI.

Afraid to question it, or speak aloud,
  I chid my trembling self with whispers low,
Upbraiding my weak courage, thus so cowed:
  'Why is my wit,' thought I, 'so dull and slow?
  —This heart was dust and ashes long ago;

'And how can dust and ashes be alive?
. My fancy by my fear is wrought upon!
The soul—the soul immortal—must survive;
　　But can a fleshly heart keep beating on
　　When pulse and blood and vital breath are gone?

'Yet since the dead,' thought I, 'are still unrisen,—
　　Since each, with folded hands upon his breast,
Is still a captive in his stony prison,—
　　Might not a Buried Heart that died unblest
　　Have liberty to rise before the rest?'

XII.

But every question woke a doleful doubt,
　　And every doubt begot a dismal fear;
Till down I knelt to breathe a prayer devout—
　　Whereat the beating grew so loud and near
　　That up I leapt, and stood attent to hear.

'Make known the meaning of thy moan,' I said,
　　'For *I*, like *thee*, have tasted human woe,
And if thou bring a message from the dead,
　　Whether from Heaven above or Hell below,
　　Whatever it may be, I fain would know.'

XIII.

The beating Heart that held me so in thrall
　　Then beat the louder; till the beaten air
Shook every shining pane and dusky wall
　　And carven pillar—whilst I listened there
　　To wait what message it was now to bear.

I waited till I feared that I should faint!
　The Blessed Virgin in her rosy bower,
And huge Saint Christopher, and every saint,
　And all the Triple Kings within the Tower,
　Seemed staring at me in that stilly hour!

XIV.

Thus spake the Buried Heart from out its tomb:
　'Begone, O breaker of my tranquil rest!
Betray me not—but leave me to my doom;
　For whether Life or Death be curst or blest,
　In spite of curse or blessing, Death is best!'

XV.

Thus did it speak; and though it spake no more,
　Yet, while the silent moonbeams round me fell,
I heard it panting nearer than before—
　Nearer and louder—beating like a knell!
　And forth I hurried to escape the spell.

Down the long aisle, and through the mighty door—
　Away from sepulchres and dead men's bones—
Into the open air of Heaven once more—
　I ran like mad—and all the while the moans
　Seemed to pursue me with their panting tones!

XVI.

The spell still bound me with its icy chain—
　Still froze me from my fingers to my feet—
Still numbed the very thoughts within my brain;
　Nor did I guess till I was in the street
　That mine—mine only—was the heart that beat!

XVII.

I laughed a moment at my silly fright,
　And felt as having wakened from a dream,
And shaken off an ogre or a sprite
　Or horrid nightmare—yet forsooth, I deem
　My search not half so vain as it may seem:

For sure am I that, by a happy chance,
　The slab I knelt on was the very stone
That hides the Heart of Marie, Queen of France[1],—
　Since now her Buried Heart forewarns my own
　That peace awaits me in the grave alone!

———•◆•———

THE HEAVENLY HOPE.

O EARTHLY sufferer, why complain?
　　Amid thy anguish, be thou dumb!
In spite of all thy present pain,
　Thy blessedness is yet to come[2].

———————

[1] Marie de Medicis, widow of Henry IV, died at Cologne in the year 1642, and her burial-place in the Cathedral is still an object of inquiry by tourists; but the story that her heart is lying somewhere in the nave, beautifully lodged in a casket designed by Rubens the artist, is probably a fancy—plausibly based on the well-known fact that Rubens—who possessed princely wealth—was generous to the ex-Queen during the poverty of her closing years.

[2] This was a frequent thought with the Nun of Avila (or Saint Theresa) during the distressing illness which caused her death.

KING OSWALD'S RIGHT HAND:
A LEGEND OF LINDISFARNE.
SEVENTH CENTURY A.D.

I.

ONCE on a time, clad like a begging friar,
  Barefoot, and pricked by many a flint and brier,
The good King Oswald (Umbria's royal saint),
Returning from a pilgrimage, grew faint—
And being yet a league from Berwick town[1]
Could walk no further, staggered, and fell down.

II.

The snowy-bearded King, despite his age,
Had no attendant but a youthful page—
To whom the Royal Pilgrim panting said:
'Here on the highway I will lay my head,
Whilst thou shalt hie thee to the town and back
To bring a crust of bread, whereof the lack
Is like to famish me, and I shall die!'
(For he had fasted for the week gone by.)

III.

Forth skipped the well-fed page with leap and bound,
And Oswald fell asleep upon the ground.

IV.

A band of Berwick beggars passed the spot,
And spied the sleeping King, yet woke him not,
But camped around him on the shaded grass,
To wait until the noonday heat should pass.

---

[1] This pretty town, lying picturesquely at the mouth of the Tweed, is locally called Berrick.

V.

The page, returning, bore a silver dish,
Whereon, still smoking, lay a barbel-fish,
Fresh from the flood, and fresher from the fire—
As tempting as a monarch could desire.

VI.

The King awoke, and gloated on the sight,
Yet for a moment curbed his appetite,
Till for such bounty in a barren place
He first, ere tasting it, should say a grace.

VII.

The beggars, whilst the monarch's head was bowed,
Came tiptoe round him in a silent crowd:
Long was his prayer, yet breathlessly they stood,
Knowing the King beneath his monkish hood.

VIII.

The Royal Saint, when he had said his prayer,
Gazed at the gazers with a searching stare,
Until his pitying eyes could plainly see
That his gaunt guests were hungrier than he.

IX.

Then whispering to his page, King Oswald said,
'No mouthful shall I taste till *these* be fed:
Share thou with all alike what thou hast brought,
Counting thyself for one, but *me* for nought:
Divide to each a morsel of the fish,
Then break to pieces and divide the dish.'

X.

Loth was the lad to do the strange command:
Whereat King Oswald, with his own right hand,
Then gave to each of all the multitude
An equal portion of the savoury food,
Not keeping for himself a scrap or bone,
But feeding every mouth except his own.
And then the silver dish, with many a knock,
He dashed to pieces on a flinty rock,
And gave the beggars, to their strange delight,
Out of the precious metal each a mite.

XI.

When each had had his morsel of the fish,
And each his fragment of the silver dish,
Forth stepped the oldest beggar of the band,
And said with tears, seizing the King's right hand
(Which thrice he kissed ere letting go his hold),
'Oh never may this bounteous hand grow old!
But be it ever, though a thing of clay,
Exempt from death, corruption, and decay!'

XII.

Years afterward (for God is slow but sure,
And heareth all the cries of all His poor)
There came to pass (oh wondrous to declare!)
A strange fulfilment of the Beggar's prayer.
The times grew evil, till the Holy Name
Of Christ the Lord was put to open shame:
The fierce King Penda and his Pagan host
Laid waste with fire and sword the Umbrian coast.
The good King Oswald, smitten through his helm,
Hero and martyr, perished with his realm:

S

His royal bones, unknown among the slain,
•Lay till they bleached upon the battle-plain.
At last, the self-same Berwick beggar-band,
Who once had eaten from King Oswald's hand,
Espied his skeleton—a ghastly thing,
And crossed themselves, and cried, 'It is the King!'

XIII.

The sign they knew it by was surer far
Than the cleft skull that showed a battle scar;
For lo! the flesh from every bone had dropped
Save from a hand whose pulse had never stopped!
It was the King's Right Hand, still warm and white!
And half the kingdom went to see the sight!—
Proud of their Martyr, as a kingly soul
Who lost a crown to gain an aureole.

XIV.

A tomb for ages marked his burial-place,
And was a shrine for all the Umbrian race.
But marble crumbles, granite wastes away,
And urns and cromlechs tumble to decay:
The tomb of Oswald fell so long ago,
That where it stood no mortal now can know;
Yet all the world may evermore be sure,
That blest is every hand that feeds the poor[1].

---

[1] The story of King Oswald's right hand, as above given, is one of the ecclesiastical narratives which were penned at Jarrow in the eighth century by the Venerable Bede, who is called the 'father of English history.' The little stone church at Jarrow—containing the cell in which he wrote his voluminous works—still stands; charmingly situated among green meadows, near the sea. It is a quaint monument of early Saxon architecture; but, more than all, it is an

THE FINMARK FAIRY [1],

OR THE GLOMMEN SPRITE.

I.

THE Fathers at Fall Saint Jason
   Have built in a shady nook
A mill where a silent basin
   Is fed by a noisy brook.

The mill, in the driest season,
   Has never been known to fail,
And all for the simple reason . . .
   But wait till you hear the tale.

II.

The tale is an idle prattle,
   Of.how, to a poet's eye,
The clouds are a Herd of Cattle
   That wander about the sky.

Their Drover is Odin's daughter—
   A maiden of high degree,
A creature of air and water,
   A sister of land and sea.

And being a hoyden airy,
   And gadding by day and night,
Some call her the Finmark Fairy,
   And others, the Glommen Sprite.

object of reverential interest for its associations with a Christian hero
who, in the affectionate regards of Englishmen, ranks with Edward
the Confessor and King Alfred the Great.

  [1] Finmark is the northern part of the Scandinavian peninsula, and
the Glommen is the chief river of Norway.

The Monks, in their pious chatter,
    May christen her as they please ;
Her name is of little matter,
    Her soul is the Summer-breeze.

III.

The herd of this airy drover
    Have neither a yoke nor bell ;
They feed on the smell of clover,
    They drink out of Meimir's Well[1].

And oft, to the peasant's wonder,
    Who watches them from below,
They bellow and roar with thunder,
    As over the hills they go.

The drover, in driving, dallies
    To rest on a mountain-ridge,
Or loiter along the valleys,
    Or linger at Heimdal's Bridge[2].

IV.

One morning the maid was fretful
    At driving her cattle round,
And slept for a while—forgetful
    To have them securely bound.

Away over hill and hollow,
    The herd, being left untied,
Were spirited by Apollo,
    With Mercury for his guide.

---

[1] Meimir's Well is the ocean.
[2] Heimdal's Bridge is the rainbow.

The cattle were slow of motion,
  And seemed to be drowsy too,
And dreaming of grass in Goshen,
  As cattle, when dozing, do.

v.

She woke, and she chid their straying;
  But since they had strayed so far,
They now were beyond obeying,
  And deaf as the morning star.

So flinging a rope around them
  (The air being very still),
And dragging them down, she drowned them
  In front of Saint Jason's mill.

She fettered their ghosts and gyved them,
  And bound them as still as death,
And suddenly she revived them,
  And loosened them with her breath.

VI.

She tethers them at her pleasure;
  They tug, but they tug in vain;
Her rope is of endless measure,
  Like Jupiter's golden chain[1].

So slender a cord or cable
  Has never been spun or set,
Except in the ancient fable
  Of Venus in Vulcan's net[2].

----

[1] This was the chain by which Jupiter could draw all the worlds up to himself, though not all the worlds combined could draw him down.

[2] Vulcan, who was jealous of the coquetries of Venus with Mars,

VII.

At times, in the finest weather,
  The cattle are far away,
And cannot be pulled together—
  And so they are left to stray.

The Fairy is sure to find them,
  And then to the mill and weir
She brings them agen to bind them,
  As soon as the pond is clear. ·

VIII.

The water, if clear, is soundless,
  For as to its depth, you know,
The bottom of course is boundless—
  A firmament lies below.

The edge of the pool is grassy,
  And bordered with maple-trees;
And under the surface glassy
  Are maples to match with these.

If ever the glass be shattered
  By leap of a lively trout,
The cattle at once are scattered,
  And tremble and hurry out.

IX.

The Fathers are fond of coming
  To sit where the mill-wheel grinds,
For always a mill-wheel's humming
  Is soothing to lazy minds.

---

wove an invisible net in which he cunningly entangled the two
lovers, and thereby brought upon them the laughter of all the Gods.

They come at the hour of matin,
  They come at the vesper-tide,—
All bringing their books of Latin,
  But flinging them there aside.

The Fathers are fat and frowsy,
  And Latin, they find, is dull;
And few of them care, when drowsy,
  To study and pore and mull.

But each with his sacred sandal,
  And each with his pious mind,
Is keen for the latest scandal,
  Or joke of a doubtful kind.

They sit with their legs extended,
  They gossip of Youth and Love,
They wish that the Earth were ended
  And sigh for the World above.

Though down in the water plainly
  They notice the cattle white,
They ogle the maiden vainly,
  Who never appears in sight.

For never shall they behold her,
  This virgin of viewless air;
And how could a maid be colder,
  Or more to a monk's despair?

x.

They gabble of Odin's daughter,
  And learnedly they explain,
That drought is a lack of water,
  And follows a lack of rain.

The mill, in the driest season,
   Keeps running without a drop,
Because (as the Fathers reason)
   It never has time to stop.

This reason is quite too clever,
   And proves that the running mill,
Not only must run for ever,
   But very much longer still.

XI.

Now peace to the drove and drover,
   And plenty to hill and dale!
—The ballad at last is over;
   And how do you like the tale?

———•·•———

CŒUR-DE-LION TO BERENGARIA [1].

(The King was in England and the Queen in Sicily.)

O FAR-OFF darling in the South,
   Where grapes are loading down the vine,
And songs are in the throstle's mouth,
   While love's complaints are here in mine;
Turn from the blue Tyrrhenian Sea!
Come back to me! Come back to me!

---

[1] King Richard I of England was a troubadour, and the author of many love-songs.

Here all the Northern skies are cold,
  And in their wintriness they say
(With warnings by the winds foretold)
  That love may grow as cold as they!
How ill the omen seems to be!
Come back to me! Come back to me!

Come back, and bring thy wandering heart—
  Ere yet it be too far estranged!
Come back, and tell me that thou art
  But little chilled, but little changed!
O love, my love, I love but thee!
Come back to me! Come back to me!

I long for thee from morn till night;
  I long for thee from night till morn:
But love is proud, and any slight
  Can sting it like a piercing thorn!
My bleeding heart cries out to thee—
Come back to me! Come back to me!

Come back, and pluck the nettle out;
  Come kiss the wound, or love may die!
How can my heart endure the doubt?
  Oh, judge its anguish by its cry!
Its cry goes piercingly to thee—
Come back to me! Come back to me!

What is to thee the summer long?
  What is to thee the clustered vine?
What is to thee the throstle's song,
  Who sings of love, but not of mine?
Oh turn from the Tyrrhenian Sea!
Come back to me! Come back to me!

THE APPLE OF CONCORD[1].

'A VIRGIN'S *Vow, sworn in Diana's fane,*
  Although by chance, and with the lightest breath,
Is still a vow, and must a vow remain,
  And binds the votaress till her day of death,
No matter who the virgin be, nor what she saith.'

II.

So ran—engraven on a plaque of gold
  That hung across Diana's Delian shrine—
A text, which maidens, kneeling there of old,
  Were bid to ponder as a warning sign
Against all heedlessness in making vows divine.

III.

One morn the maid Cydippé, with a face
  (So thought her lover) like Diana's own,
Had started for the fane with laggard pace,
  White-robed, and crowned with poppy-buds half-blown,
To vow that she would never loose her virgin zone.

Though to Diana's shrine, with jocund tread,
  Full many a maid might hasten, thus arrayed—
More glad to be a vestal than to wed—
  Yet pale Cydippé, heart-sick and afraid,
Sighed, as along the path she loitered and delayed.

---

[1] This story comes down from a great antiquity, and has been variously rendered by Ovid, Callimachus, and Antoninus Liberalis.

The youth Acantios—poor except in pri de—
  Had won her heart, and to her hand laid claim;
But angrily her sire the suit denied;
  And now all Delos to the Temple came
To see her sworn a priestess in Diana's name.

IV.

From door to altar the expectant throng
  Stood parted where the maiden would pass through;
And while they waited (for she tarried long)
  They craned their necks, as crowds in waiting do,
And gazed and gazed agen, ere yet she came in view.

So while she tarried, all who knew the tale
  Of her great love, and of its great return,
Stood wondering if her purpose might not fail,
  Or if her heart, rebellious, might not spurn
Obedience to the mandate of a sire so stern.

V.

. The youth Acantios, on that very morn,
  Had sought Cydippé, and on bended knee,
And wild with passion (for his heart was torn)
  Implored her, with a lover's desperate plea,
For love's dear sake, to disobey her sire's decree.

VI.

The filial daughter, pious and demure,
  Chaste as Diana's self, but not so chill,
Had loved her lover with a love so pure,
  That grief had made it all the purer still;
And now she said, 'I go to do my father's will.'

And so, despite the passion in her heart,
. There was no disobedience in her mind;
'Farewell!' she cried, 'We must for ever part!'
    Nor, after parting, looked she once behind,
As on and on she walked, foredoomed and not resigned.

She walked all unattended and alone,
    In sign and token, on that solemn day,
That she who was to be Diana's own
    Had turned for ever from the world away;
And down upon her head now beat the noontide ray.

VII.

Without a sandal on her tender feet
    (For barefoot must she seek the sacred pile)
She soon began to languish in the heat,
    And sat upon a shaded rock awhile,
And mourned that Love and Fate were hard to reconcile.

Down from her brow she took her sacred flowers,
    Gazed at them long, wet them with many a tear,
And put them back—thinking of happier hours,
    Gone but remembered, whose remembrance dear,
Enhanced her present woe, and smote her numb
        with fear.

Little she thought of all the waiting crowd,
    Or of her looked-for presence in the fane,
Or of her vow that must so soon be vowed,
    Or of the Goddess in whose virgin train
She must from that unhappy day till death remain.

VIII.

Cydippé's thoughts were on the desperate youth
  Whom she had parted from an hour before,
Whose image to the very last, forsooth
  (Her soul's dear idol), she would still adore
Till at the altar she must think of him no more!

She spake his name, she uttered piteous cries,
  She flung her arms into the empty air,
She looked in vain to the unanswering skies,
  She poured her spirit forth in wild despair,—
Till her tumultuous grief was more than she could bear.

But grief must still be borne, though it be great;
  And so at last, upleaping from the stone,
And fearing lest she should arrive too late,
  Cydippé hurried onward, still alone,
With thorns to prick her feet, yet uttering not a moan.

IX.

When sad Cydippé reached the Temple-door,
  The youth Acantios—sadder yet than she—
Stood at the threshold ; and the look he wore
  Was haggard, wan, and wild beyond degree!
'And is thy woe,' she asked, 'all for thy love of *me*?'

'All for my love of *thee*!' he fiercely said,
  'And if thou lift thy finger for a sign,
Here will I enter—though I risk my head!—
  And pluck thee from Diana's very shrine,
And bear thee hence away, and make thee ever mine!'

No finger bade him! And the Damozel
  * Upraised her eyes, that downward had been cast,
And gave him, with a look, a last farewell,
    Hiding no tear of all that fell so fast;
And then, with speechless grief, into the fane she
      passed.

X.

The patient priest, who met her at the shrine,
  Laid both his hands in blessing on her brow,
Held to her lips the consecrated wine,
  Asperged her, and commanded her to bow
And kiss the Earth, and speak aloud her vestal vow.

XI.

She bent her knees, but uttered not a word;
  Her heart had stopped, as if in deathly rest;
No drop of blood in all her pulses stirred;
  —When her bold lover to the altar pressed
And flung an apple right against Cydippé's breast.

It lodged a moment in her folds of snow,
  And on it, as she plucked it forth, she read
(Bewildered now with fear as well as woe)
  Pricked on the rind, a writing; and it said,
'*I love the youth Acantios, whom I swear to wed.*'

XII.

Cydippé—who had read the words aloud,
  Not dreaming what they were—now stood aghast
At what she thus unwittingly had vowed!
  And icy tremors through her body passed,
With fiery flames, as hot as from a furnace-blast.

The priest then pointed to the plaque of gold
  That hung before her on Diana's shrine,
And with a trembling voice (for he was old)
  .Declared that she had heeded not the sign;
Which slowly then he thus recited, line for line:

XIII.

'A Virgin's Vow, sworn in Diana's fane,
  Although by chance, and with the lightest breath,
Is still a vow, and must a vow remain,
  And binds the votaress till her day of death,
No matter who the virgin be, nor what she saith.'

XIV.

Thus spake the priest, heard by the eager throng
  Who filled the fane within, from shrine to door,
From door to portico, and thence along
  Beyond the porphyry pillars that upbore
The pediment, out to the open court before.

Forth sprang the youth Acantios, with a cry
  Shrill and exultant, piercing the hushed air,
While right and left he thrust the people by,—
  Leaped to the altar, seized Cydippé there,
And bore her thence,—leaving the crowd to gape and
    stare.

Cydippé's vow was sworn beyond recall,
  And she fulfilled it 'with her heart and hand:
And there was feasting in her father's hall;
  And swiftly ran the tale through all the land:
Nor shall it be forgotten while the world shall stand[1]!

---

[1] It should be added that Cydippé of Delos, the heroine of the above adventure, was not the same person as Cydippé of Argos, of whom a story is told at page 233.

AULD TAM THE GUIDE'S TALE.

A NOVA SCOTIAN ROMANCE.

A.D. 1805.

'STRAIGHT on and up, yer Honour,
   The steps are ninety-three,
And take ye to the Lighthouse—
   Or where it used to be.

' It was the auldest lighthouse
   That stood on all our shore;
The Johnny Crapeaux built it,
   And now it stands no more.

'I was the lighthouse keeper
   Afore we built the new;
And weel I kenned the laddie,
   And kenned the lassie too.

'Down through the Bay o' Fundy
   Had ebbed the mighty tide,
Till all the sunken meadows
   Were lying green and wide.

'The tide would soon be turning[1],
   When man and beast must flee,
For back would roll a billow,
   The mightiest of the sea.

---

[1] The tidal rise is sometimes sixty feet, and the tide-wave is called
' the bore.'

'And woe to the unwary
  Who loitered in its path,
For swift would be its rising
  And terrible its wrath.

'The sun was in the solstice
  Anent the end o' June;
And long afore the sunset
  Uprose a watery moon.

'The wave would swell the highest
  That day of a' the year,
And I had set my signals
  To keep the channel clear.

'First kem a flock o' sea-mews
  A-screaming up the Bay,
In token that the tide-wave
  Had started on its way.

'And then the cattle grazing
  Along the channel's edge
Began to sniff the danger
  And quit the salty sedge.

'And last the fishermaidens,
  In forty skiffs or more,
Kem rowing a'thegither
  And racing to the shore :—

'All but a skiff, whose lassie,
  Unnoticed by the rest,
Had snapped an oar asunder
  In rounding Cartho Crest.

'This maiden had a lover,
  And I could see him stand
A-waiting till her wherry,
  With a' the fleet, should land.

'At every tide he met her
  Down at the dangerous beach,
To haul her boat for safety
  Above the water's reach.

'He was a lad, yer Honour,
  To thraw a three-year ox;
Yet he would blush to scarlet
  At anything in frocks.

'His blood would always tingle
  While pulling Ilsa's rope,—
For what is Toil but rapture
  When Love is full o' hope?

'I stood upon my watch-tower
  With weather-glass in hand,
And watched while half the Ocean
  Kem swirling to the land.

'The other skiffs had landed
  Ere Ilsa's was in sight;
Whereat her red-lipped laddie
  Turned to a deathly white.

'And first he climbed the Headland,
  Where, from the hanging cliff,
He saw the coming billow
  But not the missing skiff.

'Then on to where the Lighthouse
    Looked westward to the sea
He bounded like a roebuck
    And shouted up at me :

'"Oh tell me, tell me, watchman,
    If through your weather-glass
You spy the two-oared wherry
    Rowed by my bonnie lass!"

'I had no heart to tell him;
    Yet roughly I replied,
"I see a skiff, keel upward,
    Returning with the tide."

'Nae word he spak in answer,
    But flew as if with wings,
And off he tore his tartan
    And half his woollen things.

'I shouted, "Stay, O madman!
    To leap will be your death!"
But all in vain I warned him,
    For I but wasted breath.

'The lad sprang from the summit
    Into the swash below!—
For what is Youth but frenzy
    When Love is full o' woe?

'Down in the whirling water
    Defying Death and Fate,
And diving like a dolphin,
    The lover sought his mate.

'He sought her, and he found her;
  And though the tide-wave rolled
He clasped her to his bosom
  And let not go his hold.

'Through Copaquiddy Inlet
  The eddy ran them round,
And flung them to the Lime-pit,
  And left them safe and sound!

'A wagon-load o' roses
  Were strewn along the way
To Copaquiddy Chapel
  Upon their wedding-day.

'And Copaquiddy Headland
  Then took a change o' name,—
For such a deed o' daring
  Deserved a meed o' fame.

'The rock where Tol Macgregor
  Sprang off into the deep
For love of Ilsa Garvin
  Is called the Lover's Leap.

'And if ye hae a saxpence
  For telling o' the tale,
I now will pledge yer Honour
  In Nivva Scawtia ale.'

GREAT TOM OF OXFORD[1].

A.D. 1135.

Cast in the twelfth century, and re-cast in the seventeenth, this famous bell was for six hundred years the largest in England, and still has but few superiors, either in magnitude or melody.

I.

THROUGH all the day, in Oxford town,
  There sleeps in Wolsey tower[2]
A mighty bell of old renown—
Awaking when the sun is down,
  To toll the Curfew-hour.

It strikes a hundred strokes and one,
  With measured ding and dong,—
As if the ringing, when begun,
Instead of ever being done
  Would roar the whole night long.

O roaring Tom, though thou art hung
  Within the Church's pale,
Yet every night when thou art rung,
Thou tellest with a brazen tongue
  A very brazen tale!

II.

—When Oxford town was fresh and new,
  The Church, before the schism,

---

[1] The incidents in this ballad are historical, and are verified by citations given in the Appendix.

[2] This is the tower over the gate of Christ Church College.

Gave to the Lord His homage due
In wafers and in wax, in lieu
  Of tract and catechism.

Then Rudolph was a beggar priest,
  Who loved the Church so well
That night and day he never ceased
To crave a crozier, or at least
  An abbey and a bell.

This abbey, with a faith supreme, ·
  And with a hope sublime,
He reared in many a rapturous dream,
And fancied how the spire would gleam
  And how the bell would chime.

The fane, thus fashioned of a cloud—
  An abbey in the air!—
All planned, erected, and endowed,
Arose the loftiest when he bowed
  The lowliest at his prayer.

The mighty image in his mind
  Was long a dream alone—
A filmy fabric of a kind
Not likely to be soon designed
  In solid wood and stone.

III.

'For neither stone nor wood have I,
  Nor hammer, nor a nail!'
Quoth the poor priest; and with a sigh
He put his pious purpose by,
  And felt that it must fail.

So Rudolph grew the humblest friar
  That ever shaved his crown,
A monk the bound of whose desire
Was but his little chapel-choir
  Just out of Oxford town.

IV.

Near by, and on a parapet
  Whose ruins now are grand[1],
Sir Robert d'Oyley, banneret,
Then kept his Norman banner set
  As lord of all the land.

He owned the mill at Osney pond;
  He owned the turnpike road;
He owned (so ran the deed and bond)
The whole green group of isles beyond,
  Round which the Isis flowed;

He owned each salmon that would bite,
  Each plover that was slain,
Each clover-blossom, red or white;
And almost, though perhaps not quite,
  He owned the dew and rain.

V.

The meadow fairest to his view,
  And fittest to his need,
Was where, besides the rain and dew,
The river split itself in two
  To water Osney mead.

[1] St. George's Castle.

Now there Sir Robert parked his deer,
  And there his swans could swim,
And there this worldly man could hear
(Wafted from Rudolph's chapel near)
  Full oft a chanted hymn.

He listened from the outer side,
  But never trod the inner,
For with his land and power and pride,
And other lusts all gratified,
  Sir Robert was a sinner.

And he would boastfully declare,
  In walking through his grounds,
'I would not sell this island fair
For all the Devil has to spare,
  Were it a thousand pounds.'

VI.

This thrifty, bluff, and jovial lord
  Had found the joy of life
In adding to his herd and hoard
But not in sharing bed and board
  With any wedded wife.

'A wife is good to have,' quoth he,
  'And worth her weight in gold;
But sweet is freedom to the free,
And when I wed, it shall not be
  Till I am grey and old.'

VII.

Yet when at last his back grew bent,
  And when his head grew hoar,

Sir Robert felt but half content
With taking toll and tithe and rent,
  And wanted one thing more.

Though old and rich, he lacked an heir—
  And so he wooed and won
A youthful damsel, tall and fair,
Who soon gave hope that she would bear
  The agèd sire a son.

Sir Robert rubbed his wrinkled hands,
  And blessed his honeymoon,
And thanked his stars that all his lands
Were promised thus in Hymen's bands
  A lawful heir so soon.

VIII.

But trouble, like a prickly brier,
  Juts from the rose of joy,—
And now the proud, expectant sire
Feared that the child of his desire
  Might fail to be a boy.

For both in castle and in cot,
  Alike to poor and rich,
A babe begot may prove (God wot!)
Either to be a boy or not,
  The Lord alone knows which.

In hope of tempting Providence
  To turn the doubtful scale,
Sir Robert tried, at great expense,
To bribe the Heavens to grant him thence
  As heir direct, a male.

So daily as his bride increased,
  And rounded to the view,
He spread for all the poor a feast,—
And Father Rudolph, hungry priest,
  Added his blessing too.

IX.

The bride—the mother soon to be—
  Big with Sir Robert's heir,
Had been a maid of such degree
That England's king had bent a knee
  To Edith Forne the fair.

And if King Harry[1] had possessed
  A power to kings denied,
To wed the maids they love the best,
Sir Robert would have gone unblest
  Of such a saintly bride.

In all the town no holy nun
  Nor godly devotee
Had at the public altar done
To Mary, and to Mary's Son,
  Such bowing down as she!

She helped the parish in its needs,
  And showed such special bias
For so devoutly counting beads,
That Father Rudolph said, 'She leads
  A life profoundly pious.'

---

[1] King Henry I.

X.

If in the monk's suspicious mind
  A grain of doubt had room,
It was perhaps that he divined
A worldliness in one inclined
  To wear a scarlet plume.

It was a prince's feather, bright
  As for a queen's attire:
And Edith, as she proudly might,
Wore it by virtue of her right
  As lady of the shire.

Alone, or at Sir Robert's side,
  Each day of all the season,
Whether she went to walk or ride,
She wore it as Sir Robert's bride—
  Yet for a secret reason.

The King to Edith Forne had said,
  'Take this, and though we part,
And though thou must Sir Robert wed
Yet wear my token on thy head,
  My image in thy heart.'

And so in every breeze that blew
  The lady's plume would quiver;
But though it was of royal hue,
Yet old Sir Robert never knew
  How royal was the giver.

XI.

One day, when Edith's girth was great,
  And when her time was nigh,

She took a stroll, alone and late,
In Osney mead, to meditate,
　And watch the sunset sky.

But though to watch the sunset sky
　Would oft to Edith bring
A drop of dew to either eye,
Yet now her lids were hot and dry
　With longing for the King.

She crossed her hands upon her breast,
　And sighed to see his face —
Till, as the sun illumed the West,
A bird called to her from his nest
　And mocked her doleful case.

XII.

This bird, a magpie, on an oak
　That shaded Osney mill,
Had saucy ways of hailing folk
And answering back to all who spoke,
　As any magpie will.

He fattened on the grains that dropped
　Around the miller's ricks,
And people who were passing stopped
To note a creature so full-cropped
　And tame and fond of tricks.

He dearly loved a bit of cheese,
　A cherry, or an apple,
Or a few pods of garden peas, —
And often Rudolph brought him these
　While on the way to chapel.

The pie would eat from Rudolph's hand,
  Or perch on Rudolph's shoulder:
But Edith did not understand
That such a bird was in the land,
  For Rudolph had not told her.

XIII.

The scarlet plume on Edith's head
  Flamed like the dying day,—
And so the magpie, hating red,
And being but a bird ill-bred,
  Shrieked, as a magpie may.

And Edith's scarlet plume without
  Matched with her heart within—
For there is many a dame, no doubt,
Who in a heart the most devout
  May hide a scarlet sin.

XIV.

Now Edith fair was just from prayer—
  For, at each vesper-tide,
She daily laid her unborn care
Low at the shrine—(it still is there)—
  Of chaste Saint Freidiswide[1].

(This saint was then of fresh renown,
  Not having long been dead,—
A virgin who had beaten down
A prince who came without his crown
  To steal her for his bed.)

---

[1] Spelt also Frideswide and Frevisse.

But prayer, that makes the pure so bold,
  Emboldened not the dame
Who heard the magpie scoff and scold—
For in the tattle which he told
  She heard him name her name.

XV.

Perhaps she heard some other word,
  Perhaps no word at all,
Yet at the jargon of the bird
Her soul was startled, as if stirred
  By Gabriel's trumpet-call.

'O Edith Forne! O wretch forlorn!'
  (So said the screaming pie)
'A dame were better never born
Than live to be a thing of scorn!
  False woman, fie! oh fie!

'Go moan and groan! thy sin is known!
  And it shall be proclaimed!
It shall on every wind be blown
Till thou be mocked in every zone,
  And round the world be shamed!'

XVI.

The bird, now bolder than before,
  Flew at her head, to scan
The fiery feather which she wore,
And which he pecked and pulled and tore—
  Till Edith turned and ran.

She ran with fleet and frightened feet
 To where her vesper prayer
In chaste Saint Freidiswide's retreat
Was scarcely cold—in hope to meet
 The priest still tarrying there.

And Rudolph was surprised, no doubt
 (As well he might have been),
That she, so lately rustling out,
Had turned her silken self about
 So soon to rustle in.

XVII.

'O holy father!' Edith cried,
 'I beg a boon of thee,
For as I walked the water-side
A great bird—bold, and fiery-eyed—
 Screamed at me from a tree!

'His cry was not a raven's croak,
 Nor yet an owlet's screech,
But as he chattered on his oak
I understood the tongue he spoke—
 For it was human speech.

'Full angerly and long he chid,
 And put me to the blush,
And seemed to hint at something hid,
And bade me do as he should bid
 Or he would never hush.

'But when I asked what I must do,
 His answer was not clear—
Though at my very face he flew
And thrust his beak of ebon hue
 Into my very ear.

'So come with me, I beg of thee,
From here to Osney mill,
And pray the bird upon the tree
To make his meaning plain to me
That I may do his will.

'For till he makes his meaning plain
I know not what to do,
And yet his loud accusing strain
Keeps ringing in my throbbing brain,
Piercing me through and through.'

XVIII.

Thus Edith said—with lips as pale
As if the dead should speak;
And then she covered with her veil
The red confusion which her tale
Flashed into either cheek.

XIX.

Now Rudolph, peering through the lace
Which Edith blushed behind,
Saw in the crimson of her face
The certain sign, the treacherous trace
That marked a guilty mind.

'My daughter, by my cowl and stole,
And by the rood,' quoth he,
'Thy look is full of dread and dole—
There is a sin upon thy soul—
Confess it now to me.'

XX.

At first the lady frowned a frown
  Of innocence austere,
But soon through all her silken gown
A tremor rippled up and down
  As pride gave way to fear.

At last, with all her brain aflame,
  And with a throbbing breast,
And with a tongue that shrank to name
The secret of her love and shame,
  Fair Edith thus confessed :—

XXI.

'O that, like pure Saint Freidiswide,
  Whom a prince vainly wooed,
I too, in cold and maiden pride,
With chaste refusal had denied
  A monarch when he sued!

'But ask of yonder marble dove,
  Perched on her virgin dust,
What maid, save such a saint above,
Could win on earth a monarch's love,
  And yet deny his lust?

'Before I wore Sir Robert's ring,
  Who took me for a maid,
I listened to my lord the King—
And now my sin—a living thing—
  Has made me sore afraid.

U

'Beneath my heart, from morn till night,
   From night agen till morn,
There leaps a babe, with main and might,
As if impatient for the light,
   And eager to be born.

'He thrusts me with his hands and feet,
   And waxes fierce and wild,
And burns with anger at the cheat—
For well he knows the base deceit,
   And is King Harry's child.

'The more he greatens with my girth,
   The more he scorns the lie,
And threatens that the whole wide Earth
Shall know how kingly is his birth,
   And how forsworn am I.

'But though he threaten, chide or warn,
   And though a prince he be,
I would not fear a babe unborn,
Save that the herald of his scorn
   Mocks me from yonder tree.

'For what will all the people say,
   And what my lord, forsooth,
If when they walk the King's highway
They hear a bird upon a spray
   Proclaim the dreadful truth?

'Oh would that I could cast a stone
   To crush his chattering beak
Ere yet to all the town be known
The horrid and accusing tone
   With which he dares to speak!'

XXII.

'Cast not a stone,' the priest replied,
　'Lest thou should'st miss thy aim,
And lest through all the country-side
The bird go flying far and wide,
　And tattle to thy shame.

'But let us hasten to his nest,
　And ask of him betimes—
Since now thy sin hath been confessed—
What penance will atone the best
　For such a crime of crimes.

'A sin, however deep the dye,
　If for a price compounded,
May still be hid from every eye—
For this is just the reason why
　Our Holy Church was founded.'

XXIII.

The twain then crossed, from dyke to weir,
　That meadow, green and level,
Wherein Sir Robert parked his deer,
And which Sir Robert would not hear
　Of selling to the Devil.

XXIV.

Now to the Devil (or the Deil,
　However named or writ)
A pious monk will never kneel,
Yet often slily will appeal
　To borrow subtile wit.

U 2

That Rudolph now such aid besought
  There cannot be a question,
For down he bent his brow in thought,
And from the Fire Infernal caught
  The flash of a suggestion.

At least, the glowing hope now thrilled
  The dame's devout confessor,
That any penance which he willed
Would be at any cost fulfilled
  By such a rich transgressor.

XXV.

But from so great and grand a dame,
  Trembling with guilt and terror,
What ought the Holy Church to claim
As proper price to purge her blame
  And expiate her error?

XXVI.

—To make the lady pure indeed,
  Chaste as before she fell,
The monk resolved, with holy greed,
To claim no less than Osney mead,
  An abbey and a bell!

XXVII.

On went the twain, with pious zeal,
  To where the Osney ferns
Still fringe the haunt of trout and eel,
And where the ancient water-wheel
  Of Osney mill still turns.

XXVIII.

Out hopping from his house of straw,
  Just wakened from a doze,
The bird whom Edith held in awe
Rebuked her with a churlish caw
  For troubling his repose.

Then down he perched without a fear
  On Rudolph's shaven crown,
And uttered words not very clear
Except to Rudolph's learnèd ear,—
  And plucked at Rudolph's gown.

Thrice flapped the wise prophetic bird
  The wings which he was preening,
And spake what Rudolph plainly heard,
Though Edith never caught the word
  Nor understood the meaning.

'Oh fie! oh fie!'—so said the pie—
  'What scruple hinders thee?
Shrink not to tell a cunning lie,
O beggar priest, and by-and-by
  An abbot thou shalt be!'

XXIX.

So said the pie—or so the priest
  Imagined him to say—
And the loud chatter so increased,
That Rudolph's silent scruples ceased
  And dumbly died away.

Then flapped the bird his wings once more
  And mounted to his nest,
While Edith, trembling as before,
And heart-sick to the very core,
  Stared mutely at the West.

XXX.

The West, that now was all ablaze,
  Set Osney flume aglow: .
For the clear water caught the rays
And flashed them up to Edith's gaze
  From crystal depths below.

XXXI.

The pie, by chance, let fall a glance
  Into the glassy flume,
And there, with curious eyes askance,
Saw mirrored in the clear expanse
  The lady's scarlet plume.

The scarlet plumes now being two
  (One nodding in the stream),
The pie was puzzled at the view,
And did what any pie would do—
  He gave a deafening scream.

The shriek was shrill, and seemed to fill
  The whole vast hollow sky,
For now the rumble of the mill
And other noisy things were still,
  All save the piping pie.

XXXII.

A sin awakes a thousand fears,
  And Edith in dismay,
Half frantic at the creature's jeers,
Pressed her white hands against her ears
  To keep the sound away.

But still she heard it all the same,
  For louder yet he jeered,
And chid her with such bitter blame
That, in her fright, the desperate dame
  Thus threatened whom she feared:—

XXXIII.

'Beware, O bird that canst not sing,
  How thou dost talk instead,
For thus to prate of such a thing
Is treason to our Lord the King,
  And he will have thy head!'

XXXIV.

Quoth Rudolph, 'Seek not to appal
  A pie so addle-pated,
For probably a head so small
Would fear but little, if at all,
  To be decapitated.

'But *I* can menace, not in vain,
  His very soul's salvation,
For I will bid the bird explain
His harsh portentous cry—on pain
  Of excommunication.'

So Rudolph, crucifix in hand,
  Spoke Latin to the pie,
And stood awhile as one may stand
Who, having made a dread demand,
  Awaits a meek reply.

XXXV.

The pie, unmeek, disdained to speak—
  And long the listeners waited,
·Until, in pique, he shook his beak,
And gave a shriek that seemed in Greek,
  Which Rudolph thus translated :—

'The bird,' quoth he, 'declares to me,
  That all the shameful story
Which he so trumpets from the tree
Is but a warning sent to thee
  Through him, from Purgatory.

'For Purgatory lies between
  The realms of bliss and woe,
And from its centre can be seen
The world on high, the world terrene,
  The world that lies below.

'All things that *have* been, all that *are,*
  And all that are to *be,*
The magpie knows—and from afar,
With wings as black as fire can char,
  He now hath flown to thee.

'He comes, a prophet, to foretell
  That to thy dire disgrace,
Unless thou hide thy secret well,
The eyes of Earth and Heaven and Hell·
  Shall see it in thy face.

'But thou canst hide it, if thou wilt,
  From every eye alike,
For Holy Church shall purge thy guilt
If thou wilt have an abbey built
  From here to yonder dyke.'

XXXVI.

Then Rudolph, breaking off a reed,
  Marked out upon the moor
From weir to dyke—across the mead—
The acres that the Church would need
  To make the lady pure.

Moreover, being worldly wise
  (For a true priest was he),
He pointed to the blushing skies,
And told how high the spire must rise,
  How big the bell must be.

XXXVII.

Sore troubled at the great demands
  Made by the greedy friar,
The trembling lady wrung her hands,—
For who could claim Sir Robert's lands
  Without Sir Robert's ire?

'But I will hie me home with speed
  And clasp his knees,' she cried,
'And I will plead for Osney mead:
But oh, my soul is sick indeed
  Lest I should be denied.'

XXXVIII.

Home to her tower in Oxford town
  The lady Edith sped,
And loosed the girdle of her gown,
And laid her burdened body down
  Beside her lord in bed.

Quoth she, 'What woman knows her fate
  Who has a babe to bear?
And since my travail will be great,
Death may await thy wedded mate
  As birth awaits thine heir.

'So if, my lord, thou holdest dear
  Heaven's gift to thee through me,
Make thou an offering—free and clear—
Of Osney mead, from dyke to weir,
  To Holy Church in fee.

'Make all the meadow hallowed ground,
  And lay me there with tears,
And build above my lowly mound
A lofty abbey, turret-crowned,
  To stand a thousand years.

'And in the belfry be there hung
  A bell of such a chime,
That ages hence it shall be rung,
And shall be called the sweetest tongue
  Of all the olden time.'

XXXIX.

Thus spake she to the doting man,
　Who, with his arms around her
(And wondering why her tongue so ran),
Half promised to fulfil the plan
　And be the abbey's founder.

'Swear it,' quoth she, 'that it may be
　A vow thou durst not break,
And I, thy faithful wife, agree—
Whatever thou shalt ask of me—
　To do it for thy sake.'

XL.

'I ask of thee,' quoth he, 'to bear
　No weak and puny girl,
But stalwart boy, robust and fair—
Fruit of my body, born my heir,
　And fit to be an Earl.'

XLI.

Then Edith laid the old man's hand
　Above the unborn child,
Who, like a billow to the land,
Now rolled, as when the storm is grand
　And when the wave is wild.

Quoth she, 'No weak and puny girl
　I to my lord shall bring,
Nor boy with spirit of a churl,
But man-child fit to be an Earl—
　Yea, fit to be a King.'

Her travail then, that very night,
  Rushed on with rapid throes,
Till piteous was the lady's plight,
Whose babe came leaping to the light
  Just as the morn arose.

She bore a boy—not slight and slim,
  With feeble cry and stir,
But lusty, and so large of limb
That mortal breath passed into *him*
  By passing out of *her*.

Yet ere the new-made mother died,
  She kissed the new-born thing,
While, more than with a mother's pride,
She blushed as in the babe she spied
  The image of the King.

XLII.

Sir Robert saw the lily wilt
  That bore the bud, and said
(Not guessing at the lady's guilt)
'O Rudolph, be an abbey built
  To shrine our sainted dead.

'So write for me to sign—a deed,
  Conveying free and clear
To Holy Church, through thee, the mead
In which my swans are wont to feed
  And where I park my deer.'

XLIII.

The abbey, as Sir Robert willed,
  Was modelled fair to see,
And took a thousand men to build,
And Rudolph's plan was all fulfilled,—
  For Abbot now was he!

He built, anent the altar high,
  A tomb all silver-tipped,
And brought the Lady there to lie,—
And years rolled by, and then the pie
  Was buried in the crypt.

And all the monks with one accord
  Said, 'Let the bird be sainted!'
So, on the walls, for his reward
(With other angels of the Lord),
  His effigy was painted.

XLIV.

Those monks are now in Heaven or Hell
  (Or some in each—who knows?)
And long ago their abbey fell,
But nightly yet its booming bell
  Tells how that abbey rose.

The bell that hung in Osney spire
  Now hangs in Wolsey tower,
And with a tongue that cannot tire,
Whose echo rolls through half the shire,
  It clangs the curfew-hour.

It strikes a hundred strokes and one,
  With measured ding and dong,—
As if the ringing, when begun
Instead of ever being done,
  Would roar the whole night long.

O roaring Tom, be nightly rung!
  Or if thy curfew fail,
Still be thy heavy hammer swung—
If only that thy brazen tongue
  May tell thy brazen tale!

———•◦•———

FIN DE SIÈCLE.

(EIGHTEENTH CENTURY.)

THUS wrote the merry Abbot of Saint Cyr,
  Who came (as many of his order do)
To Paris in the springtime of the year,
  Without his hood, to spend a week or two :—

'Dear Padre, through the town a river flows,
  And all along the banks on either side
Sit patient anglers, either in a doze,
  Or watching bobs that doze upon the tide.

'Full forty thousand hooks from morn till night
  Lie baited in the river every day,
Yet hardly once a year a fish will bite,
  Or if he does, he always gets away.

'So in this wicked city, O mon frère,
  I entertain the hope (if not the wish)
To pass my week as free from every snare
  And safe from all temptation as a fish.'

Thus wrote the merry Abbot of Saint Cyr,
  Whose hope (if not his wish) was brought to
      nought,—
For in his innocence, without a fear,
  He nibbled at temptation, and was caught.

DON CUPID'S TRICK.

THE little boy called Love lay dead,
  And on his tiny tomb
Some carven letters sweetly said
That for a day his heart had bled,
  And named the maid for whom.

This maid, on coming to the mound,
  Felt a remorseful pain,
And kissed his image, clasped it round,
Grew pale, and sank upon the ground,
  And shed an April rain.

Then, like a prison-bursting thief,
  Outleapt the bounding boy,
Whose stay in Hadés had been brief—
For hardly had he died of grief
  Than he arose for joy.

'What means this caper?' cried the maid,
  As in his arms she sank,
And half-delighted, half-afraid,
Began most sweetly to upbraid
  This most audacious prank.

'Fair maid, your scorn of me,' he said,
　'Was all a make-believe,
And put the thought into my head
To play the trick of being dead,
　To see how you would grieve.'

She dashed with anger from her eyes
　Her all-too-tender tears,—
And greatly to the lad's surprise,
And heedless of his woeful cries,
　She boxed his little ears.

'Back to your tomb, and there abide!
　And quit it not!' quoth she
(And added, locking him inside),
'I never loved you till you *died*
　For just your love of *me*.'

EPIGRAM

ON THE FIGHTING EDITOR OF THE MORNING BROWBEATER.

THIS quarrelsome old curmudgeon,
　Whose pen was a daily bludgeon,
　　Would laugh at the rogues he bruised,—
　　　Yet *he* (as we learn)
　　　When whacked in return,
　　Was never at all amused,
But took it in *very* high dudgeon,—
This quarrelsome old curmudgeon.

ANACREON'S DISCOVERY.

B.C. 541.

I ONCE in the Vale of Tempé
   Went roaming the whole day long
In quest of a glimpse of beauty
   To serve as a theme of song.

I looked at the mists of morning
   That seemed, as they fringed the sun,
Like fleeces that far out-goldened
   The trophy that Jason won.

I saw in the burning zenith
   The face of the bashful moon,—
Diana and great Apollo
   Saluting each other at noon.

I watched as the train of Hesper
   In timorous twos and threes
Shone down from the heights of Heaven
   And up from the depths of seas.

But ever at each new splendour
   That followed from morn till night
I felt in my soul a sadness
   From gazing at what was bright.

And ever the brightest sunshine
   Would sadden my soul the most,—
As if in the smile of Nature
   I also beheld her ghost.

x

I marvelled how sky and ocean,
  How mountain and shining plain,
Could shadow and pall my spirit
  And give me a subtile pain.

I said, 'There is something lacking
  In sights of the land and sea:
Such beauty may comfort others,
  It never can comfort *me*!'

Then, weary of foot with tramping,
  And weary of heart and head,
I fretted and yawned and murmured;
  And vowing a vow, I said:

'I never will kill a tortoise
  To make for myself a lyre
Till first I have seen a vision
  That kindles my blood with fire!'

Just then, from a lamp-lit window
  I chanced as I sauntered by,
To catch, through the vines of ilex,
  The flash of a woman's eye.

I saw it for just a moment,—
  But moments are ages long;
And now, and from now for ever,
  That vision shall be my song[1].

---

[1] Anacreon, the ancient Greek poet, was born B.C. 562, and is styled (from his birthplace) the Swan of Teos. He once received from King Polycrates a gift of five talents, and was so excited at having such a sum of money that for three nights he could not sleep. He then returned the money in full, with the message that it cost him too much trouble to keep it. Having written many songs in praise of wine, he died from swallowing the seed of a grape.

HOMEWARD BOUND.

FLY fast, O ship! the sea is wide,
  My love is on the other side:
How far the East seems from the West!
When shall I clasp her, breast to breast?

When shall I kiss her, lip to lip?
My heart flies faster than the ship!
My darling dwells beside the sea
And looks and yearns and waits for me.

Or have I stayed too long away?
The world is full of change, they say:
In all the changes that occur
What if there be a change in her!

O breeze that bloweth good and ill,
Come whisper if she loves me still!
Give answer, O ye billows blue,
And tell me if she still is true!

The heedless wind and heartless wave
Give not the answer that I crave:
What if she be as wild and gay
And full of fickleness as they!

I swear by all the heavens above
I love her with a changeless love!
Beyond where sky and ocean blend
I love her to the world's far end!

Fly fast, O ship! and to the gale
Spread every snowy swelling sail!
Then nevermore shall land or sea
Divide agen my love from me!

A TIFF IN ARCADIA.

YOUNG Florian was a love-sick swain,
    Who in his joy and pain
(For love has both) thus said and sighed
    Ere yet he won his bride:

'Ye Gods, if when she comes to-day
    Her answer still be nay,
I then will take my flock and crook
    And seek another brook.

'I will go East, I will go West,
    And never will I rest
Until I find the healing stream
    That sparkles in my dream.

'For all our shepherds tell a tale
    Of how in Tempé's vale
There is a magic fount that flows
    To heal a lover's woes.

'And once, to quench a shepherd's thirst,
    That fountain upward burst
And flowed with crystal water chill
    Until he drank his fill.

'Then straightway, like a phantom weird,
    The fountain disappeared,
And the bewildered fool forgot
    To mark the magic spot.

'That silly shepherd never knew
    Whether the rain or dew
Or melting of Mount Ida's snow
    Made the charmed water flow.

' He only knew that from the bank
   Whereon he knelt and drank
He rose refreshed, and nevermore
   Had heartache as before.

' For she who with her haughty frown
   Had crushed his spirit down,
Was from his memory swept away
   All in a single day!

' Oh would that I myself had quaffed
   That same oblivious draught,
And now were cured of all the pain
   Of having loved in vain!

' To-day she will agen be here,
   And she will mock and jeer
Till I shall wish, amid her scorn,
   I never had been born!

' Ye Gods, inspire me to forget
   All passion, all regret,—
All image of her, I implore,
   Now and for evermore!

' Yet nay, ye Gods, deny my prayer!
   She is so pure and fair
That be her answer what it will
   I must adore her still!'

—The maid, who stood behind an oak,
   Heard every word he spoke;
And forth she stepped, and blushed, and sighed,—
   And Florian won his bride.

COUNT GHORKO'S COURTSHIP.

A. D. 1742.

I LOVED Honora, and she was kind
  (Or kind for a livelong day);
She then, in a temper, changed her mind—
  For so a lady may.

She changed her mind (as a lady will)—
  She said to me, 'Go thy way!'
And forth in a fury, pale and ill,
  I went—yet longed to stay.

She watched me then from her window-pane,
  And beckoned and seemed to say,
'A wooer may woo and not in vain—
  Despite the lady's nay.'

I turned and climbed to her parapet,
  And pushing the vines away,
I captured her then—and hold her yet—
  For ever and a day!

THE TRAGIC FATE OF SOCRATES.

HIS wife was old
  And was a scold.

THE BRIGAND'S VESPER-HYMN.

A.D. 1630.

Osmin d'Ordrado was a brigand in the Pyrenees. He had no wife, but lived on a memory and a hope. In his bivouac after supper, to please his comrades, he sometimes sang what he called his vesper-hymn, as follows:—

MY darling and I together
    Stood under a lilac-tree:
She gave me her vow of betrothal
    And sealed it with kisses three.

The balms that the Queen of Sheba
    Brought Solomon from the South
Were nought to my darling's kisses—
    She kissed me upon the mouth.

And after her trine of kisses,
    I gave for her plighted hand
A ring with the stones in triplet,
    Like stars in Orion's band.

The stones were the brightest jewels
    That ever were lit with flame!
They twinkled as if they knew her!
    She gave to them each a name!

The name of the first was Honour,
    The name of the next was Truth,
The name of the last and brightest
    Was Hope as the Star of Youth.

The ring? It is on her finger,
    It burns in her graveyard clay!
She wears it arrayed for bridal—
    Awaiting her wedding-day.

The priests in their masses for her
Proclaim her a saint above!
—O darling, be Saint or Angel,
Yet *I* am thy Lover, love!

Thy lilac! It now is withered!
But ever Orion's band
Comes tripled to Heaven, to tell me
That *there* I shall clasp thy hand.

SOLILOQUY OF LAZARUS.

A FACE-CLOTH on my face? I draw no breath?
Bound hand and foot? Laid in a stony cave?
O Christ of Nazareth, I am in my grave!
Speak, Lord of Life, and call Thy dead from death!
—Thou speakest! For I hear a voice that saith
'Where have ye laid him? Lazarus, come forth!'
My tomb is cracking like the frozen North
When Spring has resurrection from the ground!
I breathe—I stir—my pulse begins to bound—
My heart leaps up against my folded hands!
Off with this winding-sheet that wraps me round!
—Weep not, O Master! I have burst my bands!
Thy Lazarus comes forth, and here he stands!

THE BARREN FIG-TREE'S REPLY.

'The time of figs was not yet.'—St. Mark.

I AM accurst—I wilt—I fade—I die!
  For hither yestermorn a Nazárene
(A God, they say, yet of a mortal mien)
Came blighting me with lightning from His eye:
And now agen to-day He draweth nigh,
  Followed by many a gazing Gergesene
  Agape with wonder that a tree so green
Should wither at a word and shrink and dry,
  Ready for axe to cut and fire to burn!
  Tell me, O Prophet (for I now discern
That Thou art more than rabbi or than seer),
  What was my fault, or my offence, or crime?
  Thou camest for my figs before their time:
How could I yield them ere their season due?
  How could I haste for Thee the rolling year?
Why didst Thou curse me then, O cruel Jew?
  Shall I be curst, yet curse not in return?
  O Teacher, Thou hast yet a thing to learn:
  I know an ancient prophecy that saith
  How Christ the Lord shall die a shameful death.
If Thou, O smiter of my bloom, be He—
Die Thou upon a thrice-accursèd Tree!

ABELARD'S FIRST HOPE.

PARIS, A.D. 12—.

THE maiden of my heart's delight,
  Who tempts me with a face too fair,
Is not a nun, yet morn and night
  She bows her pious head in prayer.

I dare not speak to her of love,
  Nor drop a hint of love's desire,
For eyes like hers, lit from above,
  Sparkle, but not with earthly fire.

I kiss her only on her hand—
  Devoutly—at her finger-tips:
What would she guess or understand
  Were I to venture on her lips?

What if the passion in me pent,
  Which I have hid for many days,
Should of a sudden find a vent
  And burst into an open blaze!

Could I—so rash a fool—be sure
  That she who is so chaste and chill,
So proud, so passionless and pure,
  Would pardon and would love me still?

I dare not put her to the test:
  I only ask a saint so fair,
Not for a pillow on her breast,
  But a remembrance in her prayer!

THE SHEIK'S ENIGMA.

THE cunning Sheik of Carmahan [1]
(A very droll facetious man
Whose wit was hard to comprehend)
Thus wrote a riddle to his friend:

'I had a Pearl of greater price
Than all the Twelve of Paradise!
This gem (my fault must be confessed)
I wore too vainly on my breast.

'For though I kept my precious prize
Enwrapped and hid from envious eyes,
Yet if my bosom had been bare,
They must have spied my jewel there.

'Once on a wild and stormy day
A whirlwind shook my pearl away:
I rushed in frenzy up and down,
And hunted for it through the town.

'I searched and searched, from nook to nook,
Yet all the while forgot to look
Within the one and only shrine
Where I had hid this gem of mine.

'All night my brain was in a whirl
Lest I should never find my pearl,
A treasure which to me was worth
All other precious things on earth.

[1] In Persia.

'The morning came and lit the skies,
And yet to my benighted eyes
The world was dark, or I was blind,
Or else a madness seized my mind.

'At last, despairing in my quest,
I dashed my hand against my breast,
And with relentless stroke on stroke
I bruised my heart until it broke.

'O happy bruise! O soothing smart!
For by the breaking of my heart
I found my Pearl just as before,
Hid in my bosom's very core!

' Now therefore tell me, if you can,'
(Thus wrote the Sheik of Carmahan,)
'What hidden meaning you divine
In this mysterious screed of mine?'

'Your precious Pearl,' his friend replied,
'Was Argazil, your youngest bride:
You quarrelled, and she ran away—
But she has since come back to stay.'

A VALENTINE.

(With a Spray of Snowdrops.)

O CHILLING maid, whose frosty smile
 Benumbs my heart and reason,
Accept in thy most freezing style
 This emblem of the season.

KING JOHN'S RIDE TO RUNNYMEDE.

It is a tradition in Oxford that on the evening of June 14, A.D. 1215, while King John was amusing the lower orders of the people with a grand fête of gross character, he received from his revolted Barons—then in arms against him throughout all England—their final and peremptory summons commanding him to meet them on the following morning at Runnymede for the signing of Magna Charta. The King's fulfilment of this summons required him to take a night's ride of four or five hours on a good horse. There is a rival tradition that he rode to Runnymede, not from Oxford, but from Windsor—a much shorter gallop. The two traditions constitute a duplicate historical foundation for the accompanying ballad.

1.

THE times were ill in England,
 And boded worse and worse—
For woe befalls a kingdom
 Whose King becomes its curse.

King John—the vilest monarch
 That ever wore a crown—
Had spread at Beaumont·Palace
 A feast for Oxford town.

(For by his wine and wassail,
 His music and his sport,
He hoped to win the People,
 Since he had lost the Court.)

So all the town was bidden,
 And all the town must go;
For whoso dared be absent
 Would be the tyrant's foe.

The brave might scorn his bidding,
  And bide his royal hate,
But all his fawning caitiffs
  Would throng his palace gate.

II.

It was that proud old palace
  Whereof is left no stone,
Yet which, in all its glory,
  Was once King Richard's own.

But sad was Merrie England—
  For death had barbed a dart,
And tipped its point with poison,
  And pricked King Richard's heart[1].

Locked in a silver casket,
  And set with jewels fine,
The Heart that was the Lion's
  Was now a Holy Shrine.

And at the Shrine the Nation
  Had prayed to Heaven, and said,
'O crown the Lamb of England
  King in the Lion's stead!'

But ere the prayer had ended
  The gentle Lamb was slain,
And to the Lion's palace
  The Wolf stole in to reign.

---

[1] King Richard I of England, while reconnoitring the Castle of Chalus in Limousin, approached so near its walls that a bowman on the parapet hit him with an arrow. The arrow was envenomed, and the wound was mortal. The chroniclers delight to tell of the King's magnanimity to the skilful archer, who on being brought as a prisoner to the royal bedside, received the dying monarch's pardon, and was, dismissed in peace.

III.

The Wolf must have his orgies—
    And so, in Beaumont Hall,
To-night he holds a revel,
    And loud will be the brawl.

Crowned with a wreath of ivy
    And clad in white [1] King John
Salutes a thousand feasters
    And bids the feast go on.

It is the King's own supper;
    And yet he scarcely sups,
But stares at the carousers
    That clink to him their cups.

It is the King's own palace,
    And where his court should be—
Yet whom does England's monarch
    Look vainly round to see?

IV.

He sees no earl nor baron,
    No knight from any shire,
No burgess from the townhouse,
    No hoary-headed sire,—

No black-robed judge nor abbot,
    No hero battle-scarred,
Nor from a college-cloister
    A scholar or a bard.

---

[1] Like all the Plantagenets, King John was strikingly handsome and imposing; and though he had now hardly reached his forty-eighth year, yet like an octogenarian he already had snow-white hair; and his festal garments were of white, to match with it. His tunic (we are told) was white damask. His gloves (which were also white) had rubies on one hand and sapphires on the other. His white baldric was studded with diamonds.

The town had wits and worthies
  (For never town had more),
But though the King had bid them,
  They darkened not his door.

They bore no more his banner,
  Nor bowed before his throne,
Nor gathered at his banquet—
  They left the King alone.

V.

Yet not alone, for varlets
  Most villainous and vile
Now sat where lords and ladies
  Were wont to sit erewhile.

For when a house grows rotten
  The vermin will intrude,—
And now the proud old palace
  Reeked with the low and lewd.

At all the ten great tables
  They crowded every bench,
And every tipsy gallant
  Drank with a wanton wench.

VI.

In spite of flute and tabor,
  In spite of mime and clown,
In spite of jest and laughter,
  The monarch wore a frown.

The merry mob grew noisy,
  And as the noise increased
The King grew mute as marble,
  While others kept the feast.

He sat as in a stupor
   Or in a dumb despair,
Each hand upon a griffin
   That knobbed his oaken chair.

He clenched the knobs with fury[1]
   As if the carven things
Might be the imps of devils,
   And bode the death of Kings.

VII.

For now the Wolf of England
   Was sickened with the fear
That once again his hunters
   Were on his track and near.

He knew that all his Barons
   Had on their oaths agreed
To muster on the morrow—
   In arms—at Runnymede.

In arms? A peaceful Council
   To meet in battle-line?
Yea, England asks a Charter,
   Which England's King must sign.

Thrice hath he scorned to sign it,—
   And now, from all his realm,
His Barons go to brave him,
   And go with sword and helm.

---

[1] There was a vein of madness in King John, for in his ungovernable rage he would roll on the ground, biting at sticks and stones, and foaming at the mouth.

If further he defy them,
  Their weapons they will draw [1],—
For Kings, though high in England,
  Are not above the law!

VIII.

—The eve is mild and misty,
  Warm with the breath of June,
And in the sky a circle
  Begins to rim the moon.

On such a night graves open
  And spectres stalk abroad,
And at the evil portent
  The coward King is awed.

—What sees the startled monarch?
  What is it makes him rise,
And thrust his hands before him
  To hide it from his eyes?

He sees a Wandering Spirit
  Whose body has not found
A grave in any churchyard
  Or consecrated mound!

---

[1] The author of *Magna Charta* was probably Stephen Langton, the Archbishop of Canterbury—the greatest statesman of his day—the chief pillar, at once, both of church and state. He was the prime mover and moulding mind of the peaceful revolution against King John—a revolution which, except for the masterly policy of Langton, might have cost a civil war. The Archbishop's chief associate was William Marshall, Earl of Pembroke—a grave and lofty-minded patriot whom Macaulay has eloquently honoured. The third principal figure in the movement was Fitzwalter, a fiery soldier—who was ready, in case of need, to take the field at the head of the joint troops of the Earls and Barons. Fitzwalter's daughter Matilda—with whom King John had had a disastrous love-affair—had been subsequently imprisoned by the

It is as fair a Phantom
  As ever trod the air,
A youth of blooming visage
  And long and golden hair.

And in his breast his death-wound
  Begins agen to bleed;
And now he points his finger
  At him who did the deed!

IX.

And now the kingly culprit,
  Dumb, yet with chattering teeth,
Stands shivering, till his sword-blade
  Rattles within its sheath!

He feels an icy coldness,
  He feels a burning flame;
For great as is his terror,
  Still greater is his shame.

He cringes to the Shadow,
  And asks with bated breath,
'Did not my two-edged dagger
  Deal out to thee thy death?

'Then tell me—since thy carcass
  Was sunken in the Seine—
How is thy ghost in England,
  O Arthur of Bretagne[1]?'

King in the Tower of London in order 'that she might tell no tales.'
During this imprisonment she died.   Her death added a personal
bitterness to her father's hatred of the King.   An analysis of *Magna
Charta* is given in the Appendix.

[1] It was the contemporary opinion of all Christendom—and no
testimony has since reversed it—that the Prince was stabbed by the
King's own hand.

X.

Then spake the Wraith, and answered
  (For so a spirit can),
'I am the Prince of England,
  Although a murdered man.

'Up from the rolling river,
  Up from my slimy bed,
I come, for England calls me!
  I hear, though I be dead!

'In England's hour of peril,
  At England's high command,
The dead are like thè living,
  And rise to free the land!'

Thus spake the bleeding Shadow,
  And melted into air,
While still the King kept gazing
  As if it still were there.

And what if all the feasters
  Had seen the filmy thing!
But no, the Prince's spectre
  Was only for the King.

XI.

Draining his trembling goblet
  To drown the fear he felt,
The tyrant spilt some wine-drops
  Against his buckled belt.

The drops were three red splashes,—
  And the King scowled, and said,
'Would that these drops of purple
  Were gouts of blood instead!—

'One from the heart of Pembroke,
  One from Fitzwalter's own,
And one from flinty Langton's
  (If blood be in a stone).

'And would that I could poniard
  Each rebel of their host,
Till every mortal traitor
  Should be a bleeding ghost!'

Thus to himself he muttered,—
  And then to all the crowd
(Who hushed their buzz to listen)
  He thus harangued aloud:

XII.

'I hate their hellish Charter—
  The Devil's own device:
So hark how I have spurned it,
  Not once, nor twice, but thrice!

'The Barons first, as Pilgrims,
  Swore on Saint Edmund's tomb[1]
That I must sign their Charter
  Or meet a Tyrant's doom.

'But I, the Lord's Anointed,
  Said to those impious men,
"Shall I, the King of England,
  Unking me with a pen?   ,

'"I would not sign your Charter
  Though Gabriel from the sky
Should cast the scroll before me
  And bid me sign or die!"

[1] In the town of Bury St. Edmunds.

XIII.

'They dogged me then to Brackley—
　Where I, who love the chase,
Kept hounds of better breeding,
　Curs of a nobler race!

'Quoth Langton, "Sign the Charter,
　Or never from to-day
Shalt thou have leave in Britain
　To bring a buck to bay!"

'I answered, "Britain's forests
　Are mine, and mine alone!
—What fool would sign a warrant
　To will away his own?"

'Quoth they, "Forfeit thy forests,
　Or forfeit else thy crown[1]!"
And off they drew their gauntlets,
　As if to fling them down.

'"Fling down instead your Charter,"
　Quoth I, "and let it rot!
For though ye threat till Doomsday,
　Yet will I sign it not!"

XIV.

'They mobbed me last in London,
　And nailed against my door
The screed which I had mocked at,
　And spat upon before.

---

[1] The forestry clause of the Charter is given in the Appendix.

'Pembroke was there with menace,
  Langton with curse and ban,
And mailed Fitzwalter, leading
  The pikemen of his clan.

'I scoffed at all their pleading;
  I scowled at all their train:
"To me," quoth I, "the sceptre—
  To you, the yoke and chain!"

'And ever as they urged me
  This answer still I gave:
"The King may be your Tyrant—
  He shall not be your slave!"

xv.

'Yet now agen these rebels,
  Who thrice have felt my scorn,
Have writ to me to meet them
  Upon the morrow morn.

'Ye gods! the quiet morning
  Shall hear a roar indeed!
A meadowful of asses
  Will bray at Runnymede!

'But let them sign their Charter
  With twenty signet-rings,—
One signet shall be lacking,
  And that shall be the King's!'

—Then from the ten long tables
  Burst a tempestuous blast
Of wild and windy plaudits,
  Each louder than the last.

XVI.

'*Who* says my Court has quit me?
  It is a *lie*!' cried he;
'The Court is ... where the King is ...
  My courtiers? ... they are *ye*!

'What though your breaths be reeking
  With smell of sink and slum?
What though your betters brand ye
  As England's froth and scum?

'The froth and scum of England
  (Like slime of other slop)
Shall not be slow in mounting!—
  Its place is at the top!

'Ye louts, ye shall be lordlings!—
  As high as ye were low!—
For whoso would be noble,
  The King can make him so.

XVII.

'My bounty shall be boundless;
  My gifts shall never cease;
For I will shear the Barons
  And give to ye the fleece!

'Ye shall have caps with feathers;
  Ye shall have boots with bells;
Ye shall have silks from Flanders
  To deck your damozels.

'So drink, ye carls and carlines!
  Drink to your King! drink deep!
The night was meant for wassail;
  The day was meant for sleep.

'Carouse from now till midnight;
　Carouse from then till morn!
This was King Richard's palace—
　The house where he was born.

XVIII.

'Why was I born his brother,
　Except to make his throne,
His diadem, his sceptre,
　His Lion Heart my own?

'His Lion Heart, though shrivelled
　Within its silver shrine,
Yet beats agen, defiant,
　Here in this breast of mine!

'So here in Richard's palace
　I swear by Richard's shade
That I will teach these Barons
　How Kings shall be obeyed!

'The lord of any castle
　Is lord of all its churls:
My castle is the kingdom—
　My serfs are Dukes and Earls.

'From *them* to *me* be homage
　And not from *me* to *them*!
Down let them kneel, these traitors!
　And kiss my garment's hem.'

XIX.

—Then once again the plaudits
　Were wild and long and loud,
Until a hush of wonder
　Fell on the startled crowd.

For now the Curfew sounded;
  And ere its clang was still
The clattering hoofs of horses
  Grew loud on Beaumont Hill.

The horsemen as they halted
  Sent up a bugle-call
That rose from moat to merlon
  And pierced the Banquet Hall.

XX.

The drunk and drowsy warder
  Who staggered to the gate,
Cried out, 'What lousy laggards
  Be ye who come so late?'

'Three noblemen of England,'
  Quoth they, 'who come to bring
A message from the Kingdom,
  A mandate to the King.'

Then Pembroke and Fitzwalter
  (Each with his armour on)
And Langton (with his crozier)
  Strode in before King John.

XXI.

.The Royal Wolf, whose hunters
  Had tracked him to his lair,
Flashed from his angry eyeballs
  A very wolf's own glare.

But at such bold intruders
  He gasped and grew afraid,
And fumbled at his sword-hilt,
  Yet dared not draw the blade.

He writhed as if the Furies
  Had lashed him with their whips—
Till sweat was on his forehead,
  And froth was on his lips.

Then reddening with his frenzy
  And whitening with his fright,
He cried, 'Why come ye hither—
  Unbidden—and at night?'

XXII.

'O King, thy angry Kingdom
  Hath sent us,' answered they,
'To bring to thee a mandate
  Which thou must now obey.

'We come while bats are flying,
  And while the owlet screams,
Lest, had we come by daylight,
  We had disturbed thy dreams.

'But sleep not thou to-morrow,
  For thou the morn shalt rue
Unless thou meet thy Barons
  At drying of the dew!

'They call their meeting early,
  Before the sun is hot—
And hot will be their anger
  If thou shalt meet them not.

'For if thou flout the Council
  That meets upon the morn,
Far better, O thou tyrant,
  Thou never hadst been born!'

XXIII.

Uprose the maddened monarch
  And strode across the floor,
And flung a casement open
  To mark the moon once more.

The silver orb had mounted
  Till it was zenith high,
And now its misty circle
  Was shrouding half the sky.

The boding sign struck terror
  Into the tyrant's mind;
He dared not venture forward,
  He dared not stay behind.

He turned him to the feasters,
  And said, 'The feast is done!'
And all the dumbstruck rabble
  Departed one by one.

The spacious hall grew empty:
  The three grim lords alone
Stood with the trembling tyrant,
  Who tottered like his throne.

XXIV.

He flung his crown of ivy
  In rage at Langton's feet,
And cried, 'Trample it, traitor,
  Thy treason be complete!

'Archbishop or archdevil,
  A curse be on thy soul!
But I will sign thy Charter—
  Fetch me the hated scroll!'

'Go seek it *thou*,' quoth Langton,
  'It seeks not *thee* agen !
It asks of Kings the homage
  That Kings have asked of men.

'This homage thou must render;
  Which if to-morrow's sun
Shall see thee slow in doing,
  Thou art thyself undone.

'So choose thee from thy stable
  Thy horse of fleetest speed,
And ride with us till morning
  From here to Runnymede.

'There, on the greenest island
  In all the river's length,
The Council of the Kingdom
  Will meet in battle-strength.

XXV.

'And first, in friendly concord
  (For they be peaceful men),
They will unroll their parchment,
  And give thee ink and pen.

'But then each belted Baron
  Must see thee sign and seal,
Or else from every scabbard
  Shall flash a blade of steel.

'So spring into thy stirrup—
  For if thou tardy be,
Another King in England
  Shall sign and seal for thee.'

XXVI.

Cried he, 'I have a stallion,
  The fleetest ever foaled,
His forefeet shod with silver,
  His hindfeet shod with gold;

'His speed is like the falcon's,
  Or like an arrow's flight,—
But, by Saint Anne! he stirs not
  Out of his stall to-night.'

Quoth they, 'Then on the morrow,
  O King, thy kingly sway
Shall have an end in England
  Ere ending of the day.'

'Bring me,' cried he, 'my charger,
  My red-roan Arab steed!
He is no English traitor,
  To fail me in my need!

'*He* never has betrayed me,
  Nor wished me overthrown!
What friend have I so loyal?
  I have but him alone!'

XXVII.

Out of the monarch's stable,
  With stately prance and bound,
Was led his horse Abdallah,
  Who neighed and pawed the ground.

The King caressed his stallion,
  Yet muttered, 'By Saint Anne!
I mount not at the mandate
  Of any mortal man.'

'Then mount at *mine,* thou tyrant!'
  Outspake a voice, whose tone
Was not from tongue of mortal,
  But was a dead man's moan.

The guilty King, who heard it,
  Made haste to give it heed;
For now the wound was gaping,
  And he could see it bleed.

And the King cried, 'O Arthur,
  Hide thou thy bleeding breast,
Or haste thee back to Heaven,
  And I will heed thy hest.'

XXVIII.

Then by the moonlit river,
  And through the dewy gorse,
King John to fullest gallop
  Goaded his fleetest horse.

And since the royal charger
  Was fleeter than the three,
The King rode as the leader,—
  For so a King should be.

XXIX.

—The moon went down in darkness
  Ere yet the East grew grey;
And on and on the monarch
  Galloped and led the way.

Through twenty sleeping hamlets
  Along the riverside
The King and his three convoys
  Kept on their nightlong ride.

No word spake he to either,
  But to his horse alone;
Who pricked his ears to listen,
  Obeying every tone.

(More royal than his rider!—
  For not the whole Earth's face
Could show a horse so noble
  That bore a man so base.)

XXX.

·—The cocks had done their crowing,
  The flocks were at their feed,
When Lord Fitzwalter's bugle
  Rang out at Runnymede.

Across the dewy island
  So merrily it rang
That half a score of trumpets
  Made answer with a clang.

The Barons all were waiting,
  Each with his weapon drawn;—
For never broke in Britain
  A day with such a dawn. ·

The larks flew back from heaven,
  The bees rushed from the hive,
The field-mice scampered winking
  To see the King arrive.

And if the King's arrival
  Had been an hour too late,
He would have lost his sceptre,
  And met a tyrant's fate.

Abashed before his Barons
  The humbled King drew near,
And though he was their monarch
  He did not seem their peer.

XXXI.

Those five-and-twenty Barons,
  Each with his armèd train,
Stood forth with banners flying
  As on a battle-plain.

Joined to the living Council
  There hovered overhead
The unseen mighty conclave
  Of England's patriot dead.

Yea, Heaven and Earth together
  Were there—a single band;
For both the dead and living
  Arose to free the land.

XXXII.

And when before the despot
  The Charter was unrolled,
Thus ran the precious writing
  In letters as of gold:

'The Baron in his Castle,
  The Yeoman at his plough,
Shall make the law of England
  To which the King shall bow.'

The tyrant signed it, sealed it,
  And knelt to it in awe,—
For Kings, though high in England,
  Are not above the law!

z

XXXIII.

From age to age in honour,
  The scroll is handed down,
A law above the statute,
  A power above the crown.

It is a Nation's refuge
  Against a despot's will:
For while the land has monarchs
  It may have tyrants still.

So, till the Earth shall perish
  The Charter must remain;
Or till in Merrie England
  There be no King to reign [1].

———◆———

LINES BY THE NEXT POPE.

'The present Prisoner of the Vatican, Leo XIII, is one of the most advanced Republicans in Europe.'—*Le Temps.*

A.D. 2000.

I BLESS the world with all my heart
    And every living thing
Except a mortal set apart
    And wrongly called a King.
—The only rightful King is He
    Who hears our Paternosters!
—The rest, whoever they may be,
    Are but impostors.

---

[1] King John, who up to the time of the signing of Magna Charta had reigned seventeen years, was so broken in spirit by the triumph of the Barons, that he died a twelvemonth afterward, aged forty-nine :— leaving behind him, down to the present day, the worst repute that has ever attached to the memory of an English King.

GRANDFATHER SILVERBUCKLE'S TALK.

(FOR CHILDREN.)

YOU clamorous little darlings
   Who clamber about my knee
And pester me for a story,
   Now what shall the story be ?

I happen to know a fable
   Not hard to be understood,
And if you will only heed it
   Perhaps it will do you good.

Since Adam and Eve were little
   It always has been the rule
That even the smallest children
   Shall never be late at school.

Now three little barefoot urchins,
   Who started for school one day,
All suddenly took a fancy
   To stop on the road to play.

They knew they were very naughty,
   For always a voice within
Gives warning to every creature
   Who goes to commit a sin.

But always the paths of pleasure
   Are tempting to tiny feet,
And off and away the urchins
   All ran to a field of wheat.

The wheat being tall, it hid them
   As if it had been a screen,
Yet ever the wee transgressors
   Were fearful of being seen.

They talked of their plans in whispers
  As low as the hum of bees,
And wisely began their pleasure
  By not being hard to please.

They gathered the great red poppies,
  They hunted the dragon-flies,
They sported till sparks of rapture
  Came flashing from all their eyes.

But bliss is a transient blessing;
  The merry are quick to mourn:
The first of the barefoot truants
  Trod suddenly on a thorn;

The second was stung by hornets;
  The other espied a snake;—
So each little heart was beating
  As if it would bleed and break.

They turned on their heels with terror,
  And fled like a herd of deer,—
For keen is the pang of conscience,
  And swift are the feet of fear.

Ere ever the dews of morning
  Had dried on a bud or leaf,
The day of the stolen frolic
  Had come in an hour to grief.

A fable should have a moral.
  The moral of mine is plain:
A pleasure that is forbidden
  Is certain to end in pain.

KOSSUTH ON GORGEI'S CAPITULATION.

A.D. 1849.

I COULD have better borne the blow
    And throbbed with less of fever
Had he, the Traitor, been my foe
And not my Captain,—whom I know
    As my deceiver.

Is ancient fealty at an end?
    Is shining honour rusted?
Alas, the blow to which I bend
Was from 'mine own familiar friend
    In whom I trusted.'

To such a blow what balm can be?
    O God, it healeth never!
For even if the land be free,
My heart, a wounded aloe-tree,
    Must bleed for ever[1]!

---

[1] Gorgei, the Hungarian General of 1848, and the friend and comrade of Kossuth, unexpectedly surrendered the Hungarian army; but it is fair to add, in Gorgei's behalf, that his surrender has been vindicated on the ground of military necessity, and as a humane measure to prevent the needless slaughter of his troops.

CALLIO'S THREE QUERIES.

A.D. 1590.

Callio was a Court rhymer in the Kingdom of the Two Sicilies.

WOULD I give up the maiden
    Whose eyes look into mine?
—Not for the King's own daughter
    With all her jewels fine!

Would I give up my treasures,
    The books upon my shelf?
—Not for the throne and kingdom—
    To be the King myself!

Would I give up the laurel
    That on Parnassus grows?
—Not for all other honours
    That all the Earth bestows!

———•———

ST. AUGUSTINE TO MONICA.

(In their Garden at Hippo.)

O MOTHER, in thy bower
    I plant for thee a flower
Which by an emblem bids the soul aspire:
For just as here, amid this muck and mire,
    This earth-enrooted Heliotrope
    Pursues with ever-wandering eye
    The flying Sun across the sky,—
So doth the flesh-encumbered soul,
    Earth-clogged, and not allowed to fly,
    Yearn upward and, through all the blue,
    Its Shining and Immortal Hope
            For evermore pursue!

THE OLD OLD STORY.

A COUPLE of robins
That perched on a tree
Said each to the other,
'How sweet it would be
To love and to marry
And always agree!'

They loved and they married:
But husband and wife
While yet in the honeymoon
Kindled a strife,
And all about nothing,
Yet spoiling their life.

They live in a garden
Where cherries are red,
They sleep in the downiest
Nest for a bed,
Yet always are wishing
They never had wed.

They bicker, they fidget,
They flutter their wings,
And this is what each
To the other now sings:
To love and to marry
Are opposite things.'

THE SILVER PENNY.

I FOUND a Silver Penny;
　'And now,' quoth I,
　'What shall I buy?
For I can buy with this
　All things, or very many—
　Even a smile or kiss.'

I spent my Silver Penny;
　'And now,' quoth I,
　'O world, good-bye!—
For, having squandered this,
　I get no smile from any,
　Nor can I beg a kiss.'

AT THE OWOYO RIVER.

To ——.

I WANDER by Owoyo stream
　To watch its wintry flow,
And fancy how its banks will seem
　When Summer roses blow.

Owoyo stream, so icy chill,
　So very like to thee,
Goes wandering at its wayward will
　Without a thought of me.

Owoyo stream, though freezing cold,
　Shall thaw its ice in June:
But oh! the Fates have not foretold
　If thou wilt melt as soon!

SUMMER AND WINTER.

A SONG.

I CROWNED her brow in Summer-time
  With roses white and red;
I sang my love to her in rhyme,
  And well my wooing sped!
      The Summer-time,
      O blessed time!
  Long after it had fled
She smiled, and told me that my rhyme
  Kept running in her head.

I struck the stars with head sublime!
  I hoped (from what she said)
To crown her brow in Winter-time
  With orange-buds instead!
      The Winter-time,
      O cursed time!
  The fool whom she has wed
Is jealous, for he swears my rhyme
  Keeps running in her head.

———◆———

TOM PEPPER'S DEFINITION.

YOU ask me, What is Love? And I reply
  That Love is Folly—by another name:—
The giving of a heart,—not knowing why,—
  And getting no requital for the same.

A CONFAB WITH A CRICKET.

(*Gryllus Campestris.*)

O CRICKET on the Hearth, the chilly dew
　　That drives thee hither to my evening fire
Will house thee here, I hope, the winter through,
　　Thou merry minstrel!—of whose strident lyre,
Although it be incessant, yet I never tire.

Thou noisy little negro of the night!—
　　Thou tiny body with a mighty soul!—
Thy key is pitched to such a shrilly height,
.　　That when thou grindest out thy carmagnole,
Thou scarest back the prowling mouse into his hole.

Thou too art thievish like the thieving mouse,
　　And wickedly dost pilfer many a crumb;
And yet thou art as welcome to my house
　　As if King Oberon and his Queen had come
To blow for me their trumpet or to beat their drum.

I love the noise of rain upon the roof,
　　Or of the horse when crunching in his stall,
Or of the shuttle in the warp and woof,
　　Or any cheery hum or cry or call—
But thou, O Cricket, hast the cheeriest tune of all!

The croaking frog, for envy of thy note,
　　Lies lurking for thee in his reedy fen,
Nor art thou safe from slipping down the throat
　　Of hungry lizard, salmon, hen or wren—
Save only in the hospitable homes of men.

And so, O cousin of the katy-did,
   Instead of taking lodgings in a tree,
Or gadding as the locust does, amid
   The moors and meadows, with the cow and bee,
Thy little head is wise to hide itself with *me*.

O chimney-haunter! sacred is the creed
   That when thou comest to the poor man's cot
Thou bringest to the inmates luck indeed—
   Health, peace and plenty—and I know not what:
And I, for one, believe it—whether true or not.

So let thy coming be a pledge to stay;
   And though thou hast a threatening pair of wings,
I prithee use them not to fly away;
   But tarry here, and while the kettle sings
Chat to me cheerfully of pleasant household things.

The fates have fitted thee for household life—
   For thou art fortunate, as I am told,
In being married to a silent wife,
   Who has no tongue to gossip or to scold—
And such a wife is rare, and worth her weight in gold.

I seldom lack a friend or welcome guest
   To grace my table and to try my wine;
But though society be of the best,
   However brilliantly the wit may shine,
I always tire of company—except of thine.

But *thou* remainest when the *rest* are gone,
   My one most lively, most loquacious friend;
And through the livelong night until the dawn,
   In language which I never comprehend,
Thou tellest me a tale that never has an end.

The meaning of thy chirp (if I may guess)
.   Is charitable: and, if understood,
Would prove intended for my happiness—
    Or, better still, intended for my good:
So sit and warm thyself—I will pile on the wood.

My rude forefathers in a rougher age
    Found in thy merry antics such delight,
That they would shut thee prisoner in a cage,
    With dozens of thy tribe, to see thee fight,
And hear thee sing in chorus on a winter's night.

But thou art safe with *me* from all restraint—
    My home is thine—each corner and each room;
And should the housemaid offer a complaint,
    I will forbid her ever with her broom
(Or with her heavy heel) to antedate thy doom.

Thou art not beautiful, I will confess;
    And when I catch of thee a hurried glimpse—
If I had never known thee, I might guess
    That thou art one of Satan's blackest imps,
Or Satan's very self—save only that he limps.

Thou nimble scion of those crickets twain
    Who at the Deluge hopped into the Ark,
Hide at my hearthstone from the winter's rain!—
    Stay till the quenching of my vital spark!—
And teach me how to take my leap into the dark[1].

---

[1] 'When the cricket *shrills*,' says Harris, 'he raises his wing-covers a little, and shuffles them together lengthwise, so that the projecting vanes of one are made to grate against those of the other.'

THE UNWILLING BACCHANAL.

A LAY OF A MIDNIGHT ORGIE.

PLACE—*Piccadilly.*   TIME—*Silly Season.*

I.

I WENT to the Cock and Hen
  One evening at ten.

I noticed a sign that hung
  On spigot and bung.

The letters were painted red,
  And temptingly said:

A GUEST WHO WILL TELL A TALE
PAYS NOTHING FOR ALE.

II.

I thought it a crazy rule
  Devised by a fool.

So, draining my flowing mug,
  I said, with a shrug,

'O publican, this is good,
  And drawn from the wood:

'But *gratis*? Then please explain
  What profit you gain!'

'On telling your tale,' quoth he,
  'Perhaps you will see.'

III.

The guests, who were jolly chaps
(A dozen, perhaps),

Said merrily, 'Let the story
Be long—and be gory;

'Begin it and take your time—
And give us a crime—

'A horror, with ghosts, to thrill
The blood to a chill!'

IV.

—I answered, 'A man of sense
Takes care of his pence:

'So listen while I relate
King Pharamond's fate.

—'King Pharamond reigned in Gaul
(If ever at all):

'No chronicles now remain
Of Pharamond's reign.

'Yet what if his town were sacked
In fable or fact?

'How oft at a tavern-table
A fact is a fable!'

V.

—My hearers had now increased
To forty at least:

The host, with his bill of fare,
Stood back of my chair,

And pointed to '*quail on toast*'—
(The cunning old host!)

'But no,' I replied, ' I *hate*
A supper so late:

'To pamper the appetite
Is madness at night:

'To guzzle and gormandize
Is what I despise:

'My tale is of Death and Doom—
So let me resume.

VI.

—'King Pharamond, it appears,
Was young for his years.

'He followed in age forsooth
The follies of youth.

'This being confessed, the rest
Is readily guessed.

'The cause of our primal woe
Was woman, you know!

'Her ways, when the world began,
Were fatal to man:

'Her ways, till the world shall end,
Will never amend!

VII.

(*'A morsel of bread and cheese,*
Mine host, if you please!')

VIII.

—'King Attila's boats in line
  Descended the Rhine.

'King Pharamond's frightened Franks
  Defended the banks.

'Defended?   Defence was vain!—
  So when it was plain

'That Pharamond's city-wall
  Was ready to fall,

'He climbed at the midnight-hour
  His citadel-tower,

'And leaned on the coping-stone,
  And said with a groan:

IX.

(*'O Thomas, this cheese, egad,*
  Is mouldy and bad!'

And Thomas (the waiter) said,
  'Your honour, instead,

'Could manage to eat, no doubt,
  A couple of trout.'

I ordered what scarce I needed,
  And thus I proceeded :)

X.

—'Of course, as the King looked down,
    He feared for his town.

'The shriek of an owl would start
    A throb in his heart.

'A swash of the flowing river
    Would give him a shiver.

'For how can a man be bold
    When guilty and old?

'A man with a sin confest
    Has peace in his breast:

'But peace is a thing forbidden,
    The sin being hidden.

'The King—who had done, in fact,
    A horrible act—

'Had now for his last resource—
    (*A lemon? Of course!*

'*It gives to the fish a relish!*)
    —The deed? It was hellish!

'The work of a fiend, I say,'—
    —(And here, by the way,

'*A hock*,' quoth Thomas, '*brings out
    The flavour of trout.*'

'*The fish*,' I replied, '*are fine—
    So bring me the wine!—*

'*And pass me the pepper—thanks!*')
    —'The King of the Franks,

'Surveying the starry vault,
    —(*And also the salt*)—

'And taking his final view,
    —(*The vinegar too*)—

'Stole up to a lonely loft,
    In which he had oft,

'On nights that had long gone by,
    Received (on the sly)

'A beautiful Gothic dame,
    Whose guttural name

'I happen, to my regret,
    Just now to forget.—

XI.

('*But oysters, as I remember,
    Come in with September!*

'*If breaded before you fry them,
    I think I will try them—*

'*A dozen of Natives—Dutch—
    Not buttered too much.*)

XII.

—'Now though, to his chamber dim,
　　At Pharamond's whim,

'His charmer would wend her way
　　At night where he lay,

'Yet always before the dawn
　　The witch would be gone.

'For then to another's bed
　　She furtively fled!

'A woman is sure to rue
　　A dalliance with two.

'The King, as you know, was one :
　　The other?—his son!

'The nature of love is fickle—
　　(*I wish for a pickle—*

'*And also the mustard—French—*)
　　—The beautiful wench

'Who thus, with her magic chain,
　　Entangled the twain,

'Had never the least desire,
　　Of course, for the sire.

'Her single (yet double) care
　　Was thus to ensnare

'The Prince for his bonny self—
　　The King for his pelf.'

XIII.

('*Is mustard improved,*' asked I,
   '*If served with a fly?*'—

Quoth Thomas, '*The fly is dead—*
   Try something instead:

'*He's dead as King Richard's hoss—*
   Try Worcestershire sauce.')

XIV.

'Remember – it all took place,
   This shame and disgrace—

'This more than disgrace and shame,
   This criminal game—

'It happened (suppose we say)
   A year and a day

'Ere Attila, Scourge of God,
   Was sent with a rod—

'A besom of Heaven—to thwack
   King Pharamond's back.'

XV.

('*This ketchup, my boy, is thick,—*
   And dry as a stick!'

So Thomas, who feared my frown,
Put craftily down

A sherry of ancient brand
In reach of my hand.

I drank it, and then for sport
I ordered a port.)

·XVI.

'A woman, at heart,' said I,
'Is fond of a lie :

'King Pharamond's crafty leman
Was woman and demon :

'For while to the King pretending
A love never-ending,

'Her heart—(for I think she *had* one,
Albeit a *bad* one)—

'Aspired to the Prince alone—
As heir to the throne.

'She said to him, ."By the powers,
This passion of ours

'"Would yield us a keener zest
If put to a test !"

'The youth, who was brave and candid,
Then boldly demanded,—

'"What test would you fain impose,
My lily, my rose ?"'

XVII.

('*A sausage were well, I think,*'
Said Tom, with a wink;

'*Or possibly you could try
A terrapin-pie.*'

My appetite strangely grew—
I ordered the two.)

.

XVIII.

—'The beautiful Goth was vicious
And over-ambitious:

'She played for the Prince's hand—
Audacity grand!

'But just as a bud is nipped
Or pinion is clipped,

'Or taper is set afire
To flash and expire,

'The Destinies dashed away
Her hopes in a day!'

XIX.

(*I ordered, just here, a sliver
Of anchovied liver.*)

XX.

—'The Prince, being warm with wine,
Had bathed in the Rhine;

'And afterward never more
  Had come to the shore.

—'Or such was the false report
  That startled the court.

'"But no," said the lady, "no!
  It cannot be so!

'"Not even his cap was found—
  He never was drowned;

'"He *must* have been put away
  By malice, I say!

'"And *who* was the Prince's bane?
  The King, it is plain!

'"Whenever I praised the Prince,
  His father would wince.

'"Oh, jealousy was the root,
  And murder the fruit!

'"And lest he should murder *me*,
  My cue is to flee!"

—'And so with her guilty gains
  She fled his domains.'

XXI.

—(And here I remark, in passing,
  That Tom was amassing

In sixpenny tips, I knew,
  The wealth of a Jew:

And knowing that I was willing
  To give him a shilling,

He artfully said, '*The house
  Is famous for grouse.*'

I nodded, and answered, '*Bring
  A breast and a wing.*')

XXII.

—'King Pharamond saw with woe
  The march of his foe.

'The War, as I said before,
  Was now at his door.'

(*One hardly can help repeating,
  If talking while eating.*)

XXIII.

—'King Pharamond gives a wheeze
  And clutches his knees!

'He wedges between them his thin
  Cadaverous chin!

'He plucks at his beard and hair,
  And says, in despair:

XXIV.

('*Oh, where is the chow-chow jar?
  How thoughtless you are!*—

'*You even forget the curry!*)
  —The King in his worry

'Is wild with the madding thought
  Of what he has wrought,—

'And thus he attempts to plead
  Excuse for the deed:

'"My son, like a fowler, set
  His cunningest net;

'"And so, as the dove was mine,
  I feared his design;

'"For youth, as the old discover,
  Is good in a lover!

'"A woman is apt to hunger
  For one who is younger!

'"Whenever the Prince was near,
  The lady would leer!

'"Whenever the Prince was gone,
  The lady would yawn!

'"Now this being hard to bear,
  I ended it there!

'"But *how* can the thing be known?
  I did it alone!

'"Yet certainly *she* must know—
  Or *why* did she go?

'"—Instead of her fleeing thus
  And making a fuss,

'"I thought she would proudly stay,
And haughtily say—

'"As soon as the hour was ripe,"—·
(*Now grill me a snipe,—*

'*Allowing, you know, each leg
The yolk of an egg.*')

XXV.

(Mine host, who had taken toddy,
Already was noddy.—

And Thomas, from force of habit,
Suggested Welsh rabbit!

*—I ordered, at Tom's suggestion,
The relish in question.*)

XXVI.

—'Now ye who attend my tale
Prepare to grow pale!

'The moon was beginning to shine
And swim in the Rhine.

'The King at the image gazed
Until he was dazed.

'It seemed to his tortured soul
A chalice—a bowl!

'He saw, as it floated up,
A death in the cup!

'The crime that he hoped to hide
  Was writ on the tide!—

'For there, in the flowing stream,
  With glitter and gleam,

'The cup, as a tell-tale, lay,—
  Not floating away,—

'Not sinking from mortal sight
  But horribly bright,

'And warning the world to think
  He poisoned the drink!'

XXVII.

(Here Thomas, the stupid ass,
  Brought *pâté de chasse.*

I didn't myself *inquire* for it,
  Nor feel a *desire* for it.

Yet, tempted by truffled game,
  I sampled the same.

—Too rich!—for it made my head
  As heavy as lead.)

XXVIII.

'The monarch begins to freeze!
  What is it he sees?

'Unchallenged by sentry-post,
  In marches a ghost!—

'And straight to the King it glides
   With terrible strides,—

'And close to the King it stands—
   A bowl in its hands!

'It gibbers, and tries to speak,
   And says with a squeak—

'(*Oh, bring me a Salad!—plain—*
   A simple Romaine.)

XXIX.

—'For what is a King? A man
   Whose days are a span!

'King Pharamond's span is narrowing!
   His horror is harrowing!

'A woman with yellow hair
   Approaches him there!

'She bends with a panther's crouch
   And creeps to his couch.

'She leaps with a panther's spring
   And throttles the King.

'"Nay, offer no piteous plea,
   But listen!" cries she.

'"I wept for my honour sold
   To thee for thy gold!

'"I never have sold it since
   To King or to Prince!

'"I searched for a Sibyl wise
  To read me the skies:

'"She said to me, 'Thou shalt bear
  A kingdom an heir:

'"The King of an Eastern land
  Shall sue for thy hand!

'"This King of the East, a Hun,
  Shall follow the sun,

'"And march on a victor's quest
  To conquer the West:

'"And *thou*, as his wedded bride,
  Shalt ride at his side:

'"For *thou* art to deal a blow
  To finish his foe.

'"So whet thee a dagger bright
  And go in the night—

'"When none shall be there to see—
  And carry thy key

'"And open, as oft before,
  King Pharamond's door,

'"And say to the reprobate--"
  (*O Tom, it is late!*

'*So mull me, before I go,
  A demi-Bordeaux,—*

'*And see that you keep the pot,
  Not boiling, but hot.*)

XXX.

—'Arrayed in her robe Tartáric
　The lady barbaric

'Cries out to the panting King,
　"I come and I bring

'"Another—beneath my girth—
　Awaiting his birth;

'"Who, ere he shall draw his breath,
　Shall leap at thy death!

'"For I, by my holy vows,
　Am Attila's spouse!

'"The deed that I do is done
　For Attila's son!"

XXXI.

—'She added to what she spoke
　The flash of a stroke,

'And Pharamond, pale and haggard,
　Exclaimed as he staggered—

'(*Now bring me a B. and S.!*)'
　And here I confess

I ordered eftsoons a second—
　(The drinks being reckoned

---

[1] This drink is called the 'eye-opener.'

In chalk, in the ancient style)—
And Tom with a smile

(For Tom was a rogue) inferred
I ordered a third!

XXXII.

He brought it—I saw him book it—
I fancy I took it!

I hadn't the slightest trouble
In now seeing double.

These Openers of my Eyes
Revealed a surprise:

The guests, to my great dismay,
Had stolen away!

The host, with a horrid sound,
Terrific, profound,

Applauded my tale of gore
With snore upon snore!

XXXIII.

I shook him and said, '*I go—
How much do I owe!*'

XXXIV.

Quoth he, as he took his chalk,
'A guest who will talk—

'(And *you*, Sir, O goodness gracious,
　　Were *very* loquacious!)—

'A talker, I say, will first
　　Feel nothing but thirst;

'But soon, in his empty maw
　　A hunger will gnaw!

'He scruples to eat at night,
　　Yet longs for a bite.

'Now merely a snack, he thinks,
　　Will do—(with his drinks);

'But no—he will stuff his crop!—
　　He orders a chop,

'Or cutlet of veal or lamb,
　　Or jigger of ham;

'Or, if he be bold and rash,
　　He ventures a hash,

'Or orders a bible-leaf[1]
　　Of *à-la-mode* beef;

'And then (with a glass of grog)
　　The leg of a frog,

'Or shrimps, or a roasted crab:
　　Till, what with his gab,

'And what with the time he takes
　　In jokes that he makes—

---

[1] On a whaling-ship, the very thin slices into which a whale's
blubber is cut are called 'bible-leaves.'

'Especially if he runs
  To villainous puns—

'He guzzles and eats until . . .
  He swears at his bill!

'Your own, as you see, is scored
  In chalk on the board:

'A guinea, by my account,
  Is just the amount:

'My figures are seldom wrong—
  Your story was long!'

XXXV.

—I found in my purse, all told,
  A guinea in gold:

The deuce! I had been a ninny,
  And eaten my guinea!

I hadn't a bare baubee
  For Thomas's fee!

I turned to the host, and said,
  'Your letters in red

'I took for a foolish rule—
  But *I* am the fool!'

———•———

THE IMMORTALITY OF LOVE.

THE Heart is fickle. Who can tell
  When Love will flit away?
The lover loveth long and well
  Who loveth for a day!

B b

AN ATTIC PHILOSOPHER'S VIEWS[1].

I LIVE in Paris—not 'in style,'
   But on a rusty little isle
Where all is quiet, save the scream
Of steamers blowing off their steam;
Or when a raft may chance to pass,
Announced by brayings of an ass;
Or when, if favoured by the weather,
The islanders all flock together
And on a Sunday dance a jig,
Or grease and try to catch a pig;

Where anglers fish from morn till night,
Encouraged by a single bite;
Where dogs are shaved in little boats;
Where babies get their milk from goats
(That freshly yield from door to door
The drink of Baby Jove of yore);

And where I rent upon a *quai*
A garret for a franc a day.

II.

I am a stranger—that is why
The price they charge me is so high:
My native neighbours shrewdly laugh,
And say I pay too much by half.

---

[1] The above trifle, not originally meant for publication, was written as a skit for a private occasion.

III.

It is the City's oldest part,
Its very core, its very heart,
And stands sequestered and alone,
And is a village of its own—
That seems removed a' thousand miles
From wicked Paris and its wiles.

IV.

A narrow strip of running water
Divides me from the Latin Quarter—
Where Babel is at times let loose,
And frisky students play the deuce,
(Though *my* secluded situation
Has kept me out of such temptation.)

V.

My palace fronts the waterside
And wears a look of shabby pride,
And feels as lofty as it felt
When there its ducal owner dwelt :
For there, with snuff-box and peruke,
Abode a high and mighty duke,
Who in his splendour raved and swore
(A hundred years ago or more)
At democrats and all the clan
Of clamourers for the Rights of Man !

How *would* he swear—how *would* he rave
Could he come hither from his grave
To find his latest legatee
A howling democrat like me !

VI.

The stony stairs, the oaken floors,
The griffins on the great hall-doors
Remain to show the high gentility
Of that decayed and old nobility:
—But dukes, I hope, have had their day,
And as a democrat I say,
I would there reigned—in all the Earth—
The one Nobility of Worth!

VII.

Five stories up above mankind
I, with my elevated mind,
Can (like a very duke) look down
On all the gentry of the town.

VIII.

Here, lodging half-way up the sky,
We dwell together, She and I—
My pretty Angelique, my pet,
My little, wanton, young grisette.

One night, amid the rain and sleet,
I took her thither from the street:
At morn, the storm had passed away
Yet Angelique desired to stay.

How could I slam my garret-door
And shut her out for evermore?
For I am weak, I will confess,
At sight of beauty in distress.

O scandal, hush, and chide me not!
For Angelique, my young cocotte,
Although she shares my garret-mat,
Is nothing but a Maltese cat.

IX.

Or not a cat, but just a kit:
And oft, to please the little chit,
'O Angelique,' I say, 'You tread
The stairways of the mighty dead:
How do you like this grand old place—
This rookery of a royal race?'

As plainly as a cat can speak,
'O beggar-bard,' says Angelique,
'Our garret is divinely nice,
For it abounds in rats and mice.'

X.

Then as she dips her nose of pink
Into a bottle of my ink,
I answer, 'O you arrant witch,
You think me poor, but I am rich:

'By charter of a window-pane
I own all Paris and the Seine!
For all the spires that I can see,
And all the streets, belong to me!

'Nor on the stream can come or go
A tug-boat with a barge in tow,
Except to haul it where my eyes
Can make a capture of the prize.

'A hundred thousand casks of wine
Along the river-marge are mine,
Which I with any friend will share
Who climbs my castle-in-the-air.

'I own a fleet of floating-arks,
Where women wash the City's sarks,
And where with elbows white as snow
They all stand rinsing in a row.

'I own (Oh tell it not in Gath!)
A ladies' public swimming-bath,
Down into which I cannot see,
But Fancy paints the sight for me!

'I own a *quai* a mile in length,
All masonry of solid strength;
Yet once a week the solid stone
All changes into flowers full blown!

'I own each pair of dripping oars
That flash between the stony shores:
I own each torch and lantern light
Of all regattas in the night.

'I own that pretty, tiny tot,
James Gordon Bennett's baby-yacht:
And also (when I have the *sous*)
I own the *Herald*, with the news.

'I own the Pantheon's noble dome,
Owned lately by the Pope of Rome
(Who now would like to get it back):

'I own the stately Tour Saint Jacque,
The finest tower in all the town!
[What fool proposed to tear it down?]

'I own a nearer, dearer fane,
For just outside my window-pane
My neighbour Notre Dame looks in
With every gargoyle all agrin!

And oft I borrow their grimace,
And mock, as they, and make a face,
And cast my most religious jeer
On all this sublunary sphere.'

XI.

I also say to Angelique,
'You are so fat, you are so sleek,
That this must be a healthy place;
And so you here shall romp and race
Till all our little purse be spent,
And I no more can pay the rent:

'To pay the rent is growing hard,
For *I*, like many a better bard,
Now write my epopees so well
That not a copy can I sell.'

XII.

She heeds me not, the little minx!
For only of herself she thinks,
And better loves her only gown
Than all the sights of all the Town!

And like my cat, one coat alone
Is all that *I* myself now own:
And even this (my Sunday best)
Has *no* red ribbon on the breast:

Yet since this gewgaw I descry
On many a greater fool than I,
It is a badge I never covet,
But in my garret am above it.

XIII.

O Paris, pompous as thou art
With pinnacle and spire and mart,
My modest isle, from coast to coast,
Has not a monument to boast.

For here no mighty pile was built
With lofty dome of glittering gilt,
Nor awful crypt of shining gloom
Empurpling an Imperial Tomb.

Here is no proud triumphal arc,
No obelisk, no public park,
No fount to cool the summer's heat,
No statue standing in the street,
No granite fortress grey and grim,
No round-tower on the river's rim,
No market-house, no long arcade,
No double-pillared colonnade,
No avenues of tempting shops,
(With other tempters for the fops,)
No gilded hell, no devil's den,
Nor even anywhere an N.

XIV.

The isle, within its civic pale,
Has just a chapel and a jail;
From both of which, for many a day,
The honest folk have kept away.

XV.

And since the isle is bare of sights,
Save only from its garret-heights,
No gangs of gawks from foreign lands
Gape here with guide-books in their hands.

XVI.

Yet all the place, from shore to shore,
Is reeking with historic lore :

Here Julius Caesar came in flight
From being beaten in a fight ;
Yet gave a different version—very !—
In writing up his Commentary ;
(For in his bragging book, you know,
He always overthrew his foe.)

Here in this once umbrageous isle
Merlin and Vivian dwelt awhile ;
And here the King of France one day
Allured Diana's self astray.

Here came the holy Genevieve
And told the haughty Huns to leave :
And *when*, since then, was known or sung
Such triumph of a woman's tongue ?

Here came Saint Denny, head in hand,
And though he never deigned to land,
He flung his sacred skull ashore,
And now the skull has grown to four.

Here Danté, when a college-youth
(Ere Beatrice was born forsooth),
First loved a lass of lesser note,
Who kept the island's ferry-boat.

Here, underneath the screening trees,
Walked Abelard with Héloise;
And here too *I* have walked with . . . well . . .
But no . . . I never kiss and tell.

XVII.

St. Louis, he whose noble fame
Gave to my little isle its name,
Came hither oft at break of day
To lay aside his crown and pray.

I wonder if the Lord still cares
(Or ever did) for human prayers?
And did He lend His gracious ear
When cruel Catharine sought Him here?

For here she came in widow's weeds,
And sat and told her blessed beads,
And shed a pious tear or two,
And passed to . . . Saint Bartholomew!

XVIII.

How small the people look below,
As they are walking to and fro?
For men with all their pride of place
Are but a puny, pigmy race;
And though the ant within his hill
(As we are told) is vainer still,
Yet as for me—above the crowd,
And looking down—I might be proud
Save only that, from lack of pelf,
I am Humility itself.

XIX.

I count my bridges—they are seven
(With Heimdal's bridge [1] besides, in Heaven).

They greatly vary in design,
And one of them is wondrous fine,
With four Zouaves of carven stone :—
Those giant sentries ! never known
On any night to fall asleep,
So faithful is the watch they keep !

Another bridge (the city's boast,
And which a Frenchman loves the most),
Was built of the destroyed Bastile—
A bridge in crossing which I feel
All tyranny beneath my heel !

I also much admire of course
King Henri Quatre's bridge and horse :
And yet for amplitude of plan,
And nobleness of arch and span,
Few bridges equal, I suppose,
The bridge of Henri's noble nose.

XX.

And where the King, with royal brass,
Still stares at all the dames who pass,
I often go, on idle days,
To rummage round the bookish *quais.*
Once, on the parapet of stone,
I found a volume of my own !

[1] Heimdal's bridge is the rainbow.

—I take it up! I fondly eye it!
I look as if I mean to buy it!
I handle it with tender touch,
And (with an accent), ask 'How much?'

'This book,' replies the bibliopole,
'Is still uncut, the leaves are whole;
For this is English, and they say
That English, Sir, has had its day:
Accept it as a gift!' he said.

Whereat I proudly shook my head.
'Oh no!' quoth I, as in the rack
I fiercely thrust the volume back;
'This author once had quite a vogue,
But then he proved an arrant rogue!
You are a fool, I must avow,
To foist him on the public now.'

XXI.

I take a ramble every day
Along the crowded Élysées;
Yet not to see the newest fashion;
But I have always had a passion
For catching glimpses of the features
Of eager hurrying human creatures!
I love to read with rapid look
That never-failing wonder-book,
The Human Face, miscalled 'divine':
For Man, I think, outranks by far
The greatest gods that were or are,
And bears engraven on his face
The history of a higher race

Than in the high Olympian halls
Made Heaven resound with drunken brawls.

So as my fellow-men go by
I love to look them in the eye,
And in their answering looks behold
Not deities of days of old—
But beings of a better grain:
For mortal men are, in the main,
Not half such thieves and rakes and pimps—
Such devils and such devils' imps—
Such high adepts in every crime
As were the gods of early time.

Or if you answer me and say
That there be better gods to-day;
Then I rejoin and I repeat,
The gods are now in every street;
For if the gods are come agen,
They are the multitude of men;

And though 'the human face divine'
Be seldom beautiful or fine,
But often ugly, I confess,—
Yet still I like it none the less,
And love to read the hope or care,
The mirth or misery, written there.

This book is ever fresh and new—
Nor does it cost a single *sou*.
—But candour prompts me here to add
That when my heart is sick and sad,—
Of all the books I seek to read
For solace in a time of need,

My book of books, to soothe my woes ...
Is one I keep at John Munroe's.

XXII.

Beneath my window is a lane
Where, every Friday, sun or rain,
A fish-wife with her cart comes by
And halts and shrieks to me on high;
And so, to gratify the wish
Of Angelique (who dotes on fish,
And who is orthodox, I hope),
I drop a basket by a rope.

My fish-wife is a jolly jade
Who rants at the decline of trade,
And scolds and says the times are bad,
The worst the island ever had;

And yet she proves by girth and band
The growing fatness of the land:
She lives so well, and is so stout,
That she has twinges of the gout,—
With husbands three beneath the ground,
And two above, but none around:
And yet the jade is not content,
But tipples till her coin is spent,
And shouts that things have gone to wrack,
And bawls to have the Empire back.

XXIII.

My wattled basket comes and goes
And brings me up my *Figaros*,
My *Matins* and my *Moniteurs*,
Until my little kitten purrs

And says that, judging by their spats,
The journalists behave like cats:
A censure which I think is true,
And yet (to render them their due)
These gentlemen, however cruel,
Are harmless when they fight a duel.

XXIV.

One day I asked of Angelique,
'What would you say, if you could speak?
For oft you mumble like a man;
So try to tell me, if you can,
What most you wish for in the world?'
Whereat her little tail she curled,
And round and round she danced and purred,
And answered, 'A canary-bird.'

XXV.

Quoth I, 'Why do you chase your tail
So vainly and without avail?
For though you follow it so fast
You never catch it at the last.'

Quoth she, 'Why do you hunt a rhyme
From early dawn till dinner-time,
And chase through half the blessed day
A thought that always flits away?'

XXVI.

—I like (and so the sculptors do)
The marble horses of Coustou
(Though peppered here and there in spots
With ugly Prussian rifle-shots).

I like the monumental maiden
Whose mighty lap is always laden
With wagon-loads of flowers and grass
To deck the memory of Alsace,
And make a Frenchman swear in vain
At never getting back Lorraine.

I like the City that is dight
The World's Metropolis of Light:
I like its various halls of knowledge,
The University, the College,
But oh I like the best of all—
In fact I *love*—the Students' Ball.

I go there always, once a week:
But not, of course, with Angelique:
I leave her with her mice and rats,
And go and dance with other cats.

XXVII.

I do not say that such a plan
Meets the religious wants of man;
But now-a-days I seldom find
A man of a religious mind:
I used to think I knew of *one*,
And *I* was *he*: but, Oh my Muse,
My beautiful and early views—
As full of moonshine as the moon,
And glowing as the bug of June—
Are muddled now, and full of doubt,
And this is how it came about:

One summer night my lamp was lit,
To which the moths began to flit:

I winced to see the greedy flame
Devour each pretty midge that came :
At last, to rid me of the sight,
I wrathfully blew out the light :
And then I railed, presumptuous man,
At cruel nature's heartless plan,
Till in the darkness where I sat
I felt upon my brow a gnat !
I slapped my philosophic head
And smote the sweet musician dead !
It was, I grant, a brutal blow
And laid my lofty logic low.

So now I think that soon or late,
With all who muse and meditate,
Whether on moths that burn their wings,
Or on the general frame of things,
Think as we will, our final thought,
Self-contradicted, comes to nought.

XXVIII.

Since hopes are slow in coming true,
My dearest wishes are but two :
And first that, with its trials past,
The French Republic is to last :
And next, that there will dawn a day
When carts will come and cart away
The heap of garbage on my *quai.*

XXIX.

O best of countries ! Darling shore,
Which I perhaps may see no more

I would that I to-day were there,
Agog in the Chicago Fair[1]!
Sweet Native Land! I love thee still
In spite of the McKinley bill.

XXX.

But now, an exile, as I sit
With no companion save my kit,—
My window, like a wizard's glass,
Foreshows what is to come to pass.

Oh, be the fancy not in vain!
For I discover through the pane,
From East to West, from North to South,
Across the open Cannon's Mouth
The Spider's Web, when War no more
Shall belch its horrid thunder-roar!

I see the Horn of Plenty filled!
I see the teeming acres tilled!
I see the toilers of the land
Each with his guerdon in his hand!
I see the crumbled crown and throne,—
While nowhere round the world is known
That tawdry, despicable thing
Which modern nations call a king!
I see the captive's broken chain!
I see a balm for every pain!
I even see a tender ruth
Upon the very tiger's tooth!
Yea, in my mirror I behold
The coming of an age foretold

---

[1] This was written in August, 1893.

Wherein (although I say not when)
The very cockatrice's den
Shall be a place where you may stand
And stroke the creature with your hand:
Though, as for me, I don't affirm
That I shall greatly pet the worm.

XXXI.

Alas! the things that we foresee
Are not the things that are to be!
The Lion lying with the Lamb
Is very pretty, but a sham!
Nor is there yet a Prince of Peace,
For Wars go on and never cease;
And still the nations groan in pain
In order that their kings may reign;
And still the world is overawed,
And cowed and crushed by force and fraud;
For Might is ever with the strong,
And Right is ever in the wrong!

XXXII.

The two great Powers of Good and Ill
Were equal once—are equal still—
And equal evermore shall be:
For Justice vaunts that she is blind,
And, caring little for mankind,
She holds so evenly her scales
That neither Right nor Wrong prevails,
And God is kept upon a level
With His arch-enemy the Devil.

XXXIII.

I often go on sunny days
To Montparnasse and Père-Lachaise,
But not to weep or mourn or sigh:
The dead are happy—so am I.

XXXIV.

And though my garret is too bare
For any but a cat to share,
Yet I shall soon remove from hence
To lodgings of a less expense.

The house to which I am to go
Is yon pavilion, grey and low,
Whose roof just makes a little ridge
Above the level of the bridge.

It is the Morgue, and in it lies,
Each day, the last new wretch that dies:

And on its hospitable shelf
I shall at last be laid myself.

O gentle neighbours, after that,
Be kind to Angelique, my cat;
Nor drive her forth upon the town,
Nor fling her in the Seine to drown!

And where I once was wont to dwell,
Nail on the wall a slab to tell
That there, the island's modest pride,
Its humble poet, lived and died.

KING HELGI TO QUEEN SIGRUN.

In the seventh year after the King's death, the Queen, on making a pilgrimage to his cairn, heard him say to her—

I.

WHEN thou art gay, my darling,
  I know it in my tomb,—
For on my breast the roses
  Then burst afresh in bloom.

II.

But when thy heart is troubled,—
  Then every withered bud
Shoots down a thorn that pricks me
  And draws a drop of blood.

THE DIVINE ALTERNATIVE.

I.

'MY child, thou art going astray!' said God,
  'So hearken, and let Me *advise* thee!'
    —His warning, though kind indeed,
    I heard—but I failed to heed.

II.

'Ungrateful!' He said (and He raised His rod),
  'To turn thee I must *chastise* thee!'
    —So then, with a scourge indeed,
    He smote me—and now I bleed.

A PLEA FOR THE SKALD AND HIS RUNES.

THE calm and cloistered poet,
    Austere and strict in prayer,
    Dwells in the upper air—
If not in Heaven itself, yet just below it.

II.

In spite of men's derision,
    Who mock him while he sings,
    He tells them of the things
Which he beholds in Valhal, in his vision.

III.

For what know *ye*, O mortals,
    Concerning Gods or Fates,
    Save what the skald relates
From glimpses through the high celestial portals?

IV.

Thence with a swift gyration
    He wheels ·his wings below—
    Till from the World of Woe
He echoes back its wail and lamentation.

V.

For by what necromancy
    Can mortals guess how dire
    Is the Infernal Fire—
Save as it sparkles to the poet's fancy?

VI.

What shall his weird recital—
His kantali[1]—his kit[2]—
His wisdom—and his wit—
Earn for the minstrel as his just requital?

VII.

—A laurel not to wither!
—Ye mortals, crown him well!
—Your fate is Heaven or Hell
According as the poet dooms ye thither!

SIC VITA.

I.

AT morn, the bridegroom and the bride
Walk from the altar, side by side,
To wander where the world is wide.

II.

At noon, beneath the fiery sun,
Their journey, though with joy begun,
Grows weary, and they wish it done.

III.

At night, amid the chilly shade,
Their welcome pillow, freshly made,
Is rounded with a pick and spade.

[1-2] It will be remembered that the kantali is the harp of Finland; the kit, the fiddle of Norway.

THE MILLIONAIRE OF MECCA.

IN THE YEAR OF THE PROPHET, 403.

I.

THE pious Arab robber, Ali Bába,
　　Whenever he had robbed a caravan,
Went always afterward to the Ka-ába[1]
　　　　And knelt and prayed
And asked a blessing on his thievish trade.

II.

　　And thus this prayerful man
(Who prospered as the righteous seldom can)
Had houses, horses, harems—all the things
Which wealth (that very dubious blessing) brings.

III.

So when in his magnificence he died,
The people pointed to his name with pride,
　　　　And raised above his bones
　　　　　A noble pile of stones,
And on it carved a writing, and it ran:

'Here rests in peace—without a mortal care—
God's favourite, Ali Bába, man of prayer.'

---

[1] The Ka-ába (or 'square-house') is a small building that stands
within the Great Mosque at Mecca, and is used as an inner temple—
or holy of holies—where the Faithful followers of Islam may not
only pray, but kiss a famous Black Stone, or aerolite, which has
been an object of veneration with Arabs from time immemorial.

IV.

One day an Angel—dropping from a cloud—
Perched on the pillar! The astonished crowd,
Who gazed agape,
Stood awe-struck at the shining shape
And hushed their hum,
And marvelled why the heavenly guest had come
And·what immortal truth he had to tell.

V.

To whom the Voice Angelic cried aloud:

'God's favourite, Ali Bába, is in hell!—
And ye who plunder Pilgrims every day,
And then in yonder Temple kneel and pray,
Shall win God's favour in the self-same way!'

VI.

Thus spake the Angel—but so long ago
That now in Mecca (as the Pilgrims know,
Who yearly throng that consecrated place)
The Angel's warning needs to be repeated,—
For now, O Allah, God of heavenly grace!
How strangers in that holy town are cheated!

A CURIOSITY IN CONCHOLOGY.

'Things durable perish, while things fragile survive. Among the suggestive treasures in the Sloane collection is an ancient and well-preserved egg from Africa, of a now extinct species of bird. The faded inscriptions on the shell are polylingual. The pyramids are crumbling, while this egg, dating from the Ptolemies, remains without a crack.'—*The Times*.

I AM of Cleopatra's time and land!
    Be careful how you hold me in your hand,
For I am frail—though, as you plainly see,
I have not proved to be as frail as she!
She was a beauty! Oh, I knew her well!
She wrote her autograph upon my shell!
The letters still remain—they are in Greek:
You see them yet—(or so does Captain Speke.)
I am a wonder never known before!—
A twice-laid egg!—(don't drop me to the floor!)
A Dodo laid me first—then Speke himself
(The noble fellow!) laid me on this shelf.

PETER THE GREAT'S MAXIM.

WHAT though the Czar be lord of half the Earth,
    Yet not his sword, his spurs, his iron glove,
His golden crown, his sacred blood of birth,
His ships, his treasures . . . are a straw in worth
    Without his people's loyalty and love.

THE AMSTERDAM FISHERMAN.

Among the venturesome Netherland boatmen in the sixteenth century, it was a custom (not yet wholly extinct) to ornament their fishing-smacks with a charm for safety in the form of a carved and gilded image of the Virgin Mary as *Stella Maris*, or Star of the Sea.

I.

OUT went the Skipper
    On Zuyder Zee:
Calm was the weather:
'Watch!' said he,—
'Watch to the windward,
And watch to the lee!
God alone knoweth
Why the wind bloweth,
Whence is the tempest,
Or where it will be!
Ora pro nobis,
Sancta Maria,
Star of the Sea!'

II.

Wild was the whirlwind
On Zuyder Zee:
Pale was the Skipper:
'Watch!' cried he,—
'Hell is in riot!
The furies are free!
Breakers to larboard!
Breakers to starboard!
Death and the Devil
Are dancing with me!

Ora pro nobis,
Sancta Maria,
Star of the Sea !'

III.

Home went the Skipper
From Zuyder Zee :
.Watching was ended :
' Pray !' said he,—
' Blest is the boatman
Who bendeth his knee !
Queen of the ocean,—
Praise and devotion,
Homage and honour
And glory to Thee !
Ora pro nobis,
Sancta Maria,
Star of the Sea !'

THE TWO HARVESTERS.

THE forests are sere and sober:
The bronze of October
Has burnished the leaves:
The harvest is ready, and will be great:
O reaper, go gather thy golden sheaves !
Go gather, I say,
Thy sheaves to-day !

To-morrow may be too late!
To-day, and to-day alone,
A mortal may call his own—
To-morrow belongs to Fate.

II.

Now Fate is a cruel crone,
    Capricious and fickle,—
    And after thy sickle
She sendeth a Scythe Unseen,
    And mortally keen,
And swinging without a sound,
And the width of the swath it leaves behind
    (If visible to mankind)
    Would girdle the world around!

III.

The Swinger who swingeth the Scythe is old,—
    Too old for a day or date,
    And bearded (they say) with grime,—
Yet ever, in spite of his frosty pate,
He serveth his Mighty Mistress well;
    For the hoary knave
    Is her willing slave
Who slashes whatever she bids him fell!

The poets in ages past have told—
The poets in days to come will tell—
    How lightly he bears
    His years and his cares!

He is hale and strong,
And he strides along
With an easy gait
At a giant's rate!

He is known in rhyme
By the name of Time,—
And he worketh the will of Fate!

IV.

He worketh for neither love nor hate,
Nor careth for good nor ill,
Nor sleepeth nor sitteth still,
For a slave is he,
And a slave shall be,
And never on Earth can he hope to be free,
For he worketh another's will.

V.

His work is to cut and kill!
His weapon is never dull—
Its temper is superfine!
He cleaveth the oak and vine—
He cleaveth the heart and skull!
For Oh with his Scythe he cutteth deeper
Than *thou* with a sickle of *thine*!
—The singer, the dancer, the laugher, the weeper,
The king and the clown,
The great and the small,—
He ever invisibly follows them all—
To slash them, and gash them, and hew them down.

VI.

And Fate—as his mistress and owner and keeper—
Whose bidding he never hath disobeyed—
Now saith to him, ' Minion mine, what ho!
      I issue to thee
      Another decree:
Go follow the mowers as now they mow!
Go follow the reapers as now they reap!
Go softly behind them, and creep and creep
   (For *thou* art a *sly* old creeper!)
Go follow them like a creeping shade!
Go haunt them and harry them with the blade
That moweth the mower and reapeth the reaper!'

VII.

 O husbandman, husbandman, close at thy heel
The Scythe that is sharper and colder than steel
    Now follows thee fast!
    —So quicken thy speed!
A fortunate mortal is he indeed
Who reapeth the harvest which he hath sown!
    Thy meadow is yet unmown!
    So hasten! The season is brief!
    The autumn will soon be past!
      Go gather, I say,
      Thy sheaves to-day!—
      For Oh, to thy rue,
      To-morrow *thou too*
Shalt be, in thy turn, a gathered sheaf l

TRANSPLANTED.

From Goethe.

' Ich ging im Walde.'

I ROAMED the forest
  In quest of nought
Save flitting fancy
  And flying thought.

A hidden blossom
  I chanced to spy—
As bright as Hesper,
  Or woman's eye.

I wished to pluck it,
  But heard it say—
'Must I be broken
  And flung away?'

Then up I dug it,
  The root and all,
To grace the garden
  Beside my hall.

There did I plant it
  In sheltered ground,
And there it blushes
  The whole year round.

A MITHER'S LUVE[1].

From the French of Jean Richepin.

ONCE a luve-sick lad forlorn
    Luved a lass who gave him scorn.
          O tol, lol, lol,
          O tol, lol, la.

'Fetch thy mither's heart to me
For my dog to eat,' said she.
          O tol, lol, lol, &c.

To his mither's house he sped—
Killed her—snatched her heart—and fled.
          O tol, lol, lol, &c.

In his flight he tumbled down,
And the heart rolled on the groun'.
          O tol, lol, lol, &c.

As the heart went rolling by,
He could hear it give a cry.
          O tol, lol, lol, &c.

Cried the heart—with anguish wild—
'Hast thou hurt thysel', my child?'
          O tol, lol, lol.
          O tol, lol, la!

---

[1] As the original was written in *patois*, the translation is given in *patois* also.

APPENDIX

———◆———

CARL OLAF'S CANTICLE.

THE political allusions in this poem will not, I hope, be regarded as ungracious; but of course I could not truthfully portray the thoughts and feelings of a Norwegian peasant, and particularly of a peasant-bard, and at the same time omit his aspirations for national independence.

Moreover, not only from a political, but also from a literary, point of view, the present attitude of Norway is independent and commanding—as the following anecdote will illustrate :—

One afternoon in August, 1893, in company with a seaside party of journalists, I witnessed from the jetty at Tréport (on the English Channel) the incoming of a Norwegian ship from Gibraltar. 'Is it not odd,' asked one of the spectators, 'that Odin's Vikings should now be hailing from the Pillars of Hercules?' 'Not so,' replied another, 'for the Pillars of Hercules are now Ibsen and Björnson !'

THE LEMMING.

The account which the late Rev. J. G. Wood, the naturalist, has given of the Lemming is as follows :—

'At uncertain and distant intervals of time, many of the Northern parts of Europe, such as Lapland, Norway, and Sweden, are subjected to a strange invasion. Hundreds of little, dark, mouselike animals sweep over the land, like clouds of locusts suddenly changed into quadrupeds; coming from some unknown home, and going no one knows whither. These creatures are the Lemmings, and their sudden appearances are so entirely mysterious that the Norwegians look upon them as having been rained from the clouds upon the earth. Driven onwards by some overpowering instinct, these vast hordes travel in a straight line, permitting nothing but a smooth perpendicular wall or rock to turn them from their course. If they should happen to meet with any living being, they immediately attack, knowing no fear, but only urged by indiscriminate rage. Any river or lake they swim without hesitation, and rather seem to enjoy the water than to fear it. If a stack or a cornrick should stand in their path, they settle the matter by eating their way through it. The country over which they pass is utterly devastated by them. . . . These migrating hosts are accompanied by clouds of predacious birds, and by many predacious quadrupeds, who find a continual feast spread for them so long as the Lemmings are on their pilgrimage. The fish come in for *their* share of the banquet, and make great havoc in their columns. The reindeer is often seen in chase of the Lemmings. The termination of their extraordinary migrations is generally *in the sea*, where the survivors of the much-reduced ranks finally perish. It is fortunate for the country that these razzias only occur at rare intervals, a space of some ten or fifteen years generally elapsing between them. The Lemmings feed on grass, reeds, and lichens. They are obstinately savage creatures—swarming in the forest, sitting two or three on every stump, and biting the dogs' noses. The irritable little animals will not permit a passenger to move by them, but boldly dispute the right of way, uttering little sharp squeaking barks.'

'Fimbulwinter,' says Prof. R. B. Anderson, 'is the great and awful winter of three years' duration, preceding the End of the World.'

'Hammerfest,' says Lord Dufferin, in his *Letters from High Latitudes*, 'is scarcely worthy of my wasting paper on it.'

'The Dalesmen of Norway and Sweden,' says Sir George Dasent, 'may be reckoned among the most primitive examples of what is left of peasant life.'

MR. FROUDE'S NORWEGIAN REMINISCENCES.

Mr. Froude, the historian, who has twice explored the Fiords of Norway in a private yacht (and who has written a charming narrative of each voyage), found that the Sogne Fiord, at a point a hundred miles from the sea, was 700 fathoms in depth: and, he says, 'We have to account for chasms which, if we add the depth of water to the heights of the mountains above it, are 9,000 feet from the bottom to the mountain-crest.'

The following particulars are from the same pen :—

'We went up into the North Fiord—of all the Fiords the most beautiful. The cataracts were in their glory. I counted seventeen all close about us where we anchored. We landed for our frugal luncheon—dry biscuits and a whiskey flash—but we sate in *a bed of whortleberries*, purple with ripe fruit, by a cascade which ran down out of a snowfield. . . .

'We brought back our basketfuls of trout, and Norwegian trout are the best in the world. . . .

'On a single cottage-roof you may see half a dozen trees growing ten or fifteen feet high. . . .

'The Norwegians depend for their existence on their sheep and cattle. Every particle of grass available for hay is secured; and grass, peculiarly nutritious, often grows on the high ridges, 2,000 feet up. This they save as they can, and they have original ways of doing it. In the Geiranger it is tied tightly in bundles and flung over the cliffs to be gathered up in boats below. But science, too, is making its way in this Northern wilderness. The farm-houses, for shelter's sake, are always at the bottom of valleys, and are generally near the sea. At one of our anchorages, shut in as usual among the mountains, we observed one evening from the deck what looked like a troop of green goats skipping and bounding down the cliffs. We discovered through a binocular that they were bundles of hay. The clever bönder had carried up a wire, like a telegraph wire, from his courtyard to a projecting point of mountain: on this ran iron rings as travellers, which brought the grass directly to his door. . . .

'The flowers everywhere were most beautiful; and the wild roses were the fullest, reddest, and most abundant that I had ever seen. . . .

' In the boats we sat, tormented by flies such as are seen nowhere but in Norway. There is one as big as a drone, and rather like one, but with a green head, and a pair of nippers in it that under a magnifying-glass are a wonder to look at. This, I suppose, is the wretch described by "Three in Norway," who speak of a fly that takes a piece out of you, and flies to the next rock to eat it.'

The Alhambra.

It has a place not only in Spanish but in American history.

This colossal palace—which the Moors built at Granáda in the twelfth century, and which was the residence of their kings for two hundred years—was besieged by Ferdinand and Isabella, and surrendered to them on January 2, 1492.

As an immediate consequence of this capitulation, Christopher Columbus was enabled to set sail from Palos on August 3, of the same year, in search of the new continent, which he found on October 12.

But if the Moors had held out at Granáda a few months longer, the Admiral's voyage would necessarily have been postponed beyond the ensuing winter—and might, in that case, have never been made at all.

In the grounds of the Alhambra, tradition points out the spot where the defeated Moorish king, Boabdil, on the day of his surrender, sat and wept—till he was rebuked by his mother Ayesha in the memorable words, ' You do well to weep as a woman over what you have failed to defend as a man !'

It is now the gay custom of the peasantry around Granáda to have a mid-winter frolic by climbing to the Alhambra on each recurring 2nd of January, in order that every maid who hopes to be married during the year may strike a silver bell that hangs in the Torre de la Vala. The maid who makes the bell ring the loudest is to get the best husband! So the bell is kept jingling fiercely during the whole day of the pic-nic—and the merry noise has been heard at Loya, twenty-nine miles away !

A WORD OF ACKNOWLEDGEMENT.

The credit of popularizing the Norse Mythology in the English-speaking world is due, in a great degree, to the venerated Benjamin Thorpe for his literal rendering of the Eddas; to Eirikr Magnússon of Cambridge; to Sir George Dasent; to Willard Fiske for his invaluable labours at Cornell University; to the copious and interesting manual by Prof. R. B. Anderson of the University of Wisconsin; to Prof. Hjalmer Hjorth Boyesen of Columbia College; to the essays of Max Müller; to the *Corpus Poeticum Boreale* of Gudbrand Vigfússon and F. York Powell; and (last but not least) to the poems of Longfellow and of William Morris.

———————

GREAT TOM OF OXFORD.

'William the Conqueror ... bestowed Oxford Castle on Robert D'Oyley, a favourite follower.'—Moore's *Historical Handbook of Oxford.*

'Robert, a nephew of the first castellan, wedded Edith Forne, a concubine of Henry the First.'—John Richard Green's *Early History of Oxford.*

'This Robert d'Oilley, the 2, had a wife caullid Edythe Forne, a woman of fame, and highly estimid with King Henry, by whose procuration Robert wedded her. . . . Edythe usid to walke out Oxford Castelle to solace, & oftentymes when yn a certen place in a tre as often as she came a certen Pyes usid to gather to it & ther to chattre & as it were to speke onto her. Edythe much marveling at this matier was sumtyme sore ferid as by a wonder. Whereupon she sent for one Radulf a chanon of St. Fredeswide's, a man of a vertuous life, & her confessor, askyng hym counsel, to whom he answerid after that he had seene the fascion of the Pyes chattering only at her cumming that she should build some church or monastery

in that place. Then she entretid her husband to build a priorie, &
so he did, making Radulph the first prior of it.'—Leland's *Account of
Oxford and Oseney Abbaye.*

'This lady used to please herself, when living with her husband in
the castle, with walking by the riverside, and under the shady trees.
Frequently observing the magpies gathered together on a tree by the
river, making a great chattering as it were at *her,* she was induced to
ask Radolphus, a canon of St. Frideswide, and her confessor, the
meaning of it. Madame, says he, these are not Pyes ; they are so
many souls in Purgatory, uttering, in their way, their complaints
aloud to you . . . and he humbly hoped, for the sake of the love of
God, she would build a church,' &c.—Anthony à Wood's *Ancient
and Present State of Oxford.*

'Little does the traveller imagine as the train passes by the
cemetery, just outside the Great Western Station at Oxford, that he
is going over the site of what was one of the grandest monastic
piles in England.'—Goldie's *Bygone Oxford.*

'Oseney Abbaye was the envy of all other religious houses in
England and beyond the seas.'—Sir John Peschell.

'The monastery had magnificent towers . . . and the rows of
pinnacles which adorned them were so grand and pleasing that
strangers from far and near came to take drafts of the same.'—
Anthony à Wood.

'In the abbey church was buried Edyth Doyly, circa 1152, on the
North side of the altar in a religious habit.'—Ibid.

'There lyeth an Image of Edyth of stone, in the Abbite of a Vowess,
holding a Hart in her right Hand, on the North Side of the high
altare. . . . The inscription was Memorabilis Matrona Deo devota. . . .
The cumming of Edyth to Oseneye, and Radulph waiting on her,
and the Tre with the chattering Pyes be painted in the Waule of
the church, over Edyth Tombe in Oseneye priorye.'—Leland.

'Here was a large and melodious Ring of Bells, the best as was
thought, in England ... deep and very musical . . . so famed for
their tunableness that foreigners traveling in England went to here
them chimed. . . . These bells, at the pulling down Osney cathedral

or abbey, together with a large clock-bell hanging in the same tower, were translated to Christchurch, and put up in their steeple, where they yet remain. . . . Thomas, recast in 1630, now called Great Tom of Christchurch, and said to be the largest bell in England, is six feet in diameter and eighteen in compass.'—Anthony à Wood.

'St. Frideswide, patroness of Oxford, was daughter of Didan, prince of Oxford. Algar, prince of Mercia, smitten with her beauty and virtues, and not being able to overcome her resolution of chastity, gave so far a loose to the reins of his criminal passion, as to lay a snare to carry her off. The virgin escaped his pursuit. After her death, in the eighth century, she became the patroness of the City and University of Oxford.'—Butler's *Lives of the Saints.*

KING HELGI TO QUEEN SIGRUN.

A similar song exists in the folk-lore of Denmark, and was done into English, many years ago, by Dr. Prior.

KING JOHN'S RIDE TO RUNNYMEDE.

MAGNA CHARTA.

The British Museum possesses (and shows to strangers) what is popularly called the original parchment of *Magna Charta*, with the signatures and seals of King John and his Barons. But there were *several* originals. These were sent at the time to different parts of the kingdom, and were deposited in the Cathedrals. The best-preserved, and now the most legible, of these several original parchments is the one at Lincoln Cathedral. Unfortunately the one in the British Museum is greatly faded—not only by time, but by water and fire.

The great political upheaval in England in the thirteenth century (the bloodless revolution whereof *Magna Charta* has ever since been the venerated memorial) was nothing less than the change of the English Government from an absolute to a limited monarchy.

The Norman Kings of England, from William the Conqueror to John, had reigned without statutory restriction or legal responsibility. The royal power had never been constitutionally defined, and each successive descendant of the Conqueror had tacitly assumed that the Sovereign of England had an unlimited prerogative. In fact, there was almost nothing to curb or fetter the King's will.

After 150 years of such unlicensed kingly power, the King's authority became—in the hands of King John—no longer endurable by the English nation.

With a unanimous movement the Barons of England, in a body, together with their stalwart and angry yeomanry, with arms in their hands, demanded from the King a written charter which should expressly circumscribe—through all future time—the powers of the English crown, and check its encroachment upon the just liberties of the realm.

In the quaint and monkish Latin of their day, they wrote a document for the King to sign and seal—a document ceding away, from that day henceforth and for ever, all further claim or pretence by any King of England to arbitrary power. This was *Magna Charta*, or the Great Charter.

King John at first, and for many months, refused to sign it.

At three different places—namely, at St. Edmundsbury, at Brackley, and at London—he was confronted by his Barons, who repeatedly and angrily thrust the Charter before him and demanded his signature under a threat of armed compulsion.

His peremptory and offensive refusal on each occasion is easily accounted for by an examination of the Charter; it stripped him clean of all his despotic assumptions, and rendered the King's will wholly subordinate to a written and supreme law of the land.

It tied his hands with many cords. The Charter contained sixty-eight sections, each of which was a limitation of his prerogative as an absolute monarch. A few of these sections will serve as illustrating the spirit of the whole document.

Section·1 says: 'The English Church shall be free, and shall have its rights intact, and its liberties uninfringed upon.' And the King is made to renounce expressly all royal interference with the free election of bishops.

Section 2 provides that a feudal estate, on the death of its owner, shall pass promptly to its rightful heir, without detention by the Crown, and without spoliation for the Crown's exchequer.

Section 8 estops the King from compelling widows to give their hands and lands in marriage against their will.

Section 17 declares that courts of justice, instead of being put to the trouble of following the King's progresses, shall be conveniently held in a fixed place.

Section 20 says: 'No freeman shall be amerced save upon oath of upright men from the neighbourhood.' [This put an end to all arbitrary royal fines—which, in that age, had grown to colossal proportions.]

Section 27 provides that the King's constable shall not take the yeoman's corn without paying for it.

Section 30 says: 'No sheriff or bailiff of ours shall take the horses or carts of any freeman for transport, unless by the will of that freeman.'

Section 31 adds: 'Neither we nor our bailiffs shall take another's wood for castles, or for other private uses, unless by the will of him to whom the wood belongs.'

Section 33 says: 'Henceforth all the weirs in the Thames and Medway, and throughout all England, save on the sea-coast, shall be done away with entirely.' [This was to prevent exclusive grants of valuable fisheries to royal favourites.]

Section 36 declares: 'Henceforth nothing shall be given or taken for a writ of inquest concerning life or limb; but it shall be conceded gratis, and shall not be denied.'

Section 39 (and this is the most important section of all) says: 'No freeman shall be taken, or imprisoned, or disseized, or outlawed, or exiled, or in any way harmed—nor will we go upon him, or send upon him, save by the lawful judgements of his peers, or by the law of the land.'

Section 40 adds: 'To none will we sell, to none deny or delay, right or justice.'

Section 47—known as the forestry clause—says: 'All forests constituted as such in our time shall straightway be annulled.' [This estopped the King from arbitrarily taking possession of any coveted district of English greenwood and turning it into his private hunting-ground.]

The above extracts are sufficient to show the legal meaning—and also the political value—of *Magna Charta.*

It is the most celebrated of all English State-papers.

'It is still,' says Hallam, 'the keystone of English liberty. All that has been since obtained is little more than confirmation and commentary. And if every subsequent law were to be swept away, there would still remain the bold features that distinguish a free from a despotic monarchy.'

THE END.

OXFORD: HORACE HART, PRINTER TO THE UNIVERSITY

Lightning Source UK Ltd.
Milton Keynes UK
UKHW012235110219
337137UK00006B/1110/P